CH009004439

About the Author

Born in Enfield, North London, in 1956, Sid grew up there and in Edmonton before moving to Hertfordshire.

Having started work in London in 1973 at the Stock Exchange and subsequently with HM Customs and Excise, Sid moved back to Hertfordshire in 1978.

After thirty years with the fire brigade, Sid started to work as a diving instructor moving to Mallorca, living there for five years and then to Egypt for a year.

Now back in the UK and living in Dorset, Sid is involved with maritime archaeology and local history.

Can You Smell Smoke?

Recollections of thirty years of fire
service
1978 - 2008

Can You Smell Smoke?

Recollections of thirty years of fire service
1978 - 2008

===============

Sid Payne

Olympia Publishers
London

www.olympiapublishers.com
OLYMPIA PAPERBACK EDITION

Copyright © Sid Payne 2017

The right of Sid Payne to be identified as author of
this work has been asserted in accordance with sections 77 and 78 of the
Copyright, Designs and Patents Act 1988.

All Rights Reserved

No reproduction, copy or transmission of this publication
may be made without written permission.
No paragraph of this publication may be reproduced,
copied or transmitted save with the written permission of the publisher,
or in accordance with the provisions
of the Copyright Act 1956 (as amended).

Any person who commits any unauthorised act in relation to
this publication may be liable to criminal
prosecution and civil claims for damage.

A CIP catalogue record for this title is
available from the British Library.

ISBN: 978-1-84897-758-7

First Published in 2017

Olympia Publishers
60 Cannon Street
London
EC4N 6NP

Printed in Great Britain

Dedication

Happy memories of
John Miles, 1939 - 2010
Mick Barnaby, 1955 - 2011
Alan Morgan, 1951 - 2015

CONTENTS

INTRODUCTION

I have been meaning to write this book for years. It was going to be a retirement job, but I don't seem to have retired yet. Since I left the job I have been abroad working as a diving instructor and I haven't found the time to get started. Anyway I am back in the UK now and the diving work here just isn't as frenetic.

Ever since my first shift at Potters Bar fire station I have recorded every call I went on and kept scrap books and other documents and photographs. When I retired in 2008 I went to live in Mallorca and in 2012 moved to Egypt for a year. Unfortunately during that year, a lot of things went missing in Mallorca and included were some of my early notes.

So anyway I think this is probably as accurate a story of fire service life as you can get and although not always politically correct I hope it will be of interest.

Of the thousands of incidents I went to, the majority were of a minor nature; false alarms, car fires, rubbish fires, grass fires, people locked in or out etc. etc. I have mentioned just a few, the more interesting ones.

I have tried not to write it too much in an emergency service jargon so that hopefully it will make sense to everyone.

As you read the story you will come across fire service related terminology and I have put a number of reference tables at the back of the book so if you are not sure have a look there.

Everything may not be in exact chronological order but it's as good as I can remember. There are a lot of names mentioned and I trust no one will be too upset with my recollections. I should point out now that I am rubbish with names and of the hundreds of people I met during my thirty years I cannot remember half of them. I have tried hard to put names to faces but in most cases have failed miserably.

Don't forget that these are my memories, as I recall them.

To be honest in thirty years working with the fire brigade in Hertfordshire there were very few people who I didn't particularly like and no one as I recall who really annoyed me. Not bad when you consider how many people crossed my path over the years.

Someone asked me once, how, many people actually work for the Hertfordshire fire brigade, I replied, "oh, about half of them!"

Anyway enjoy the trip down memory lane.

Sid Payne,
Dorset, 2015.

1. THE EARLY YEARS: 1977-1980.

1978. JOINING AND TRAINING.

It was November 1977 and I was working with HM Customs and Excise and serving as a lance corporal with C company, 4th (v) battalion the Royal Green Jackets operating from Sun Street drill hall in the City of London.

The news was full of the impending national strike by the country's fire brigades and around the 14th November I was at the drill hall when a dozen or so "firemen" arrive. They came with a couple of Green Goddess fire engines and were, I think, Royal Air Force lads dressed in duffle coats, wellington boots and steel helmets. Anyway they made themselves at home and for the next two months were rushing here and there on emergency calls with varying degrees of success.

As a 21-year-old, bored with office life, the excitement of the fire strike was very attractive and during those two months I decided to apply to the Hertfordshire Fire Brigade for a job. I remember telling my mum the plan and without even looking up she said, "Are you sure son, you'll get awfully dirty!"

Anyway I duly sent off my application and was pleased to receive a reply from the Staff Office of the brigade asking me to attend for an interview.

And so a few weeks later I found myself with a number of other hopefuls at Hertford fire station attempting tests of English and mathematics and tasks including wiring an electrical plug and reforming pieces of cut card into a square… all tricky stuff! The physical side of things comprised of carrying one of the other hopefuls around the station yard on my shoulders and running up and down the four floors of the station staircase, up ladders and over roofs etc.

Sometime later I had another letter, this time confirming my acceptance in the post of recruit fireman and, feeling pleased with myself, I resigned from HM Customs and the Territorial Army and prepared for a career change. In a few months I had gone from Lance Corporal Payne 24351708 to Recruit Fireman Payne 339.

I reported for my twelve weeks basic training as part of Recruit Squad 2/78 at Hertfordshire Fire Brigade headquarters on 7th April 1978 and spent the first few days drawing my fire kit from County Supplies at Hatfield, signing up for the Fire Brigades Union, the pension scheme (a great move) and meeting my fellow recruits and instructors. As a course we were fairly enthusiastic but as firemen none of us got very far up the ladder (so to speak). Dave Greaves managed to attain the rank of sub officer and I seem to recall had many women problems along the way. Phil Grey and myself rose to the heady heights of leading fireman, me late in my career and Phil by taking the brigade photographer's job. Of the others, they all left the job as firemen after thirty years, going out on the sick or in other circumstances; the others being Paul Bromwich, Gerry Baugh, Trevor Jopling, Geoff Puddy, Mick Coyle, Tom Weir and Jack Wood.

We did have one other starter but he left on the first day after hitting himself in the face with a jet of water from the hosereel. The outgoing Training Officer was Station Officer Alan Wallace with Station Officer Mick Howell and training Sub Officers Mick Clarke and Ray Harper. It was like good cop/bad cop with Mick being a nice softly spoken man and Ray being the loud obnoxious one who got under everyone's skin!

Our first practical session was marching; we all looked the part in our double breasted Lancer fire tunic, yellow cork helmet, yellow plastic leggings, leather fire boots and polished axe and black belt. Gerry Baugh, who had been in the Merchant Navy I think, and wearing the weekly course leader white belt, volunteered to show us how to march. **"RIGHT MARKER,"** bellowed Sub Harper and off went Gerry tick-tocking (same arm, same leg) his way across the yard to the amusement of all. Training proceeded apace with escape ladder drills, pitching various other ladders, pumping and road traffic accident procedures all interspersed with academic classes. I always seem to recall the emphasis in those days was on the practical rather than the theory.

To give you an idea, here is a breakdown of our training for week seven.

Monday: Standard messages and coded stops, combined drills, escape drills (rescue using a short extension ladder), pump drills and maintenance.

Tuesday: Water tender and pump drills, building construction, pump operation, pump drills and maintenance.

Wednesday: Introduction to Porto Power, fixed installations, standard tests, combined drills, physical training and maintenance.

Thursday: Foam drills, practical firemanship, escape drills (rescue from a small window), knots and lines, private study and maintenance.

Friday: Written assessment, practical assessment, lower down by line, interviews and maintenance.

Two other characters appeared after a few weeks both trying to join the training school staff. Sub Officers Ian Chapman (Chankers) and Roger Gurling. Ian eventually got the job and after that the end of week exams got easier because he would tell us the answers; and I will never forget Roger's opening line when he took us for some drill. We were all lined up in fire kit and he snapped to attention and said "Right, I know I'm f*****g ugly but we're going to drill anyway", you just had to like the man!

One morning I overslept and arrived late. I covered my hands with grease from the engine and said my car wouldn't start. Still got a huge bollocking from the governor, Mick Howell, who had probably heard it all before, anyway I wasn't late again.

We moved around for our training with some being done at Hertford fire station, some at Welwyn Garden City where the ten of us were accommodated in a broom cupboard and St Albans where the old Divisional Commander's house had been altered to be the Breathing Apparatus Training Centre.

Our appliances (fire engines) were a couple of old pumps, a Bedford TK Water Tender Escape and a Bedford J5 Water Tender Ladder both from the early 60s. Considering what we ended up with in 2008 our uniform and equipment in 1978 was really quite primitive although we were expected to do the same tasks with it, as I said previously – practical people.

The training passed quite quickly but it was bloody hard work with a lot to take in. My final written exam average taken on 8th June was seventy-three point two percent; oral exam on 13th June eighty-three percent and final practical exam also on 13th June seventy-eight percent. Anyway at the end of the twelve weeks all of us had managed to get through somehow and we started to prepare for our pass-out parade.

15th June, the big day arrived at Hertfordshire Fire Brigade headquarters and everything was polished, painted and gleaming. At 2.15 p.m. our guests, family and friends were welcomed by the Chief Officer and together with all the fire brigade dignitaries were shown up to the mess deck and then onto the roof covering the wash down area behind the appliance bays.

We marched out with our training subs, came to a halt in front of the assembled guests and came to attention for inspection by the Chief Fire Officer Ted Faulkner.

Mr Faulkner was a real gentleman and a fireman's fireman, respected by everyone in the service, and I have some good stories about him later in this narrative.

Following the inspection, we doubled away and began our display. We did four drills and all went well apart from the third one. The drill was to pitch the escape ladder to the fourth floor of the tower with a hose line (a jet) hauled aloft by a line and got to work, a 464 ladder pitched to the third floor with a hose line carried aloft and got to work and two jets on the ground floor. Up on the fourth floor I threw the line bag out of the window, it got snagged and shot back in the third floor window and down to the ground floor inside the tower, shit! A short break ensued while the crew on the third floor hauled the line back up, threw it out again and down to the ground. I don't think anyone noticed.

I passed out as a probationary fireman, fantastic.

To celebrate our triumph, we organised a couple of piss ups one at a local Hertford pub which we managed to keep quiet from Ray Harper, and one in the bar at Hertford fire station. I have a great photograph of the course lined up bent over mooning with Chankers Chapman striking a great pose in the centre of the group. What a night that was. Some girls turned up I don't know if someone brought them or they were booked but I remember one of the lads was asked, "who had them after you?" to which he replied "Hertford White Watch I think"!

Following on from all this we started on our two weeks breathing apparatus (BA) training at St Albans.

Hertfordshire Fire Brigade. recruit squad 2/1978.
Back Row, L to R: Paul Bromwich, Mick Coyle, Phil Grey, Tom Weir and Geoff Puddy. Middle Row: Me, Dave Greaves, Trevor Jopling, Jack Wood and Gerry Baugh. Front Row: Sub O Ray Harper, Stn. O Mick Howell, Stn. O Alan Wallace and Sub O Mick Clarke.

Recruit Squad 2/78: L – R: G. Baugh, T. Weir, D. Greaves, G. Puddy,
M. Coyle, Me, P. Grey, T. Jopling, J. Wood, P. Bromwich.
Pictures: HFRS

1978. MY FIRST POSTING.

We had been told prior to the pass-out where we were to begin
our careers and I was to be posted to the Red Watch, Potters
Bar. This was about a twenty minute drive from my home in
Cuffley, so that was okay. I had some time off before joining
my new Watch and so decided to call in at the fire station to
introduce myself.

The Watch had just finished drilling and were in the tower
when I arrived. The crew on duty were Sub Officer Norman
Davis and firemen Alan Morgan, Gary "Stavros" Norris and
Roger Church. All really nice blokes. Norman was a bit of a
worrier, Alan one of the funniest men ever, Gary would leave
notes on the telephone so we would know what to say if
anyone phoned up for him and Roger, another funny man,
who later left the job under a cloud.

As we were talking the bells went down and the crew
turned out to a bedroom fire in the hotel located at Bignalls
Corner, South Mimms on the A1(M) motorway.

I followed the pump for a look (well I was a lot keener
then).

And so at half past eight on the morning of my first shift I arrived at the station for my first day, full of anticipation and hopes for the future in the fire brigade. At nine a.m. we lined up, in full fire kit, the off-going watch was dismissed and Sub Officer Davis allocated us our riding positions on the appliance, and as the new boy I would be number five. That meant I would sit in the middle in the back and not get to wear BA for at least six months, really until I could prove myself to the others. All the equipment on the pump was checked, the driver, Gary, was responsible for the appliance itself, lights, fuel etc.

At that time someone would have to stay on the appliance, listening to the radio, as the control room went through each wholetime appliance call sign to check the reception starting with 010 Hemel Hempstead's WrL right up to 330 Letchworth's WrL. Potters Bar being 150.

Up to the mess deck for tea.

Potters Bar was in B Division with our headquarters station at St Albans. The Division was under the command of Divisional Officer Martin assisted by Deputy Divisional Officer Baker and ADOs Miles, Peto and Wheeler. B Division consisted of twelve stations, six wholetime and six retained. Potters Bar was a one pump station and also housed the ambulance station with its one ambulance, both sitting side by side in the bays. It was a two storey building with, as well as the bays, the ground floor had a watch room, station/sub officers dormitory, locker room, toilet block, ambulance station and basement. Upstairs was the kitchen, mess deck and bar, offices, rest room and dormitory. The pole house was situated outside the dormitory and came down in the locker room on the opposite side of the bays to the pump. At the front was a house occupied by ADO Hugh Wheeler who sported a huge handlebar moustache. At the back was the drill yard, tower, BA charging room and hose store. Our appliance was a Dennis F series (HBM 770N).

During the day we had a cook, Shirley, who when Blue Watch were on duty spent most of the time sitting in a sink of water, courtesy of John Ratty and a cleaner, Peggy, who spent her time sweeping with broom handles that had cock heads carved on the end thanks to Alan Morgan.

Over tea I met the other two members of my watch. The guvnor, Station Officer Pete Lester, a mechanic by trade, although at the time I was driving a 1960 Ford Anglia so most repairs could be done with a lump hammer! And finally there was Leading Fireman (L/Fm) Dave French, a tall, strange character whose bedding was christened *The Old Grey Weevil Nest* from which he rose phoenix like in the mornings, usually with an erection.

> Just before lunch the bells went down, the lights came on and the tannoy crackled into life. The Geordie voice of the control operator (whose name I forget) told us "Fire call, fire call, order your appliance to a rubbish fire, Cranbourne tip, Cranbourne Road, Potters Bar". So off I went on my first call as a fireman, onto the pump, the doors swing open and we are heading up the road with the blue lights flashing, the bell ringing and sirens blaring.
>
> Trying to get dressed in my fire kit as the appliance swung along, through the red traffic lights, overtaking – by the time we arrived at the incident I was kitted up and ready for action. There was a huge pile of rubbish, including building materials well alight. The others were quite happy for me to grab a hose line and run it out to the fire, Gary, the pump operator chasing me along with the water so that when I connected my branch to the end of the hose the water gushed from the nozzle onto the fire. Fantastic, after an hour or so the fire was out and I was covered in dirt and muck (as mum had predicted) and as I rolled up my filthy hose I couldn't help but notice four other squeaky clean, smiling faces.

Back at the station the hose, being canvas, had to be cleaned and hung up the tower to dry (guess who did that) and the appliance restocked with clean hose (guess who did that) and once my kit was washed (guess who did that) and I was respectable (guess who did that) it was lunchtime.

And so the first day ended at six o'clock in the evening and with each of my first four duty shifts yielding one call per shift. I was off to a good start, with another call to Cranbourne tip and two false alarms.

Gary, Alan and Roger all lived in Cheshunt (Gary only some of the time if his notes were anything to go by) and had to pass through Cuffley on their way home so after a day at work we would all stop off at the Plough for a pint and a chat.

I started on the forty-eight hour a week shift system and we worked two day shifts from nine in the morning until six in the evening, two night shifts from six until nine and two days off. To complicate matters, whatever shift fell on a Friday we only did one of, plus a rota day programmed in. An average day shift consisted of checking the engine, tea, an hour's drill, tea, station work, lunch with tea, checking/testing fire hydrants, fire certificate inspections or other station work, tea, volleyball, tea and home. A night shift involved checking the pump followed by tea and opening the bar at seven thirty, a few beers then bed. To be fair that is a very frivolous look at our shifts but one which has become the view of most people over the years. In actual fact sometimes we missed out the tea before home!

1979. TIME FOR A BATH!

During May 1979 our Dennis appliance broke down and was replaced by a Dennis D series WrT (NRO 582L). A couple of days later this too broke down and was replaced by an old Bedford TK WrT (VAR 101E). This pump was so small it couldn't take most of our equipment. As we finished stowing it and putting it on the run we were called out to a chimney fire and on our way to the incident we were overtaken by a cyclist!

On another call a few days later we were turned out to Highland's Hospital, Worlds End Lane, Winchmore Hill. Three or four London pumps were in attendance, they had all new and shiny ERF appliances and we arrived coughing and spluttering in our old Bedford, causing some wry smiles from our London colleagues!

Other entertainment on a night shift would be to watch the show put on by the woman in the house behind the fire station.

She would regularly strip off for our benefit and the appeal of it was reflected by the large number of telescopes and binoculars to be found in the Watch mess cupboards. One night I recall Alan got on top of a spare appliance parked at the back of the yard and at the height of the show he sat up and lit her up with the spotlight on the roof of the pump.

Charades was also popular with my interpretation of *Sat-turd-day-night-fever* followed by *Clothes-down* getting rapturous applause. *Come-dancing* was also a good effort and very well presented. However, don't think it was all just fun, oh no. We also carried out some serious experiments like if you spent the entire night shift farting into a jam jar, in the morning if you put a small hole in the lid and lit it would it make a passable night light?

Monday 16th July 1979 2240 hrs and the tannoy came to life,

BEEP, BEEP, BEEP "Order your appliance to an RTA persons trapped, Coopers Lane Road, Potters Bar". This was one of those unforgettable moments in any fireman's career, the first time you hear those words "persons trapped", meaning that one or more persons were unable to get out of the wreckage of the vehicle. Real life and death stuff, what you join the job for but still not knowing how you will react to it.

We made good time to the incident, maybe a ten minute drive at that time at night. The road was fairly narrow and winding with woods on either side.

The ambulance was already in attendance. We saw on arrival that a car had left the road, travelled a short distance, turned over and impacted a tree with the passenger side severely crushed. A girl had escaped from the car, the driver was trapped and it wasn't readily apparent if there was anyone else in the vehicle.

ADO Hugh Wheeler arrived to take charge. We got to work to release the driver and I was told to get into the back of the upside down car to assist with the casualty.

The Emergency Rescue Tender arrived from Hatfield.

I felt around the passenger side and found the top of the head of a second casualty still in his seat. The ambulance crew chose to concentrate on the driver who was alive and could be released fairly easily. The driver's door was popped open and he was removed from the car.

The twenty-year-old passenger was believed to be deceased and the officer in charge decided to pull the car away from the tree using a Tifor winch and turn it back upright prior to releasing him. He was well trapped and it took some time to remove him from the wreck.

At last he was recovered and taken to Chase Farm Hospital by ambulance where he was declared to be dead, his seventeen-year-old girlfriend was detained overnight with cuts and the twenty-six-year-old driver was admitted with shoulder and back injuries.

There are two things to remember here having read about this RTA.

Firstly, that the equipment we had to deal with incidents such as this was very minimal. We had a tool made by Black Hawk called Porto Power which was used in the car industry to repair vehicle body work. It was a hand pumped hydraulic jack with various attachments that enabled you to push, pull, spread and lift things. It all came in a fairly large and heavy wooden box and every fireman would have heard the instruction during a drill session with Porto Power to "crush that box!" We also had a Tifor winch, which was a manually operated winch using a wire hawser for pulling or lifting. Apart from this high tech equipment we had a hearth kit which contained hammers, screwdrivers, saws, pliers etc… an everyday tool kit in fact.

Secondly, the ambulance crew were trained in first aid but were not paramedics and therefore would deal with the casualty as best they could but the priority was to get the patient to hospital for treatment.

Finally, and bizarrely, when on retiring, I moved to Mallorca to live and work. I met a man, same age as me, and I saw him a number of times as he came from Potters Bar. On one occasion I mentioned the fire brigade and it transpired that he and the driver of the car that crashed were friends and he had seen him on that night in 1979!

The *Potters Bar Press* of 30th November reported on the Hornsey Coroner's Court inquest.

The passenger had died from a fracture dislocation of the neck and although the driver thought he had suffered a tyre blowout, the investigating police officer disputed this and stated that the car had left ninety-nine feet (thirty metres) of tyre marks and these were not due to skidding.

On Friday 27th July 1979 the *Potters Bar Press* reported on the appearance of a twenty-seven-year-old lady driver at Barnet Crown Court on Monday 23rd under the headline:

"Driver crashed into front of boutique."

We had attended this incident on the morning of Monday, May 14th.

Her car was parked on the side of the road in Darkes Lane, Potters Bar. Before she went to drive off she had failed to remove the crook lock, which was attached to the brake pedal, and she drove across the road, unable to steer or stop, onto the pavement and through a plate glass window of the shop!

She told the court that she was not used to fitting the anti-theft device and that it was dark when she did so. The device was no longer fitted to her car to avoid a similar accident happening again. Priceless!

Another fun event was a bath race organised by the London Fire Brigade and held at Danson Park in Welling, south east London.

Alan and I decided to enter.

We started to collect things by begging and borrowing our basic needs, for example a bath! We were donated two fibreglass baths, fibreglass and resin, paint and some wood and aluminium. The design was to cut one end off of each bath and then join the two baths together with the ends turned upside down and fixed to a top deck as fore and aft cabins. An aluminium bar with tyre inner tube floats formed a stabilising outrigger and was fixed to the front. Painted red and complete with blue lights and a two tone horn powered by a car battery it did look good.

Time for a trial run. We contacted the manager of the Potters Bar swimming pool to arrange a visit. Alan and I, helped by Sub Officer Roy Square, loaded up the bath into the station van and we drove up to the pool. With great expectation we assembled the components and launched *Lorrianna* onto the calm waters of the pool. The boat was named after my future wife Lorraine and Alan's wife Diana.

At first all went well as we paddled up and down the pool carrying out various manoeuvres and testing our lights and horn. Alan then had the idea to check our stability by rocking the bath from side to side, bad move. On the fourth or fifth rock the aluminium bar buckled and snapped and the bath capsized and with blue lights flashing descended to the bottom of the pool, (ironically my marriage only lasted slightly longer before also sinking without trace). That was bad, with battery acid leaking into the water but it was just about to get a whole lot worse. The paint on our boat unfortunately wasn't quite dry and a kind of red oil slick began to spread out from the wreck on the bottom. Roy legged it as Alan and I managed to recover the bath, get it into the van and beat a hasty retreat leaving the pool manager with a red oily pool and red footprints covering the poolside. Anyway the upshot was we upgraded our aluminium bar to steel so it was a worthwhile test but strangely we never got invited back to the pool.

A reporter came to the station the week before the race and on Friday August 31st the *Potters Bar Press* featured a photograph of us in the bath and said, "These intrepid Potters Bar firemen Sid Payne and, behind him Alan Morgan have made this remarkable craft to compete in a bath race on a lake in Bexleyheath, Kent, on Sunday".

Me and Alan in the bath together.

At the lake on the day of the race, Sunday 2nd September, we set up our bath with Roy back in attendance. There were some incredible creations, a huge pirate galley from Aylesbury fire station, a German U-boat with marching music from Bow, a pink and yellow sea dragon and the Titanic (which sank twice). All in all one hundred craft from eight counties took part. The rule was that a domestic bath had to be included in the design and touch the water. Compared to some our bath was very small and this didn't bode well for the forthcoming naval engagement. The race itself was several circuits of the lake but once the claxon sounded to start the race that was pretty much forgotten as battle was joined. Weapons of choice were water cannon, soot and flour bombs and red dye with old scores being settled and new ones being formed.

We managed to keep out of the way and completed the course and I think I am correct in saying that ours was the only bath still floating at the end.

The Bexleyheath and Welling Observer of Thursday, September 6th 1979 reported the event as follows "…but for sheer mad, off-the-cuff entertainment, the one hundred craft in Sunday's bath race would be difficult to beat. Firemen in fancy dress from all over the country were treated to soot, flour and red dye fights, duckings, sinkings and even kidnappings as they dotted the lake in their craft, some built to win, others for visual impact, and the rest just for fun".

A good day out all round and the London Fire Brigade raised around £10,000 for the benevolent fund.

Back to reality.

After months of training in the BA procedures, another first. I was finally riding the pump in the number four seat!

One afternoon all the training was finally to be put to good use.

BEEP, BEEP, BEEP, "Fire call, fire call, order your appliance to Trusty Cycles, Potters Bar". There were four of us on duty with me and Roger as BA wearers. As we approached the factory the staff were evacuating the building so things looked promising (for us that is). As we entered the building in BA with a hosereel jet it became apparent that it probably wouldn't be needed.

The sprinkler system had activated and was progressively flooding the factory floor and soaking us.

At the seat of the fire we found that the boxed bicycles had been stacked so high as to be almost touching a halogen floodlight mounted in the roof. The heat from the lamp had set the top box on fire which in turn had then actuated the sprinklers.

The sprinkler system was turned off and then the job became a clean-up operation and instead of being hot and smoky I was cold and damp!

Like all fire stations Potters Bar had its characters. Probably chief among them was Blue Watch Station Officer Ralph Hentall, a man who cut the feet off of his socks as they made his feet sweat and just wore the bit up his leg! When the American Skylab space craft crashed back to Earth in July 1979, just to be on the safe side, Ralph spent the entire shift in a large metal wheelie bin and one day he came in announcing he was a butterfly and instructed his crew to keep all the windows and doors closed so that he couldn't escape. Ralph was a champion power lifter and held the veteran's world record. He also carved love spoons and once walked to

Downing Street to present one to Prime Minister Margaret Thatcher.

Another strange one was Tony Tate who once arrived a couple of minutes late one morning, just after the pump had turned out to an incident. Without batting an eyelid, he picked up his boots and leggings, tunic and helmet and ran out of the station in pursuit.

One morning I saw in the station diary the following entry:

"The gloves in the drawer are L/Fm Pennyfather" not great English I agree.

Underneath Ralph Hentall had written "I am pleased that L/Fm Pennyfather has found his vocation in life, I myself am thinking of becoming a stapling machine."

Another adrenaline rush call came in just after 0700hrs on October 6th 1979

BEEP, BEEP, BEEP, "Fire call, fire call, order your appliance to Alston Court, St Albans Road, Barnet, house fire, persons reported."

A "persons reported" call gets everybody moving up a gear, it means we are on our way to a fire in which somebody is involved or unaccounted for.

Prior to our arrival passers-by had tried to call for help from a phone box opposite but it was out of order, others alerted the residents and one tried to gain access to the flat by breaking the glass panel in the door but was beaten back by the heat and smoke.

We were part of a four pump attendance together with London Fire Brigade appliances from Barnet and Mill Hill and Borehamwood from Hertfordshire. On arrival smoke and flames were issuing from a back window and BA crews from London were already working jets into the flat.

Alan and I had rigged in BA enroute to the job and were deployed to search for the missing person; we checked the bedrooms and also the loft space. We found nothing and as the smoke cleared we came back to the kitchen where the body of the occupier, a fifty-year-old bachelor, had been found curled up in a small cupboard

> under the sink only a couple of feet from the door and safety.
>
> The bedroom was badly damaged by fire, smoke and water. The flat below was damaged by water.
>
> Potters Bar 150 was released from the incident and we returned to station.

The *Potters Bar Press* for November 9th 1979 reported on the inquest held at Hornsey Coroner's Court on 8th.

The victim had more than one hundred and fifty wine bottles in his kitchen and a blood alcohol level of 198ml of alcohol to 100ml of blood. The investigating fire officer had stated that two electric fires were found alight in the bedroom and he considered that it was these that ignited combustible material on the bed, starting the blaze.

The Police Inspector said that the telephone was off the hook, suggesting that the victim had attempted to ring for help before being overcome by fumes. The pathologist told the court that death was caused by carbon monoxide poisoning.

Our station ground was surrounded by fire stations at Borehamwood (station B14), situated down the A1 to the south west and Hatfield (B18) to the north. To the east was Cheshunt (B16). To the south we bordered London, with Barnet (J29) one way and Southgate (J28) in the other. If we needed assistance, then these would be the first stations to be called in to help and of course vice versa. Borehamwood, Cheshunt, Barnet and Southgate were permanently manned stations the same as ours and Hatfield was day-crewed which meant at night the firemen would be called from their houses around the station.

Quite often we would meet up with Borehamwood Red Watch to play sport either at the station for volleyball and tennis or a park somewhere for a football match. I recall one occasion where we met up at a local playing field to play football in fancy dress, God knows what the public thought although the match attracted a lot of attention!

Talking of Borehamwood, one night we had a standby from there to make us up to five riders. His name was Phil and he hadn't long been in the job. Later that evening we were all in the television room when I started playing up to Alan, he caught on and responded accordingly. Before long we were holding hands and cuddling on the settee. Phil didn't quite know what was happening and was getting a bit hot under collar. Alan had gone into the dormitory and pushed our beds together and had even managed to find a daffodil in a vase! To be honest it was getting a bit out of hand and ended up with a naked Sid Payne riding a naked, squealing Alan Morgan around the dormitory whipping him with the daffodil. I don't think Phil got much sleep and went back to Borehamwood wondering what the hell that was all about and incidentally left the brigade soon after.

It was a definite case of the lunatics running the asylum, which brings me on to another subject.

In our area there were a number of old nineteenth and twentieth century mental hospitals, including Napsbury in London Colney, Hill End in St. Albans and Harperbury and Shenley in Shenley. They kept us very busy, most of the time with false alarms but with a few good fires thrown in for good measure. Shenley in particular was a regular run out. One call springs to mind. The automatic fire alarm (AFA) had gone off and as usual Borehamwood, St. Albans and us had responded. As we pulled up in front of the main block we were met by man wearing a white coat and with a stethoscope around his neck. We followed him into the hospital and through a number of doors and wards occupied by vacant looking inmates whose eyes followed you somewhat menacingly. After a few more rooms and corridors, we exited the building close to where we entered, we looked to our guide for an explanation and he promptly sat down in a puddle. "Back away slowly lads" suggested the guvnor.

On the other side of our patch out towards Enfield was a more open home for the mentally handicapped called Barvin Park. We got a call there one sunny afternoon to a fire in the grounds. While I was putting a bit of water on to a pile of smouldering cut grass I was hit on the back of the head by something. Bending down to pick it up I found it to be a screw- in plastic dart flight! I threw it back and before you knew it battle ensued, firemen on one side and residents on the other. We had our hosereel and they had their dart flights and handfuls of grass and for twenty minutes we indulged in good humoured war games. I always thought it a bit strange that they had the job of assembling darts!

During the couple of years I spent at Potters Bar the Watch underwent a few changes in personnel.

By May 1979 Norman Davis retired and moved up to Northamptonshire and I didn't see him again until he turned up at my retirement party. He was replaced by Sub Officer Ray Harper who had followed me from Training School where he was a pain in the arse but was a completely different man out on station. Fm Dave Baker re-joined the Watch following a period of sick leave. By February 1980 Pete Lester had been promoted to ADO and was replaced by Station Officer Dave Price. I liked Dave a lot although he frightened the life out of me when we got a call during the night and he appeared with no front teeth.

And Dave French retired to become an insurance salesman; we bought him a briefcase I recall. Our new L/Fm was Nigel "Piggy" Tombs, again a really good bloke and leading hand, sadly he killed himself some years later to the sadness of all of us who knew him.

One other character definitely worth a mention was Fm Gary "Biggles" Williamson who had arrived by January 1979. Biggles sported a great handlebar moustache and one to rival Hughie Wheeler. He was always good fun to be with, great sense of humour. I can remember vividly Biggles' first night shift and it still brings a smile to my face. The date and nature of the call escapes me now but we had all gone to bed when at around two in the morning the alarm went off. Alan, Gary Norris and I were up, dressed, down the pole and onto the pump in good time but no sign of Biggles. Norman joined us, still no Biggs. We got rigged in fire gear, the engine was running, still no Biggs. Norman sounded the horn, still no Biggs. We were just about to leave him and go when he appeared coming across the bays. He was fully dressed in undress uniform including tie and peaked cap and carrying his bedding over his arm! As he got up into the fire engine he dropped his money and got off again! Norman's language was choice! A sight that hasn't left me in thirty-five years. He moved onto Green Watch when it was created later in 1979 and joined me again at Stevenage a few years later.

Towards the end of the year I applied for my Heavy Goods Vehicle (HGV) licence and started my driver training in October.

One of the brigade driving instructors was Sub Officer Don Huddle and I had a great two weeks out and about. The vehicle we used was one of the brigade's Salvage Tenders (ST) and so we were on call during the course.

It was quite handy for me because I got married on 27th October and needed to move to a new house. With Don and the other trainee we picked up a load of furniture from Cuffley and took it up to Needingworth in Cambridgeshire, job done.

Other trips out included a visit to Don's mum in south London and a fish and chip lunch in Southend.

On top of that we attended two operational calls one being a big mansion house fire in Thorley just outside Bishop's Stortford.

Although I enjoyed my time at Potters Bar I was starting to get itchy feet. There were a couple of reasons for this. Firstly, Potters Bar was a fairly quiet station and I wanted more excitement, more death and destruction. Secondly at that time I was living way north in a village in Cambridgeshire and it was taking me an hour or more to get to work and back. So I had my eye on Stevenage, a busy two pump station and twenty minutes closer to home. I also looked at a move to Letchworth which was even further north but like Potters Bar was fairly quiet. So I applied to transfer to Stevenage fire station and duly submitted my request.

In 1979 we had a particularly harsh winter with a lot of snow and ice making it difficult to get to work sometimes. I can still see Pete Lester getting on his motorbike to go home, heading out of the car park, straight through the fence and finishing up in next door's garden.

A week or so later we were in Cuffley on a call and, once dealt with, started the treacherous trip back to station. Driving slowly down the slope of Tolmers Avenue, Stavros Norris wasn't doing too badly in the conditions. Near the bottom of the road the pump started to slide and slide and continued to slide; in fact it slid right across Tolmers Road at the bottom of the hill and into the garden of the house opposite finishing up against the front door. After a long struggle the pump was recovered and we made it back to the station.

Red Watch Potters Bar, Jan. 1979: L – R: G. Williamson, Me, R. Church, Stn O P. Lester, Sub O N. Davis, G. Norris, A. Morgan.

1980. OFF TO PASTURES NEW.

And so at the end of March 1980 I said my farewells to Red Watch, B15, Potters Bar

As I said, I was sad to leave, it was a good station and a good Watch, and I had learned a lot there...

And so hello to White Watch, C 23, Stevenage.

Red Watch, Potters Bar, Feb. 1980: L-R: Me, G. Norris, D. Baker, L/Fm
N. Tombs, Stn O D. Price.

White Watch, Stevenage, Mar. 1980: Back L-R: Stn O W. Chandler,
L/Fm J. Miles, R. Ellis, M. Currie, I. Clinton, S. Bygrave, Me, Sub O D.
Magill. Front: E. Baker, M. Barnaby, B. Hillier.

2. STEVENAGE: 1980-2001.

1980. A BUSY TIME.

I arrived at Stevenage fire station for my first shift, White Watch's second night, on 3rd March 1980.

Stevenage had two fire engines and twelve firemen and turned out around two thousand plus times a year.

As usual we paraded in the bays to be given our riding positions for the shift. Let me introduce you to the Watch: -

WrE (call sign 230): Officer in charge Stn Officer Wally Chandler, driver Fm Mick Barnaby, BA 1 L/Fm John Miles, BA 2 Fm Robbie Ellis and no. 5 Fm Simon Bygrave.

WrL (call sign 231): Officer in Charge Sub O Dave Magill, driver Fm Ian Clinton. BA 1 Fm Barry Hillier, BA 2 Me, no. 5 Fm Malcolm Currie.

Sick that night were Fm Eddie Baker and Fm Ron Keep.

We checked our equipment and the pumps before heading up for a tea. After a drill session the evening passed with me trying to get to know the station and new routine. That meant getting a tour of the station from Barry Hillier and an introduction to the Watch from Wally Chandler followed by a chat over a beer or two.

Dinner, beer, snooker and bed.

0636 hrs BEEP, BEEP, BEEP "Order both appliances to Colestrete, Stevenage, house fire, persons reported." Mobile to incident at 0637 hrs. It's only round the corner (apparently), Barry and I rig in BA as quickly as possible and by the time we arrive at 0639 hrs we are both ready. The WrE crew take a jet into the house and we back them up with a hosereel. Stn Officer Chandler sends an informative message "House of two floors, 7m x 7m, quarter of top floor alight, 1 person unaccounted for".

The house is heavily smoke logged, John and Robbie tackle the fire, we drop our hosereel and start to search the bedroom for the casualty. As I feel along the bottom of the bed a foot appears in front of my mask, getting Barry's attention we prepare to recover the casualty. The victim, a twenty-five-year-old woman, is severely burned from the waist up and it is decided to leave her in situ.

Prior to our arrival the victim's four-year-old daughter was taken from the house by a passing milkman with burns to her legs and feet.

At 0703 hrs ADO Den Brooker sends the stop message "Private house, 7m x 7m, twenty-five per cent of first floor severely damaged by fire, one female child conveyed to hospital by Herts ambulance, one female person believed deceased in back bedroom of first floor, 1 jet, 1 hosereel, four BA".

We were back to the station just after 0900 hrs and handed over to Green Watch who carried out two re-inspections during the morning with Stn Officer Robin Rowles-Smith closing the job down around 1230 hrs.

During the day a post mortem on the victim revealed that the cause of death was strangulation and so I was now part of a murder investigation. You had to feel sorry for her parents who found this out on Tuesday evening when Anglia Television news reported it.

I don't recall whether I had to come back to the station later that day or if the police interviewed the Watch on our next duty day, anyway we gave statements and had our fingerprints taken.

In September the man convicted of her murder was given two life sentences.

What an interesting start to my career at Stevenage.

Stevenage was in C Division which covered north Hertfordshire, largely rural with a number of large towns, the biggest of which was Stevenage with some 80,000 residents. There were eleven stations, six wholetime and five retained.

Stevenage also had the Divisional headquarters situated in the old DC's house at the back of the station. The DC was John Read, DDC Ron Ambrose with ADO's Den Brooker, Colin Pond and Ron Gibson. "Bunny" Warren was the Staff Sub Officer and, I seem to recall, had a bit of a clumsy streak. I once watched him cross the short distance from the station to division dropping two bottles of milk three or four times breaking both before he gained the safety of the house.

As mentioned the appliances were a Dodge WrL which was very high and unstable on corners but by June had been replaced by a new Dennis RS series (GPG 836V). The WrE was an AEC (UUR 105K) in which the crew sat facing backwards, not the driver! It was a pain in the arse to drive, having to double declutch, and if you missed the gear change you may well have to stop and start again! Embarrassing with the blue lights and horns going! We also had a flatbed lorry for transporting the divisional foam stock cans or the shear legs (large metal tripod with a block and tackle for lifting) and like all the other stations, a utility van.

The station was quite large also incorporating the Herts Ambulance station. Our bays could accommodate three appliances and also on the ground floor were the Watchroom, three dormitories, washroom and emergency generator room. Upstairs was the Mess deck, kitchen, bar, two offices, pole house and a study room.

At the rear was the Divisional headquarters, county workshops, the AFS bays, smoke house and tower, hose store and BA compressor and store.

On my first shift at Stevenage Ron Keep was off sick with his dodgy ankles. Ron had more nicknames than anyone else, some of which were Nobber, Winker, the One and Skewer Head.

He came back to work on 10th March.

We were on nights on Friday 4th April 1980 playing bridge when the bells went down. Off went Nobber, leading the charge from the mess deck, he reached the top of the stairs and tripped over his own feet and fell halfway down the stairs, ending in a heap holding his ankles. Nine other firemen following took it in turns to tread on Skewer Head as we headed for the bays and another fire.

When we got back Ronnie the One had ankles resembling beach balls and another two and a half months off sick.

We had nine bridge players and we always tried to get up on the mess deck to set up two games before Budget Magill could join in! No other reason than it used to piss him off. Budget? Because he was the Social Club Treasurer.

With Nobber going off sick it hastened my move to be an operational driver. After passing the HGV course you had to drive the fire engine under supervision for a number of hours prior to being allowed to drive to incidents on the blues.

White Watch Stevenage only had three drivers Mick Barnaby, Ian Clinton and Nobber. With Nobber out of the frame I found myself pushed to the fore in June when the Division just didn't have enough drivers to go round. And so I started to drive earlier than forecast, fantastic I loved driving (and crashing). So on 12th June I was driving the WrL, 13th the WrE and 14th and 15th the WrL.

On 26th June 1980 I received a certificate from the Fire Services Central Examination Board stating that: having already passed Part I (the written technical papers), completed the examination by passing Part II (the practical test) and is now…

QUALIFIED FOR PROMOTION TO THE RANK OF LEADING FIREMAN

Ha, a lot of bloody good that did me, I never did manage to pass the Sub Officer's exam and despite attending for promotion interview four or five times it was to be another twenty-one years before I got to be a leading fireman!

How times change. In the 80s when I went for interview, the promotion panel consisted of the ACO, SDO fire prevention and the three DCs, enough to make you shit yourself before a question was even asked. When I got promoted in 2001 the panel was a Stn Officer, someone from

Control and the Equal Opportunities woman who kept correcting me when I referred to the men on the watch. What nonsense.

Night shift, 11th September, ten on duty, a night destined to be my busiest ever with eleven calls in the fifteen hours. Both pumps were busy during the evening followed by the lull before the storm. Late dinner and bed.

I was driver/pump operator of the WrE and not long after midnight we were called out to Penn Road where we found a car and garage well alight, both being severely damaged. Minutes after we turned out, a second call came in for the WrL to attend Wilkins' greengrocers, Bedwell Crescent were there were some wooden vegetable crates on fire.

Not long after that a police patrol in the town centre spotted a fire at the rear of True Form shoe shop.

231 was mobilised to a rubbish fire at 0249 hrs leaving the station a minute later. At 0253 hrs an assistance message from Sub O Magill, "make pumps two"

0254 hrs, BEEP, BEEP, BEEP, "Order your WrE to True Form, Queensway, Stevenage, fire."

We were in attendance at 0256 hrs at the rear of the shop in Market Square, the WrL was sent round to Queensway at the front of the shop.

The fire was amongst some rubbish piled up at the back door and had burnt through into the shop itself.

0259 hrs, Stn O Chandler, "A building of 1 and 3 floors, ground floor heavily smoke logged, 1 jet, 4 BA."

0307 hrs, Stn O Chandler, "Make pumps 3 for BA."

0310 hrs, Hitchin WrL mobile, Sub O Lemm in charge.

0312 hrs, DO Ambrose mobile.

0319 hrs, Stn O Chandler, "Make pumps 5."

0320 hrs, Hitchin WrT mobile, Fm Wickham in charge.

0324 hrs, Old Welwyn WrT mobile, Sub O Kendal in charge.

0325 hrs, Hatfield Control Unit mobile, Sub O Ambler in charge.

0325 hrs, Hatfield ERT mobile, Sub O Kitchener in charge.

Max Bygrave and Barry Hillier were the BA crew working the jet from my pump, in through the back door, and up onto the first floor.

We were losing this fight, from a rubbish fire half an hour ago we now had a serious fire on our hands.

0334 hrs DO Ambrose, "A building of three floors in shopping precinct, 12m x 30m, ground and first floors alight, three jets, 6 BA."

Thick black smoke and flames were punching out of the front and back windows and the next minute Max and Barry came flying out of the door chased out by the intense heat and a molten rubber waterfall of melting rubber boots following them down the stairs!

Slowly we got the upper hand with a "fire surrounded" message sent at 0450 hrs and finally at 0510 hrs the stop message was sent, DO Ambrose "A terrace building of 1, 2 and 3 floors, 40m x 12m, used as a shoe shop, ground and 1st floor and part of 2nd floor severely damaged by fire, five jets, 10 BA, 'D' delta, FPO required."

However, the biggest disaster was that the Canteen Van from Hemel Hempstead blew a gasket enroute and didn't arrive with the tea and burgers until gone 0600 hrs!

230 and 231 returned to station at 0643 hrs for a well-deserved breakfast and a tidy up.

What a night that was.

The Stevenage Comet of the 17th September said that fire chief, Ronald Ambrose, who was in charge of the operation said, "There was a possible connection between the three fires, which were all of doubtful origin." He explained that, "because of the stock, there was a lot of toxic fumes and dense black smoke, and flames were coming out of the first floor level to five or six feet up. It took an hour and thirty minutes to get it under control – it's a long time since I've seen a fire as intense in that type of building. It is fair to say it was the most severe fire we've had in the town centre."

One of the bonuses of a two pump station is that there is more scope for sport. We would always have at least eight firemen on duty and sometimes twelve. Volleyball was the game of choice but only if the weather was clement. At the end of the day shift after all the routines were done or at the beginning of a night shift before drill, on would go the trainers and up went the net. The only rule was in and out and that was debatable.

Otherwise pretty much anything was acceptable. We had a few injuries but more of that later.

If it was raining we would play football or hockey in the bays, same rules applied. Again, injuries were not uncommon; I remember that whilst playing in the bays at Welwyn Garden City Vince Mazio suffered a bad injury when he put his arm through the window in the bay door.

1981. AN ARRESTING SIGHT.

Early in 1981 on Sunday the 18th January we managed to annoy the Chief Officer.

It was a night shift, the previous evening, the 17th, and after a fairly uneventful evening I was enjoying a night's sleep.

A mile or so away at the Old Bury, Rectory Lane, Stevenage the owner was doing exactly the same, unaware that a fire had started in one of his barns. Just before four a.m on the Sunday morning he was woken by the sound of wood crackling, he told the *Stevenage Comet* (Wednesday, 21st January) "there was a loud noise – it was the roof going. When I raised the alarm the fire and emergency services were here within minutes."

Back at the fire station the alarm sounded, the lights came on and ten firemen were on their way to his assistance. I was driving the WrL with Sub O Magill in charge and Max, Barry and Malcolm in the back, we followed the WrE out of the bays and onto St Georges Way. Through the town and right onto Rectory Lane, smoke and flames could be seen rising from behind St. Nicholas church up in front of us.

A bit of a hold up, both pumps using two tone horns to clear the way.

On arrival there was a large, old barn well alight, one pump drove up to the barn and got a jet to work, my pump setting into a hydrant and supplying the fireground pump.

Wally made pumps 3, Hitchin were mobilised to help.

The crews set up a curtain spray between the fire and nearby out-houses and a second jet was played onto the fire. Not much else to do now except keep at it, slowly knocking it down.

The fire was under control quite quickly but there was an attendance of at least one appliance at the farm, damping down, all through the rest of Sunday and part of Monday. The barn, sixty bales of straw and hay plus farm tools were all destroyed in the fire.

Continuing with his statement to the *Comet*, the owner went on "There were twenty-five bullocks next to the barn that were running about in panic, and I had to release them into a field. The blaze raged quite fiercely but was brought under control within about fifteen minutes of the firemen's arrival." He went on to say "Their hard work certainly prevented the fire from spreading to nearby out-houses. Tractors in an adjacent barn were also saved. The timber barn was around 150 years old and is irreplaceable. But a similar structure could cost in the region of £10,000."

At that time the Chief Fire Officer Ted Faulkner lived in Rectory Lane and telephoned the station before we went off duty at nine to give Wally a real telling off– "What's the idea of waking me up at four in the morning with all that bloody noise, keep it down next time!"

In February strike action reared its head again with the announcement that our pay formula was to be scrapped and no further wage increase due until 1983! We were due a five point eight per cent rise in April as the second stage of the agreement which settled the 'emergency calls only' dispute last year.

The two-part increase was calculated on a pay formula drawn up after the 1977 strike and now the Government want to scrap it in favour of annual negotiations starting in 1983. Some things don't change.

Here are three other incidents worth relating that took place in the summer of 1981 although I can't remember all the details.

We went to a pig farm in Ardeley on a make-up where there was the report of a barn on fire. The barn contained pigs and was severely damaged in the fire. Despite our best efforts we lost 300 pigs. The pigs nearest the seat of the fire were reduced to nothing and the further away they were the less burnt they were. A vet was on site with a rifle shooting those still alive but in a terrible state and running around the yard.

On Wednesday 3rd June the headline in the paper read –

"AM I ALIVE?" ASKS WOMAN RUN OVER AT TOWN STATION.

The previous Monday we had turned out at around 2100 hrs to a report of a person under a train at the railway station in Lytton Way.

Apparently the thirty-year-old woman had jumped in front of the high speed train as it pulled into the station to make a scheduled stop. However, she fell between the rails and although the first four carriages passed over her she escaped without injury. She looked up at one of her rescuers and asked "Am I alive?" to which he replied, "Well I am so you must be."

She was taken to hospital suffering from shock and was detained in the psychiatric unit.

Another job one evening, involved a man trapped in a culvert in Fairlands Valley Park. There was a storm drain into which a man had crawled and which terminated in a small chamber with access to the outside at shoulder level and ground level in the park. Across this outlet was a scaffolding bar to prevent people getting in (and indeed out). Our man had tried to climb out through the hole and got stuck, trapped between the pole and the wall of the culvert. Barry Hillier and I were the lucky ones and took a hacksaw and some lighting with us into the storm drain and through to the chamber and began to cut through the scaffolding pole. What makes this job memorable is that a policewoman turned up outside the chamber and squatted down to reassure the casualty. She was wearing a skirt, stockings and suspenders and the whole thing was illuminated in our lamp, it took us ages to cut that pole, "no hurry lads," whispered our trapped but smiling casualty.

Sunday 2nd August and a trio of lizards had us rushing to a house in Grace Way, Stevenage.

The three reptiles, Squirt, Ziggy and Tix had been left in the kitchen while the owner and her sister had lunch, but when they returned only two were visible. Squirt, a female iguana had found a vent behind the tumble dryer and decided to investigate the cavity wall.

Guided by some scratching we made a small hole in the wall and luckily for us the lizard's tail was hanging there. Also in attendance was a reptile expert and she looped a snake stick around its tail to keep it still while we made a second hole a foot or so higher up. After a long operation Skewer Head finally recovered the lizard and held her on his chest. "Is it dangerous?" asked Nobber, "No" was the reply and as if on cue Squirt climbed up The One's tunic and sank its claw into his ear lobe, latching on and drawing blood. There stood Ron with what looked like a large, reptilian, bling earring hanging from his ear, he had a way with animals!

Sometime in 1980 I had managed to get a brigade house through the Council essential workers' scheme and had moved into Austen Paths, Stevenage with Lorraine. Around the middle of 1981 I went on nights and forgot my sandwiches which she duly brought to the station.

In the morning I went home and she had gone and I only ever saw her once more some months later.

Still I had some good nights out with Nobber at the 'grab a granny' night at the Grampian Hotel in Stevenage.

During this time we really had a great Watch.

The Guv, Wally Chandler, was old school, he didn't do anything he didn't have to, he gave me a really bad report one year that got me a stern talking to from the DC Ron Ambrose. Another thing about Wally was that whatever time of night we got a fire call he always managed to have a roll-up going by the time he got on the pump. His other party piece was to set a fire in the smoke house and put a few handfuls of magnesium swarf in the cradle with the burning wood so that when we hit the fire with a jet of water the magnesium would react with the water and explode!

The Sub was Dave "Budget" Magill who was always carrying around his treasurer's briefcase like the Chancellor of the Exchequer.

John Miles, the leading hand, also known as the Silver Fox or One Note I liked a lot although he could be a miserable bugger and would often have a cob on. Having said that, he had a great sense of humour. Every morning he would spend ages in the washroom splashing water about, if asked where he was the reply would be in the bird bath.

Eddie, or "Taddie", Baker had transferred in from York where he was based at Tadcaster, and was at the York Minster fire or so he told us, in fact he seems to have been to every type of fire ever invented.

Mick Barnaby was a funny bloke. I remember we had a fancy dress disco at the station and he came as Bob Marley. During the evening I was standing next to him in the toilet, his get up was perfect he had even blacked his cock!

Max Bygrave was good fun and a keen footballer, he played in goal for local sides and the brigade and we had some good games over the years. He went on to be promoted way up the ladder.

Ian Clinton wasn't on the watch long but he lived up in Cambridgeshire and we often shared lifts to work. Ian was promoted and left us in June. He came back some years later as our Station Officer.

Malcolm Currie was a strange one, going under the name of "Tiger Lily" and always had a couple of bags of nuts in his shirt pockets on which he constantly snacked.

"Poodle" Ellis was a bit of a union man and would regularly argue the toss. Poodle because his hair resembled that of a newly groomed dog of a certain breed. During a water fight he ran up on to the mess deck with a bucket of water where Wally was sitting reading the paper, "Not on the mess deck Robbie," said Wally without looking up, a confused look crossed Robbie's face and bosh, Wally got the bucket full. A drenched Wally went home to change and we didn't see him again for a couple of hours!

Another good story is that Poodle was out at a fire over Hatfield way, at a place called Tyttenhanger Green. He asked Control for directions to the incident and when asked for his location to be spelt phonetically he took a deep breath and started his reply: - "T… err… tango… india. No… I… NO… yankee… errr… tango, tango… hold on… erm… err… no, echo! Errr… HANG ON I'LL MOVE!"

Baz Hillier was my regular snooker doubles partner and could cheat with an astounding finesse. I went to Greece on holiday once and told him that everyone there was called Spiros, from that day we would both refer to each other as Spiros. He had a huge beard when I joined the Watch presumably a knock on from his Navy days where he was a submariner.

Nobber, I have mentioned earlier. One afternoon we were coming back to the station and as we came down one side of the dual carriageway he saw his car driving up the other side, we gave chase and got it back, but the thief ran off!

One last thing before we leave 1981 and we are not even on duty but it just has to be mentioned.

The *Comet* ran the following headline on December 2nd.

FIREMAN STARTS BLAZE AT FARM

John Miles is working on his car at Aston Park Farm, Stringers Lane, Aston where he also keeps his daughter's horse.

He said, "I was working on a car I was doing up, when I switched on, fuel came out of the exhaust and set the baled straw alight. I've been to a lot of fires but never one of my own".

In desperation he tried to fight the fire but had to admit defeat and call out the fire brigade. Two pumps from Green Watch Stevenage and one from Hertford attended the fire and no doubt had a great time taking the piss. To make matters worse Don Huddle (driving instructor) kept horses and other stuff at the farm.

John's car, a horse box owned by Don and straw and hay owned by both of them was destroyed and the barn was gutted causing hundreds of pounds worth of damage.

As you can imagine this kept us amused for years and John and Don never spoke again.

1982. A BRUSH WITH DEATH.

It was around this time that I met a pretty, young ambulance woman who was also stationed at Stevenage. My first date with Patsy was at a school in Letchworth for a Country and Western night with Nobber and Mick Barnaby.

We got together and married in 1984.

At work on Friday 26th February 1982 and we are sitting down for an afternoon cuppa and looking forward to a game of volleyball before going off duty. I am sitting facing the windows overlooking St Georges Way and along Monkswood Way when something in the distance catches my eye. I get up from the table and go to the window. Over towards the Hertford road there is a huge pall of smoke rising from behind all the buildings and trees between the fire station and whatever was on fire. I turn to the table and say, "I think we should get rigged we'll be going out in a minute" and start to cross the mess deck to the stairs amid shouts of "sit down" and "bollocks".

BEEP BEEP BEEP "Fire call, fire call, order both appliances to Shephall Manor School, Shephallbury Park, Stevenage, school on fire."

I am on the WrE, BA with Spiros Hillier.

1608 hrs. 230 mobile, Stn O Chandler in charge, 4 riders.

1608 hrs. 231 mobile, L/Fm Miles in charge, 5 riders.

1608 hrs, 321 mobile, Sub O Dolan in charge, 4 riders.

1608 hrs, 114 (HP) mobile, Fm Burden in charge, 2 riders.

Three minutes later we are pulling up in front of the school, the Stn O wants a guide line laid out from outside up to the upper floors. As we start that and lay out a hose line, the Stn O sends "make pumps 4."

1613 hrs, 310 mobile, Stn O Lill in charge, 4 riders.

As the fire was venting through the roof we were laying the guide line for no real benefit and so we dropped it, donned our BA, and worked our hose line up to the second floor. It now became apparent that the school caretaker and possibly a couple of children were unaccounted for and as we started to attack the fire other teams began a systematic search of the upper floors while the police searched the ground floor and surrounding area.

1616 hrs, ADO Gibson sends, "make pumps 5 persons reported."

1617 hrs, 201 mobile, L/Fm Smith in charge, 4 riders.

1619 hrs, 185 mobile, L/Fm New in charge, 2 riders.

1620 hrs, OC mobile, Sub O Ambler in charge, 6 riders.
On the second floor the area on fire, a workroom, was well alight and the heat was intense. We got into cover behind a wall and directed our jet through a door and onto the fire. Outside we could hear St Albans HP setting up and suddenly Wally Chandler appeared, "come on you two,

---

move up" and he pushes us right up to the door, "bloody hell that's hot" he says and disappears. Barry and I move back again. Spiros grabs my arm and points up to the ceiling where a crack has appeared and is widening as it moves along the ceiling towards us. Barry indicates to me to drop the hose and we move quickly in the opposite direction.

Within seconds there is an almighty crash and the roof collapses into the second floor and we are showered with debris and a huge lead water tank is left suspended above us caught up in the timbers of what is left of the roof. We manage to recover the hose and continue to fight the fire and a short time later we are relieved by another BA crew just as my DSU (alarm) operates. Spiros and I go back outside and change our BA cylinders ready for another go.

ADO Gibson had sent an informative message at 1626 hrs "A large country mansion of 3 floors used as a residential school. Fifty per cent of roof well alight, rest of building heavily smoke logged. 2 children unaccounted for, 2 jets, 6BA."

Barry and I went back in after a break to relieve the other BA crew again.

This time we faced a different but equally dangerous foe. We started to press forward once more but, unbeknown to us, another BA crew was coming up a different set of stairs in front of us. It was Tiger Lily and he opened up his jet and knocked my helmet clean off my head, great stuff. I give Malc a blast for good measure.

ACO Burke, the new incident commander sends "4 additional pumps required for BA."

1705 hrs, 240 mobile, L/Fm Franklin in charge, 4 riders.
1705 hrs, 311 mobile, Sub O Clark in charge, 4 riders.
1705 hrs, 300 mobile, L/Fm Cotton in charge, 5 riders.
1705 hrs, 190 mobile, Sub O Sheppey in charge, 4 riders.
1801 hrs, SI mobile, L/Fm Patmore in charge, 2 riders.

Firefighting continued until we were relieved by our Blue Watch at 1830 hrs, the stop message being sent at 1837 hrs.

ACO Burke "A building of 2 and 3 floors, 45m x 35m, top floor severely damaged by fire, remainder of building by heat, smoke and water, 6 jets, 10 BA, 3 HRJ in use, all persons accounted for."

Shephallbury Manor Fire.
Picture Archant Newspapers

Back at station we cleaned up and got off home.
Pumps were on site all through the night damping down and carrying out salvage work.

Back on duty the following morning Wally and a crew went out to relieve Blue Watch, Sub O Milton and 231 at 0905 hrs.

At 1158 hrs Budget Magill and a crew of four relieved them and finally 231 went out again at 1427 hrs and at 1618 hrs Stn O Chandler sent the message "All cool no further visits."

An entire wing of the Victorian building housing the school was pretty much gutted and the damage is estimated at £500,000.

This fire was the fifth to occur in a school in the town in the past few months and the police launched an investigation drafting in officers from all over the county to assist.

One last thing as I've just mentioned Alan Patmore, from Hitchin, he was on the salvage tender, remember? A big man, and it has to be said somewhat overweight. Years later the brigade had a crackdown on some of our larger members and they were taken off the run while their fitness and health was assessed.

I was at fire brigade headquarters for some reason and went up to the third floor and there was Alan... and the conversation went as follows: -

Sid: "Hello Alan how's things?"

Alan: "OK thanks Sid, you?"

Sid: "Fine thanks, what are you doing here?"

Alan: "Oh I'm the floor warden."

Sid: "What's that all about?"

Alan: "Well it's my job to make sure there are no more than two of us fat bastards on the same floor at any one time!"

A rainy night and Wally devised a drill/race between the two crews in the bays. The idea was to get from one end of the bays to the other, using only the equipment on the appliances and with no one touching the floor. Great let's have a bet, a pint of beer to the winners.

Five minutes to make a plan and off we went. The WrL crew set off in a flurry of activity, building platforms out of boxes and crossing gaps with ladders while the WrE crew watched with admiration. Just before they could put in their final piece of equipment in place and finish the course we got the salvage sheet off our pump, unfolded it and laid it on the floor and walked across to victory! Upstairs to claim our reward.

Wednesday 17th March was Robbie's last duty shift with us before he transferred to Worthing fire station, West Sussex Fire Brigade. With a few bank holidays to take he left on 30th March. We all went down to the Old Town for his farewell drink. A good few beers later and Robbie was handcuffed to a street sign post with his trousers round his ankles. Amidst all the merriment a police car pulled up and the officers asked to see some form of ID, someone had the foresight to explain it was a fire brigade night out, they thought about it, looked at each other, shrugged, said "oh" and drove off!

By May our AEC WrE the "Fighting 105" (UUR 105K) was placed into the reserve fleet and we took delivery of a new Dennis RS series WrE (SPM 139X).

In June the county was ravaged by fierce storms that kept us busy for a few days. On Saturday the 5th we were called out to Marymead Drive, where two houses had been struck by lightning. Around 1930 hrs the chimney on one of the houses took the full impact of the strike, shattering it and causing bricks to fall into both gardens. Four holes were ripped in the roof dislodging slates and damaging a roof beam. Next door the family car was hit by falling roof tiles and the whole house shook, "it was like a bomb going off and I was very frightened when we saw the chimney fall past the window." Television sets in both houses went up in smoke and the electricity supply was affected. We attended to make both properties safe.

After Robbie left, the Watch only had ten men and so we needed a bit of fresh blood. This came in form of two new arrivals. Firstly, Ian "Soapy" McCarthy who I think had been off sick from Red Watch and came back to work with us prior to going back to his watch (but I could be wrong). Secondly a new recruit from Training School, Dave Rees. Dave fitted in with the Watch straight away and over the years we became good friends. He joined us having had to lose weight to get into training school and when he arrived he cut a sylph-like figure. However, after some huge breakfasts and dinners, a whole French stick at break time and a few beers in the evening it wasn't long before he was back to his pre-service self and earned himself the nickname of the "Stomach" or "Stum Bob".

Both he and Ian started on our second day shift, Monday 5th July.

And it was ten days later that they were both on duty on the night of Wednesday 15th July.

At 0620 hrs the following morning a police patrol car was driving along Six Hills Way, Stevenage.

Another night's sleep is about to be rudely interrupted.

0625 hrs, BEEP, BEEP, BEEP "Order both appliances to St. Nicholas School, Six Hills Way, Stevenage, school on fire."

230 with Stn O Chandler, 231 with L/Fm Miles and Hitchin's pump mobile to incident.

When we got there there wasn't much to see, some smoke coming from the front door and the windows. Two BA crews were sent in with two jets supplied from the WrE via a hydrant. Inside the hall there was zero visibility, thick black smoke and it was very hot.

Here my recollections differ from the records. I am down in the rota book as driving the WrL but am sure it was this fire where Fm Hillier and I were in BA. We worked our jet in under the stage which served as a storage area containing amongst other things a large number of physical training mats that were smouldering and giving off huge amounts of black smoke.

The fire was under control in about an hour but there were a lot of hot spots to get at and we were cutting away and damping down until we were relieved by the oncoming watch.

The school hall, which the night before had been the venue for the school end of term concert, and the dining room were completely destroyed, the hall was a jumble of blackened child sized chairs standing in pools of water. The windows were blown out; the stage had been half consumed in the fire, burnt out spot lights and the charred remains of curtains hung from the ceiling.

It was a great setting for a watch photograph!

This was now the sixth school fire in the town in a year although this one was not suspicious and was later put down to an electrical fault, causing £30,000 worth of damage.

St. Nicholas School fire: Back L-R: Mick Barnaby, Barry Hillier, Dave Rees, Ian McCarthy. Front L-R: Max Bygrave, John Miles, and Me.

Picture: HFRS

On Sunday 24th we went over to Hemel Hempstead on relief for a fifteen pump school fire.

At the fire at Adeyfield School, fifteen fire engines and over eighty firemen needed over four hours to extinguish the blaze. Five firemen were injured during the incident, none seriously.

We were on nights on 13th December, the following morning at 0621 hrs …

"Order both appliances to Stevenage Railway Station, Lytton Way, Stevenage, person trapped under train."

230 with Stn O Chandler with a crew of 5, mobile to incident.

231 with Sub O Magill with a crew of 4, mobile to incident.

185 with a crew of 2, mobile to incident.

After an initial assessment on the platform, the Stn O asked for some equipment via the packset radio. Back in the car park we got hold of a trolley and loaded it up with Porto Power, wooden blocks and the hearth kit.

On the platform the casualty was trapped between the running board of the train's last carriage and the platform, he was conscious but very quiet and in shock. Around fifty or sixty people were asked to get off of the train to lighten the load. We tried to ease the pressure on the casualty using our Porto Power but it really wasn't up to the task and we needed to wait for the arrival of the ERT with its more powerful jacking equipment. Using their air bags and Porto Power we managed to tilt the train by about six inches and cutting through and removing a part of the running board the casualty was released after just over an hour at 0738 hrs.

He had a very severe, round, "platform shaped" laceration to his waist/buttocks and needed internal stiches.

It is thought he was running for the train when he slipped on ice.

1983. "I'D LIKE TO REPORT AN ACCIDENT".

As far as I remember each of the four wholetime, two pump stations had a WrE and a couple of spare WrEs made up the fleet. There were also a number of independent escape ladders. The CFO swore by them and wouldn't let them go.

Someone had the bright idea of getting all these appliances together to see which ladders fitted which appliances. And so on 21st January 1983 the *Great Gathering of Escapes* took place at St Albans fire station.

The great gathering of escapes.

It all started off Okay but gradually descended into chaos. Escape ladders were taken off appliances and are tried on others. The trouble was after half an hour or so as the escapes weren't numbered no one knew which ladder came from which fire engine and all the mountings are slightly different. It was an unbelievable farce, the firemen having great fun and the officers getting more desperate by the minute. Eventually the status quo was restored and everyone went away happy.

Lots of fires through the year but nothing much to report. Usual stuff, car fires, children locked in bathrooms, oil spillages and floodings. On Thursday 25th August we were called to a grass fire on the A1(M) motorway followed by another one at the Oval and, while returning from an AFA, a third grass fire in Fairlands Valley.

October 1983 was a busy time for a number of different reasons.

In the early hours of 6th, Dave Rees and I wearing BA joined firemen from Hitchin and Baldock in fighting the biggest town centre blaze to break out in Hitchin for years. Garages, workshops and locally parked cars all went up in smoke in a fire that raged for several hours in Bancroft.

We took our break, courtesy of a well-known pie maker in Bancroft who made us tea. I declined the offer of a pie after watching a lad with his tattooed arms buried up to the elbows in a huge basin of white mincemeat.

15th October and Tiger Lil's finest moment. We were called to Photo Trade Processing in Argyle Way, Stevenage where one of the processing machines had caught fire. I was driving the WrL and took the pump into the fenced off yard and we had a jet run out into the building with Nobber and Taddie in BA. Wally called for me to get Malc, who was driving the WrE, in to the yard as well to give us his water, I told him this but he drove past the entrance up to the junction. Wally was shouting abuse and pulling at the chain linked fence that separated him from Tiger, undeterred Malcolm then turned left onto the dual carriageway and disappeared from view. He had to go up to the next roundabout and all the way back past the fire before he can turn again to get to Argyle Way. But instead of going to Argyle Way he came back up the dual carriageway with no access back to the fire. Wally ran to intercept him but Lil drove straight past again. I was creased with laughter as Malc drove off up the dual carriageway with Wally running after him making a huge, double handed wanker sign. I love this job.

Later in the month of October my driving leaves a bit to be desired.

We had been called to an AFA at Taylor Instruments in Gunnels Wood Road. I pulled into the car park and the crews set off to locate the problem and check the building.

As per usual I started to turn around to facilitate our exit as soon as the job was resolved. The problem was on this occasion I failed to see the huge lighting pole on my nearside. There was an enormous crash and the pump shuddered to a stop. I got out for a look hoping it wouldn't be too bad. Oooooops, the whole of the cab was damaged, both doors were buckled and unable to open and both steps were broken in two, apart from that I had come off quite light.

Anyway as Wally and a policewoman approached the good side of the appliance, I wound down my window and said "Guv I'd like to report an accident."

The upshot was I got another bollocking and Wally had to ride in the back on the trip back to the station.

A spare appliance was collected from St Albans and all the kit swapped over.

Oh well shit happens!

I was sent, through the internal mail, a drawing of a tank with an escape ladder on! I blamed Hitchin!

Definitely has the stamp of Dick Dolan, the Sub Officer at Hitchin Fire Station.

A great time-saving innovation arrived on stations around now. Plastic hose! This replaced the canvas hose we used previously.

It didn't need drying and after a fire it could be washed and rolled up straight away and re-stowed on the appliance.

Finally, in October, two more firemen left the Watch. Mick Barnaby left on 6th, although I can't remember why, and Max Bygrave on the 13th as he got a promotion to L/fm.

And one joined, Fm Steve "Froggy" Cotton who had his first shift on Thursday day shift, 22nd December.

White Watch, Stevenage, Oct. 1983: Back L-R: Stn O W. Chandler, D. Rees, B. Hillier, M. Barnaby, E. Baker, R. Keep. Front L-R: Me, S. Bygrave, M. Currie, L/Fm J. Miles.

1984. THATCH, LIGHTERS, CHIP PANS & CIGARETTES.

At the beginning of the year, in February, we had a change of Sub Officer, Budget Magill went onto Blue Watch and the Blue Watch Sub Mick Milton came over to us. I can't really recall why but at the back of my mind it had something to do with a fireman from Bishops Stortford arriving on the watch. He was being charged with something. Radiators come to mind (why?). Mick was there to keep him in order.

On the 4th April Fm Pete "Airfix" Dartford (the model fireman) turned up for his first shift. When I first came to Stevenage I had seen Pete over at Baldock where he was a kind of adopted fireman, a station mascot if you will, he had his own uniform and everything. Anyway all that aside, Wally certainly didn't like him and while he was in charge Pete was never going to be promoted. However, as soon Wally retired

Airfix was off and he went on to become the CFO of Staffordshire Fire and Rescue Service so fair play to him, he will finish with a bigger pension than me!

Around April we were playing volleyball and I went up for that delicate little tip over the net. On the other side Tiger Lily jumped and with a big ham fist hit the ball downwards, breaking two of my fingers. "Ouch," said I as I set off around the yard cursing and swearing and screaming with pain.

Anyway Wally got the hump and banned us from playing volleyball. The following day we had a football match, a much safer option.

During the game I floated a lovely cross towards the goal, up went Dave Rees and Malc, both with a view to getting a header on it. There was a sickening thud as their heads clashed and blood spurted everywhere.

Off they went down to the Lister Hospital. Tiger Lily had eight stiches in his head and Stum Bob had two in his.

Wally said, "I suppose it's back to volleyball then."

I didn't go off sick until a week later when I was plumbing in a shower at home and every time I knocked my fingers I would perform the same rite of running around swearing. Thanks Lil.

On Friday 13th April we were called out to a three pump fire in Weston.

The following week the *North Herts Gazette* carried the headline: -

"HEROES OF COTTAGE BLAZE DRAMA"

Weston sits between Stevenage and Baldock and is on Baldock's station ground. The fire was at the unoccupied Culverin Cottage in Fore Street and the thatched roof was on fire.

Three thatchers happened to be working nearby, re-thatching a house and they immediately pitched a ladder to the roof and started to remove the thatch creating a fire break.

With the attendance of the brigade the thatch was removed and dampened down and firefighting was conducted inside the cottage where the ceiling had collapsed and some damage had occurred to the roof timbers.

During April the station had five vehicles on the run. We had our usual Dennis RS series WrE and a new Dennis SS series WrL (A318 NRO) together with a new Bedford TL flatbed lorry (PBH 630W), a new Bedford TL salvage tender (FMJ 797Y) and a Ford utility van (A190 MNM).

The Dennis SS differed from the RS in that it had a tilting cab.

Spiros Hillier had been slow to start driving, and in October the previous year had finally become operational. Here we were a few months later and he was asked to move the WrE. In gets Spiros, does his checks, starts the pump, mirror, mirror, into reverse and I was upstairs in the kitchen when I heard the crash as Baz reversed the WrE straight into the side of the WrL.

Excellent stuff, the only person I can recall to put two appliances into workshops in one go. That's class.

That, however, left us the job of locating two spare pumps from around the brigade and changing over all the equipment.

Towards the end of May, Ron Keep transferred to Hatfield. Shame, I liked Nobber.

24th June, Sunday afternoon …

BEEP, BEEP, BEEP "Order both appliances to Ridlins End, Stevenage, house fire."

I am driving the WrL with Sub O Milton in charge and Fm Hillier and Cotton in the back. WrE with Stn O Chandler in charge with L/Fm Miles, Fm Dartford and Fm Currie.

Prior to our arrival a woman and her son had escaped from the house.

I had never seen a house on fire quite like this; the whole thing was alight with smoke and flames coming out of every door and window.

Two BA crews were committed to the fire with jets while I set into the hydrant supplying the WrE, Fm Currie was the BA Control Officer. The fire was intense and it was some time before the crews could start to move up the stairs and finally extinguish the blaze.

Lots of damping down and salvage work before we could wind up the job.

The fire was started by a five-year-old boy who set fire to a piece of paper with a lighter and from that small start the interior of the house and all the contents were destroyed.

At Stevenage station during week day shifts, we had a cook, Iris and her sister and assistant, Barbara. When Iris retired Barbara was promoted to be the cook. She was good, but to be honest a bit out of her depth, she was also a bit naïve and gullible but would always do anything that was asked of her. I remember her once cooking a big pot of stew and then separating out all the ingredients into different serving bowls! And then there was the time the Mess Manager sent her out shopping and asked if she could pop into the butchers to get two pounds of clitoris. Barbara came back with nearly everything but apologised as the butcher said they were all out of clitoris!

We always invited her for our Christmas lunch and did the cooking and she loved it and always had too much to drink. I liked Barbara.

Barbara's daughter, Carol, often used to come up to the station to help her mum. Carol went on to join the Herts Ambulance Service and rose to the rank of Station Officer.

Big day on 17th July 1984. My old Potters Bar colleague Gary "Biggles" Williamson joined the Watch.

On 25th July we attended a house fire, persons reported at Lonsdale Court, Lonsdale Road, Stevenage.

A sixty-one-year-old man had been overcome by smoke from a chip pan fire and was sitting on a chair outside supplied by a neighbour.

He was confused and semi-conscious and unknown to us had suffered a heart attack. John Miles held his BA mask over the casualty's face and operated the constant flow valve to try and flush some of the smoke out of his lungs, he replied with a cough and then threw up in to John's mask. With the fire extinguished, we made-up and went back to station. The casualty was taken to Lister Hospital where he was said to be critically ill.

And John set to scrubbing his face mask!

Another new member on his first duty day, 5th October and straight from Training School, Fireman Mark Lee.

In the early hours of Saturday 10th November in Angle Ways, Stevenage, a lad has been out celebrating his seventeenth birthday and returned home, eventually. He went to bed and had a last cigarette. His mother said on Monday "he had come in awfully late, and was not quite awake. The fire burned his bed and he's got a nasty burn on his elbow."

The seventeen-year-old had set fire to his bed and thought he had put out the fire, opened a window to clear the smoke and went downstairs. The smell of burning woke his parents who got their three other children to safety as we turned up at the address.

I was wearing BA with Steve Cotton and the fire was extinguished using a hosereel. The bedroom was severely damaged by fire and the rest of the house by heat and smoke.

The occupier went on to say "My first thought was that he was in there, it was terrifying. It's not the fact that it happened, it's the thought of what could have happened."

Not long after nine a.m. on November 30th, a mum is setting off from her Canterbury Way home with her two kids on the school run. On their way to the St John Southworth School in Bedwell Crescent they turn into Verity Way. Heading in the opposite direction is a Green Line single decker bus......

We are still in the bay's checking the appliances when…

BEEP, BEEP, BEEP "Order your WrL to Verity Way, Stevenage, RTA person's trapped."

231 mobile to Verity Way with Sub O Milton in charge.

Fm Williamson is driving with myself, Fm Baker and Dartford in the back.

A Renault 5 has been in collision with a single decker bus and a Vauxhall Cavalier. Two children have been rescued from the car by passers-by and a woman is trapped in the wreckage of the car. A hosereel is run out in case of fire and the vehicle is stabilised using wooden blocks (chocks). Stn O Chandler arrives in the station van.

Inside the car the steering column had been forced down in between the front seats and the woman driver, who was conscious throughout, had been pushed to the right, against the door. We get to work to release the casualty by opening the driver's door using Porto Power and the "A" posts are cut to allow the roof to be bent back to give us access to the car interior. The driver is removed on a spinal board and transferred to the ambulance.

We make up and clean up the debris on the road.

The *Stevenage Comet* for Wednesday December 6th ran the headline:

CHILDREN HURT IN NIGHTMARE ON WAY TO
SCHOOL.
MUM IS TRAPPED IN CRASH HORROR.

The family was taken to the Lister Hospital where the driver has an operation to put a steel pin in her elbow and has stitches in her forehead, arm and leg. Her four-year-old son has forty stitches in his forehead and his six-year-old sister has a cut forehead stitched, a grazed leg and an injured back.

Normally the Stn O rides the WrE as this appliance, with the escape ladder, is deemed to be the rescue pump, if we get a call to an RTA the Stn O would swap with the Sub O as the WrL carried the hydraulic rescue equipment. On this occasion Mick Milton shot out quickly not giving Wally a chance to get to the bays in time, which is why Wally arrived in the van.

Our watch used to have sweets and chocolate bars for sale and at some point I took this job over. It was called the "Nutty Locker" and I turned it into a bit of a business. I had a contact who worked for a confectionary company, and managed to get boxes of crisps and other tasty, savoury treats. At one point I was supplying our Social Club, several other stations' Social Clubs as well as a few local pubs. I had a special jar full of gob stoppers but labelled "COB STOPPERS – FREE TO THE NEEDY" and when anyone had a cob on out would come the jar, the usual recipient being the Silver Fox Miles.

While on the subject of food, each Watch had a Mess Manager who would be responsible for organising the meals and collecting the mess money and the tea boat, at the time ours was Max. Some of the lads would eat an enormous breakfast but a few of us only had toast. When Max put the tea money up, we rebelled and formed a breakaway group, called the "Tea and Toast Boat Union" the T.T.B.U. and adopted the Robertson's Golly fireman as our badge. We each had a membership card with an enamel Golly badge. We kept the tea money the same to prove our point and the four of us, me, Taddie, Tiger Lily and Spiros enjoyed various teas, nice uncut loaves of bread and even whisky marmalade. Grown men!

TTBU membership card.

1985. LET'S WET THE BABY'S HEAD.

I think around the beginning of the year we had the new teleprinter system installed in the Watchroom. From now on as well as the voice over the tannoy we would also be able to read a printout which told us the address and map reference (as per the Hertfordshire Street Atlas), which appliance was to attend and the type of incident.

January and February were bitterly cold.

People go away for Christmas and the New Year, turn off their central heating and if they haven't lagged their water pipes they will freeze. As the water turns to ice it expands and splits the copper pipe and subsequently as the temperature warms up, it thaws out again and the water escapes from the pipe causing a flood.

We had a busy day on Friday 18th January. In Fairview Road, Stevenage a pipe had burst in the loft of a house causing damage to the bedroom, landing, stairway and kitchen and also ruined carpets.

Later the same day a young couple came home to their three storey block of flats in William Place. Their ground floor flat was flooded, a pipe had burst in the loft and the water had run down through the two higher unoccupied flats damaging all three.

The following month gallons of water flooded an empty house in the grounds of Mary Barclay House old people's home in Hitchin Road, two neighbouring flats in Wisden Road were flooded to a depth of three inches and lifts in the town's multi-storey car park were out of action due to burst pipes.

White Watch, Stevenage, Feb. 1985: Back L-R: L/Fm J. Miles, D. Rees, E. Baker, M. Lee, G. Williamson, Sub O M. Milton, B. Hillier. Front L-R: P. Dartford, S. Cotton, Stn O W. Chandler, M. Currie, Me.

It's lunchtime on 23rd April 1985 and a drama is unfolding at The Roebuck shops in Broadwater Crescent. *The Stevenage Gazette* of the 26th reported on the incident.

A twenty-year-old Hitchin man is confronting his seventeen-year-old ex-girlfriend.

He drags her, screaming, at knifepoint, to the back of the precinct, an eye-witness said "he had the girl on her knees and he was standing behind her with a knife at her throat." A have-a-go hero stepped in to help and the assailant lashed out at him with his knife, slashing his jacket sleeve. When he was told that the police have been called, he dropped his weapon, got into his red Datsun car and drove off hitting two parked cars and a wall. He drove from the scene at speed pursued by the have-a-go hero in his car. A police patrol car arrived at the Roebuck shops and joined the pursuit.

The high speed chase heads out on the Hertford Road past Bragbury End and as the twenty-year-old takes a bend on the wrong side of the road he careers in to the path of an oncoming twenty-four-ton Volvo ballast lorry…

BEEP, BEEP, BEEP "Order your WrL to Bragbury End, Stevenage, RTA persons trapped."

Down to the Watchroom to pick up the sheet from the teleprinter.

Stn O Chandler, Fm Rees, driving and Fm Cotton, Lee and Payne in the back.

Also mobile is the ERT from Hatfield with two riders and DO Alan Wallace.

On arrival it appears that a lorry has hit trees by the side of the road but on further inspection there is a car between the front of the lorry and the trees.

The wheelbase of the Datsun can only be a metre or so long from bumper to bumper.

Ten or fifteen metres behind the lorry is the impact point with no skid marks visible from either vehicle prior to impact; in the road is the car's passenger-side door.

The lorry has then braked and pushed the car the ten or so metres into the trees.

The only part of the driver that can be seen is his right arm which is visible through the driver's door window.

We are faced with an almost impossible task to free the trapped man.

The lorry is winched back a few metres to reveal the front of the car which is crushed beyond any recognition

A doctor on scene declares the driver to be deceased.

We slowly start to cut and prise apart the wreckage of the car until finally after an hour or so we can peel back the front of the bodywork and parts of the engine to reveal the interior and the casualty therein.

He and the wreckage are pretty much indistinguishable and after some more cutting away we can at last remove the body from the vehicle.

He is transferred to the Lister Hospital by undertaker's hearse.

The road is closed for most of the afternoon as the police carry out their investigations.

At the beginning of May I had to report to the DC, Ron Ambrose, for some review or other and Wally had given me a bad report for a reason that escapes me now.

Anyway I duly went in my undress uniform and took my bollocking like a man, the DC wasn't a man to argue with.

"Payne, you're dismissed," he barked.

As I went to leave he said, "Sid, come here", I went back to his desk, "I hear you've just had a baby",

"Yes, sir" said I.

"Well let's wet the baby's head then!" He got us a couple of cups of tea and we drank Gary's health. As I left he said "My regards to Patsy."

A proper fireman was Ron Ambrose, who, I think knew his men, and you knew where you stood with him, he never seemed to bear a grudge, once he'd had his say it was all forgotten.

On Thursday 4th July at 1735 hrs the brigade received a call to Printar Industries, Mead Lane, Hertford where the lagging around a 10,000-gallon bitumen tank had caught fire. The fire spread to a further seven tanks.

Four pumps from Hertford, Ware and Hoddesdon attendedand at 1740 hrs the assistance message "foam required" was sent.

One minute later the bells went down at the station requesting G4 and 231 to mobilise.

The foam is stored in twenty-two litre cans and has to be loaded onto the lorry whenever needed along with the firefighting equipment, an FB10 and round the pump proportioner and the FB KR4-33 and in-line foam inductor.

At 1750 hrs 231 is mobile to standby at Hertford station and G4 is mobile to the incident at 1751 hrs arriving at the fire at 1806 hrs.

Fire crews worked in shifts spraying the tanks with cooling water all through the night the last appliance leaving the scene at 0900 hrs on Friday morning.

Around this time something very strange happened during a day shift.

We were all out playing volleyball when, from the direction of the station, Wally Chandler was heading our way. He was wearing a pair of shorts and trainers and looked as if he was coming to join us for a game, a previously unknown event. Anyway he came on to the court, struck a pose, and the ball was served. As we played around him he reached into his pocket, pulled out his baccy tin and rolled a cigarette… "Well, that's enough of that" he said and lit up as he slowly walked back to the station!

Presumably for a shower.

At a meeting of the Herts County Council's Fire and Public Protection Committee on Tuesday 24th September they decided to spend a bit of money! At the end of the year the station was to receive a new appliance, a £170,000 Dennis/Simon Snorkel hydraulic platform. To this end all the drivers on the station had to be taught how to drive and operate the vehicle. The Green Watch Sub O Trevor Evans and driving school's Don Huddle were trained to be HP Instructors and took us out over the next few weeks to train at various locations. We used the HP from St Albans and had it on the run at Stevenage for the duration of the training.

On one of the first outings with Don, I managed to rotate the booms before raising them and wiped the blue lights clean off of the roof. It must have happened before as he had a car boot full of spares!

A further £15,000 was to be spent converting the brigade workshop at the back of the station into a bay to house the HP.

In September I bought my own fire engine, a 1941 Austin K2 hosereel tender (GLE 441). It was built for war-time service with the National Fire Service and stationed at Padstow in Cornwall.

I picked it up from Cranfield airfield in Bedfordshire and started the drive back to Codicote. Unfortunately, the core plugs in the engine had rusted out and I had to call at random houses every few miles to top up with water!

Around September/October time we received a new fire helmet to replace our cork Cromwell one. As before the helmet was manufactured locally in Wheathampstead. The Firepro helmet kept the traditional shape but was made of Kevlar, a hard plastic/composite material.

White Watch, Stevenage, end 1985: Back, L-R: Me, S. Cotton, P. Dartford, M. Lee, M. Currie, Stn O J. Story, L/Fm J. Miles, Front, L-R: D. Rees, G. Williamson, E. Baker, B. Hillier.

At the end of the year our guv Wally Chandler retired and had his retirement do in the bar at the station.

He was replaced by Stn O John Story, another good guv to work with.

On 4th October at 0200 hrs we went to a make-up at Wymondley Hall Farm, Little Wymondley. High winds whipped up the flames as we battled through the night to bring the blaze under control. By the morning a 400-year-old tithe barn was reduced to a smouldering ruin in the fire, which also severely damaged other farm buildings as well as animal feed and straw. The total damage was put at £30,000.

Police have launched a major investigation into ten mysterious farm fires in North Hertfordshire during the past year, costing the farming community nearly £80,000.

We were sitting round the table on the Mess Deck having a cup of tea when something came in. It was dressed in a brown suede leather jacket, tight trousers, shiny winkle picker shoes and what appeared to be a huge quiff on his head.

Some of the older members drew an intake of breath, accompanied by mutterings of "bloody hell" and "what is it?"

It spoke, "Hi, I'm your new recruit." it said.

That was our introduction to Fm Chris Strickland who started his career on 5th January 1986 with us on White Watch, Stevenage and went on to be the DCO of Cambridgeshire Fire and Rescue Service. Initial impression aside, a nice man.

Quite clearly without my input, neither he, nor Pete Dartford, would have amounted to anything!

The Rota Book.

This is an extremely important book in which the lucky incumbent records who does what on each shift. In this way everyone gets a go at driving or wearing BA etc. On top of the operational duties he also records kitchen duties, Watchroom duties and petrol man. Also if a fireman goes out on standby it goes in the book.

When I joined the Watch, Spiros ran the book and if you watched closely you could see that if there were any unwanted jobs to do such as exercises, L/Fm's drills or fire safety visits Spiros only did enough to get by. So when he gave up the book I grabbed it.

Strangely if you look in the back there are some more outlandish rotas, for example: -

The Taller than five feet two-inch rota.

Zippy's Sulk rota.

The Reversing the Escape into the Water Tender Ladder rota.

The Keeping Secrets rota.
The Cob and Depression rota.
The Happy rota.
Guvvy's Bad Book rota.
This one courtesy of another watch: -
The Wanker rota.
All Watch members – Number of riders = number of wankers.
And my favourite –
The Cripple rota:
Guvvy – bugleoctomy. Fm Keep – ankles x 3 and nits x 1000.
Sub O – zit, wrists and big toe. Fm Baker – legs and ankles x 2.
Fm Payne – digits x 2 and glands. Fm Hillier – knee and old age.
Fm Rees – head (stitches x 2) and ear.
Fm Currie – head (stitches x 8), ankle, knee and nasty stubbed toe.

On 10th November I took my HrT on duty with me and parked it in the bays.

During the day we got a call to a rubbish fire and we all got on the HrT and almost turned out but thought better of it.

GLE 441 at Stevenage.

1986. A BIG, NEW, SHINY TOY TO PLAY WITH.

On the 5th February at 1532 hrs…

> "Order both appliances to, Sayers Way, Knebworth, explosion."
>
> Knebworth is a village a couple of miles from Stevenage and an eight or ten minute drive.
>
> I am driving the WrE and as you go into Knebworth, the road does a dog-leg under the railway bridge, on this occasion I misjudged it and removed the nearside wing mirror on the bridge wall and made John Story jump!
>
> The detached house has a single storey extension on the front, and it is this that is on fire.
>
> Two BA crews with hosereels enter the property and extinguish the fire.
>
> Outside an ambulance is requested for a sixteen-year-old girl suffering from minor injuries. She was sitting in the room when the log-burning stove blew up in her face. The force of the blast lifted the roof of the extension and destroyed all its contents; the girl did well to escape without serious injury.
>
> The stop message is sent by Stn O Story "A private detached house, ground floor extension 6m x 4m severely damaged by fire and explosion, 4 BA, 2 HRJ in use."
>
> The structure is made safe and we head back to the station.

By March all the drivers had been trained to drive and operate the new hydraulic platform, and the non-drivers trained to operate the cage. Our new appliance is finally on the run, it is a Dennis/Simon Snorkel hydraulic platform (C342 WHA).

New HP at Stevenage, March 1986.

It is the third HP in the brigade and will cover the north of the county, the others being based at Watford and St Albans. It can reach to a height of thirty metres/100 feet and can be used for rescue or as a fire fighting platform.

It is, what we call alternate manned, which means that in the event of a call out it is crewed by two of the WrL crew.

A fire in Walkern gets Chris Strickland his nickname. We have been called to a chimney on fire in a row of cottages, WrE mobile with Sub Officer Milton in charge with Roy, Chris and me.

At the house we start to attack the fire as per usual with the chimney rods from the hearth. The rods are connected and extended up into the chimney, water being applied via a stirrup pump and bucket to a nozzle at the top (where the brush would be on a chimney sweeps rod).

However, luck is not with us and the fire won't go out.

Back outside we pitch the escape ladder to the ridge of the roof and send the sprog, Chris, aloft with a hosereel to try and get at the fire from the top of the chimney.

Chris identifies the pot above the fire and Mick gets him to put a little bit of water down the chimney. When it gets to the hearth it should start to cool as the fire goes out. But no water is coming down. Chris gives it another squirt, then another and then another. Nothing so Chris gives it a blast.

The problem is that he has assumed the pot with the smoke coming out is the one on fire, not considering that the next door neighbour could also have a fire alight.

The front door of the adjacent property opens and the occupier emerges like a black Homepride flour grader. The final blast of water dislodged years of soot into his living room. Chris's new nickname... Sooty!

Saturday June 14th Stevenage fire station open day.

Another fire in Knebworth revealed the flaw in Biggles' driving. On 1st August we were called to a field fire involving a hundred acres of standing barley worth £20,000.

The "make pumps six" message brought additional resources from Hitchin, Welwyn Garden City and Wheathampstead.

The fire engines were working around the fire trying to contain it using hosereel jets while other firemen chased the fire on foot using beaters to smother the burning crop.

Biggles went back to the hydrant in Oakfields Avenue to fill the tank with water and connected a hose from the engine to the standpipe in the hydrant. In his excitement he drove off not realising that the hose was still connected and pulled the standpipe out of the ground causing water to gush out uncontrollably until someone turned off the hydrant.

A bit later we passed him driving up Knebworth High Street with the hosereels, which hadn't been made up properly, flailing about like the scythes on a Roman chariot.

It took two hours before we had the fire, and Biggles, under control.

I think that it's about time I mentioned Pat Priestman.

Pat loved the fire brigade and we all loved her.

She lived in Knebworth and ran the Knebworth Park Show Jumping Club. A couple of times a year she organised a horse show with all the proceeds going to the Fire Brigades National Benevolent Fund.

Over the years she raised thousands of pounds and we always supported her efforts by taking a fire engine up to Knebworth Park which was on our station ground.

However, Pat's other job was as a roly poly stripogram and any excuse and those tits would be out and then it was every man for himself!

Whenever we got a new recruit or an out duty on the watch the Stn O would have them in his office for a chat and if she was about he would introduce her as his wife.

As the shift progressed she would play up to the poor unsuspecting soul and we would take great delight in watching them squirm as they were slowly undressed while trying unsuccessfully not to upset the Stn O's wife! Then in the blink of an eye Pat would have her pups out and the victim's face would be in there for the treatment.

We also knew that once they were out, we would all be in for the same.

She would turn up for parties etc. on station. In fact she turned up at John Story's birthday as a nun, sat on his lap, tits out, read him a poem and then picked him up in a fireman's lift and carried him off.

She had a soft spot for Mick Milton. He was the only one I knew who could lift her.

At her funeral some years ago a phenomenal number of people turned up to pay their respects to a well thought of woman.

What a shame that the hierarchy dropped her after it was deemed politically incorrect to be seen with a stripogram.

My old fire engine is due a makeover.

It started life in 1941 as an Auxiliary Towing Vehicle with the National Fire Service and was based at Padstow in Cornwall. An ATV was a basic box van used to carry a crew of firemen and their equipment with a trailer pump towed behind. After the end of the war in 1948 the NFS was split up and returned to the control of the local authority and so my fire engine had become part of the new Cornwall County Fire Brigade. At some point later it was fitted with a 100 gallon water tank, a hosereel drum and had two holes cut into the sides which were fitted with rollers so the hosereel could be deployed on either side.

I wanted to restore it to that condition and so on Friday 18th July I drove it to the paint shop at Redlands Ltd in Waterford. Two mates from the village had offered to rub it down and respray it for me. They were Brian Lawrence and Terry Day. It was duly rubbed down and masked for spraying.

The following day it was sprayed.

On the Sunday however it wouldn't start and we decided to tow it back to Codicote. Terry found a tow line (much too short) and we set off (much too fast). What a trip, it was, without a doubt, the fastest GLE 441 had ever gone!

I fixed on the Cornwall County Fire Brigade transfers and it looked a treat.

On Saturday 9th August Truro fire station in Cornwall had an open day and I thought I would take the engine and maybe drive it down to Padstow.

Anyway, best laid plans and all that, we got as far as Andover before the fuel pump broke and we came back to Codicote on a low loader, courtesy of the RAC.

It was around this time that I broke another fire engine.

It all started with a call to Benington where a tractor was towing a trailer loaded with baled straw.

Unbeknown to the driver, the straw had caught fire and was falling off of the trailer. I was driving the WrL and when we caught up with it we had about half a mile of grass verge and hedgerow alight.

We followed the route of the tractor using a hosereel and beaters to extinguish the fire.

Once the fire was out we started back towards Stevenage. Between Benington and Aston the road goes down into a valley and back up the other side with a little stream running along the bottom.

Mick Milton turned to me and said, "I bet you can't reach fifty by the time we get to the bottom."

I looked at him and started off down the hill. We were doing quite well, and I looked like completing the challenge.

At the bottom the road took a little dog-leg and I had to slow down a bit. Anyway, we hit the stream with a bang and as we came out the other side the pump took off and all six wheels left the ground, I could turn the wheel with no effect! We crashed back down to the road, all hitting our heads on the roof and I regained control of the pump.

Mick looked at me and said, "Forty-nine, bad luck!"

The rest of the journey back to the station was uneventful and back at the station I parked the appliance back in the bays and we went up for tea.

A bit later when I went back down to wash the engine, it was leaning alarmingly over to the right, with the remains of the leaf springs lying on the floor.

Another search around the brigade for a spare appliance and it was time to change over all the equipment again.

Forty-nine... I can't believe I didn't make fifty!

With my fire engine resplendent in its new livery I took it to a number of events.

Hitchin Fire Fayre on 27th July, Standalone Farm in Letchworth at the beginning of August, Watford Fun Day on 7th September and pictured here at the Welwyn Garden City Water Carnival on 14th September.

Saturday evening on 22nd November and we are on the way to the A1 (M) junctions 7 – 6, for a particularly grisly incident.

The police have closed the four-mile stretch of the motorway form Langley Sidings (Stevenage south) to the Clock (Welwyn).

A sixty-three-year-old man travelling on the south bound carriageway had broken down and as he tried to cross the north bound carriageway, presumably to find an emergency telephone, he was hit, initially by two cars.

"Many other vehicles including lorries and coaches also hit him," said a police spokesman.

The casualty was quite literally all over the road. The undertakers were in attendance, the police were investigating the cause and we had been called to clear the road. We worked along the carriageway using a hose reel to wash down the roadway.

The motorway was closed for two hours.

Hey guess what, I am being temporarily promoted to Leading Fireman for a two month tour of duty at C24 Hertford fire station.

I started there on 1st December 1986.

Hertford was also the Fire Brigade headquarters and had the control room up on the fourth floor.

It had one wholetime pump, a Dennis SS (A250 HPE) and one retained pump, a Dennis RS (HPL 60V).

White Watch had six members.

The officers were Stn O George Presland and Sub O Joe Bibracher with firemen Dennis Wilson, Brian Porter, Steve Childs and new boy Andy Bell. All in all, a good Watch.

Sunday 14th December 1986 was going to be a busy day.

In the morning we joined crews from all over East Hertfordshire and British Rail to take part in a big exercise in the Ponsbourne tunnel near Bayford railway station.

The *Cheshunt and Waltham Mercury* of December 19th stated, "They (the firemen) had to walk all the way from the station and 150 yards into the gloom of the tunnel itself to bring out four victims of a mock railway accident." They went on, "Breathing apparatus was used as if the tunnel were filled with smoke and improvised stretchers were made from fire brigade ladders to bring dummies out."

Anyway it was soon over and we were back on station just after lunch.

Being a Sunday we settled down for a quiet afternoon in front of the TV.

1539 hrs BEEP, BEEP, BEEP "Order your appliance to the Maltings, St. Margarets, Stanstead Abbots, fire."

1543 hrs, 240 mobile to incident, Stn O Presland in charge.

1544 hrs, 251 mobile to incident.

1545 hrs 171 mobile to incident.

We are in attendance at 1547 hrs and at 1548 hrs Stn O Presland sends "make pumps 4" and at 1551 hrs "make pumps 6."

We are the first pump to arrive and have a huge Maltings building alight with the railway on one side and the River Lea on the other. Our first task is to prevent the fire from spreading to the unburnt part. As the following pumps start to arrive we get jets in place on both sides of the building to try to achieve this. Me and a retained Sub O work our jet on the railway side of the building.

1552 hrs Harlow 1 (Essex) mobile to incident.

1552 hrs 160 mobile to incident.

1553 hrs 241 mobile to incident.

1554 hrs 234 mobile to incident.

Stn O Presland sends at 1559 hrs "make pumps 10."

1600 hrs 230 mobile to incident.

1602 hrs 190 mobile to incident.

1603 hrs Harlow 2 mobile to incident.

At 1604 hrs British Rail were requested to isolate the electrics on the line.

1606 hrs 161 mobile to incident.

At 1616 hrs Stn O Presland sent the first informative message "A range of single storey L shaped Maltings well alight – 5 jets in use."

ADO Gifford asks for me so I search him out. He wants me to liaise with the HP and prepare a site for it. It was in attendance at 1618 hrs and we positioned it at the corner of the building in an attempt to stop the fire from spreading to the part of the maltings so far uninvolved.

1620 hrs ACO King takes charge with Oscar Control as the control point. Lightweight pumps were set into the River Lea and jets got to work on the buildings. The fire is through the roof and we are showered by bricks and tiles as it falls in on itself. A small fire can be seen at the base of the roof on the iconic tower.

From ACO King "refreshments asap for approx. 60 persons."

Over the next hour or so we watch as the roof of the tower burns and eventually topples over and collapses.

At 1731 hrs ACO King, "Informative message, an L shaped building approx. 140m x 45m of one and two floors and basement used as general warehousing and garaging for light vehicles, well alight, roof off, seven jets, three ground monitors, one HP supplied from seven portable pumps set into open water."

It is really a case of standing back and pumping water onto the fire and slowly we start to get the upper hand and at 1832 hrs the stop message is sent "As informative with correction to size of building 112m x 63m, sixty per cent of building destroyed by fire."

We were eventually relieved by our oncoming watch and went back to the station to clean up and get off home.

Crews stayed at the job into Monday damping down.

The owners of the Maltings said that they had lost equipment and vehicles worth £80,000 but couldn't estimate the cost of rebuilding.

The Hertford to Liverpool Street rail services were disrupted for two hours.

In a letter dated 17th December, from the company that owned the Maltings, Rialto Builders Limited, the Chairman said:

"I know that you had perhaps as many as seventy-five firemen in attendance and that more than a dozen fire appliances were present to deal with the conflagration and, although the main part of the building was beyond salvation, your men did stop the fire from spreading to one section of the Old Maltings and that was no mean achievement in itself.

It is very reassuring, albeit in unhappy circumstances, to experience at first hand the professionalism, commitment and incredible organisation that is on call, twenty-four hours a day, seven days a week, to serve the community in Hertfordshire at times of disaster... etc. etc."

CFO Faulkner replied on the 19th December:

"Thank you for your letter following the fire at The Maltings, Stanstead Abbotts. It was very kind of you to write in such warm terms (no pun intended!)"

Fantastic sense of humour.

Stanstead Abbots Maltings fire.

Hertford Fire Station.

My two months at Hertford passed very amicably and all too quickly, it also being the first time I worked with the retained.

The boys were good; I didn't really get to know George, but again an old style guvnor like Wally. I liked Joe the Sub O, his girlfriend (later wife I think) was called Fifi (French?) and she would often wear very short skirts which was always popular when she played pool! Of the firemen Dennis was a nice bloke and a solid fireman, Brian was in his last few years in the job and was a great one for manners. He was a very calm and steady man and nothing would ever seem to annoy him. However, put a wet teaspoon in the sugar bowl and he would go berserk! Steve Childs had health issues and he worried me terribly while I was there, he had a stomach problem, never being able to keep his food down, he died before his time a few years later. Andy was a nice chap but being new had yet to make his mark.

I always enjoyed temporary promotion and found the snap decision making very stimulating. I liked to be put on the spot and it was a real rush going to an incident in charge with everything going through your mind. Anyway over the next few years I had quite a lot of leading fireman work, mostly at Stevenage.

There is a fine line to tread between being in charge and working with the watch that gets you the respect you need for both you and them to perform well. I found that if you stood up for your men against authority and didn't ask them to do things that you haven't first proved you can do (or at least try), then when you asked them to jump when it mattered they wouldn't let you down.

1987. TROUBLE WITH THE FRENCH CUSTOMS (BLOODY FRENCH).

One last incident worth a mention before I leave Hertford.

Around 0500 hrs on Thursday, January 15th, people in Ware were woken by "explosions and bangs like fireworks going off!"

The following day the *Hertfordshire Mercury* ran the headline:

BLASTS ROCK WARE BUILDERS' MERCHANTS
GUTTED BY FIRE

I was on duty at 0900 hrs and we headed out to the fireground to relieve the night shift at Graham Ltd, Marsh Lane, Ware. It had been a ten pump fire at its height including the HP from Stevenage. The entire building, warehouse, showroom, offices, several vehicles and garage were all completely destroyed in the fire.

An eye-witness said, "After hearing explosions I looked out of my window and took photographs of the flames. They were huge. Every time the wind blew the flames turned to black smoke and shot up again as the wind dropped."

We were there for four hours, putting out hot spots, turning over and damping down before handing over to another relief crew.

Picture: Hertfordshire Mercury

And so I said goodbye to Hertford, thanks lads.

Early in the morning of Tuesday 3rd February we attended another big fire in Hitchin, this time in Churchgate Arcade. The fire had started in the Chelsea Coffee House, which incidentally, had been subject to a break-in attempt the night before. The fire wrecked the café and broke into C & A Singer, a fabric shop, next door, which was also destroyed.

Two fire engines from Hitchin and two from Stevenage with DDC Colin Pond in charge rushed to the scene to fight the fire. Five BA teams using jets and hosereels had the fire under control by 0330 hrs and had the fire extinguished after four hours.

DDC Pond said, "The fire had started at the front of the shop near some seating, but the cause wasn't known."

Other Firemen joined us around this time and certainly by April, the following had arrived. Roydon "Elmo" Mitchell, a man who could put his hand to anything and good fun, Paul Hardy who was only with us for a year before being promoted to L/Fm at Rickmansworth and Mick Lawrence.

We lost Fm Taddie Baker who retired (I think) and Tiger Currie who got a L/Fm job somewhere (sale of nuts behind the bar drops dramatically!).

On Saturday 19th March, John "One Note" Miles organised a car wash at the fire station in aid of the Zeebrugge Ferry Disaster Fund. If you don't recall, this was a disaster in the English Channel when the roll-on roll-off car ferry Herald of Free Enterprise capsized moments after leaving the port of Zeebrugge in Belgium on 6th March. 193 passengers and crew were killed.

In the *Express* of April 9th it was reported that we had raised £572.60. John said "we were very pleased. We did not really think we would get as much as that. We were targeting about £300 and anything over that was going to be a real bonus."

In April I managed to get hold of an old Merryweather manual fire engine that dated from the 1830s. I have no idea where it came from now but it was languishing somewhere in dusty corner of the brigade.

It was in a really bad state and I stripped it right down replacing the rotten wood, repairing the wheels and making new leather washers before a repaint and reassembly.

Once finished it produced a reasonable jet. It was a good attraction at open days or station visits when we would get eight or ten kids "hands on" pumping the handles.

3rd May, my second son, Matthew, born in Stevenage.

On 6th June Roydon and I took the steam fire engine, which we had just acquired from Baldock, and the manual pump to the fire show "Deltafire" held at Twickenham in London.

Deltafire, Twickenham, May 1987.

Old Welwyn Fire Station, June 1987.

And on 20th June I took my fire engine and the manual pump to Old Welwyn fire station Open Day, (above).

I went to school in Potters Bar and there had a couple of pen friends at the school in the twin town of Viernheim in Germany, a few miles east of Mannheim on the River Rhine.

My friend Norbert Maliske had a relative in the fire brigade there, Michael Ahnert, and through him I had received an invite to attend the 100th anniversary celebrations of the Viernheim Fire Brigade.

I decided to attend with the manual pump, got it a trailer and with some Benevolent Fund souvenirs I set off on 24th June.

I boarded the ferry at Dover and crossed to Calais, and that's where it started to go wrong. Bad news, the French Customs wouldn't let me take the manual through and continue my journey as they considered it may be for sale. Bloody French!

The only option was to return to the UK. I went back on the next sailing and drove to Dover fire station where I was hoping I could leave the pump for a while. Good news, the Sub O there, whose name was Guy I think, agreed to let me park it and put me up for the night in a spare bed in the dormitory.

So the following day I crossed the Channel again and this time drove through France as quickly as possible, on through Belgium and into Germany at Aachen and then down to Viernheim.

I stayed with Michael and he outlined the plans for the weekend. He took me down to the fire station to meet CFO Günter Brechtel and to have a look round.

Saturday evening there was to be a huge back-slapping night, with speeches, entertainment, beer, Oompah bands and sausages. It was held at the Viernheimer Eissporthalle (Ice sports hall) in the town.

Prior to the start of the evening there was a display of fire appliances and equipment in the car park where I set up a stall to sell the fire service souvenirs I had brought with me.

It was a fantastic, typically German night that went on into the early hours of Sunday. The entertainment covered everything from singers, acrobats, magicians and bands, all accompanied by beer and more sausages.

The *Viernheimer Tageblatt* (a newspaper) of Saturday 27th June reported on the night – "ein ganz besonders herzlicher Willkommesgruß widmete Günter Brechtel einem Feuerwehrkameraden aus England, Sid Payne aus Stevenage (County Hertfordshire) nahe Potters Bar, der eigens zum 100 jährigen Jubilärum der Viernheimer Feuerwehr anreiste."

Which roughly translated says –

"Günter Brechtel gave a most cordial greeting to a fire brigade colleague from England, Sid Payne from Stevenage (County Hertfordshire) near Potters Bar, who had travelled specially to be at the 100th celebrations of the Viernheim Fire Brigade."

The following afternoon was the parade. I was resplendent in a Victorian fireman's uniform with brass helmet (which I had brought with me to wear with the old manual pump), and was asked to go on the rostrum with the great and good to view the parade.

At 1400 hrs the procession set off led by a command vehicle and followed by three horse drawn coaches carrying six fire brigade veterans. It was a huge parade taking the best part of an hour to pass the dais, over 2000 firemen from fifty-three fire brigades with sixteen fire brigade bands and vintage and modern appliances. As the end of the parade passed, the dignitaries joined in to march to the Festival Hall. So I brushed shoulders with the CFO of Viernheim Fire Brigade, the District Fire Brigade Inspector, the Mayor, the Leader of the Council, representatives of the Federation and the State and a representative of the Chamber of Fire Insurance Office.

And as reported in the *Viernheimer Tageblatt* of 29th June –

"…under Schirmherr des Jubiläums, Kreisbrandinspektor a. D. Hans Schwöbel, last not least Brandmeister Sid Payne aus Stevenage nahe Potters Bar bei London."

The Saluting Base in Viernheim.

White Watch, Stevenage, June 1987: Back, L-R:
M. Lawrence, P. Hardy, C. Strickland, Sub O Milton, G. Williamson, B.
Hillier, D. Rees, Stn O Story.
Front, L-R: L/Fm J. Miles, Me, M. Lee, P. Dartford, S. Cotton.

I don't remember the date exactly but it was in the early 80's that I saw a letter from another German town. The Ingelheim-am-Rhein fire brigade in Germany asking if anyone would like to go to an anniversary they were having.

I wrote to them asking if they would like to exchange a fire helmet with me, and from that small beginning a great friendship developed.

In the middle of September, I had some more temporary promotion, this time it took me into the Fire Prevention Department, once again at Hertford.

It really wasn't my thing but it was considered to be an advantage in the quest for a permanent leading fireman's job (again, a lot of good it did me!)

A week or so before I started I telephoned the FP department and spoke to ADO Sid Gifford, a very likable man and as un-fire brigade as you could imagine. The conversation went something like this:

"ADO Gifford speaking."

"Good morning sir, my name is Payne I am joining you for a six week secondment next week and was wondering if there is anything special that you consider I should bring,"

"What to bring, mm well I don't know, that's a good question old dear, mm let me think, ah well old dear, I think… erm, what to bring, let me see… er mm… I tell you what old dear, bring a pencil."

So off I went, with my pencil (and a spare, I didn't want to get caught out).

It was an okay time and I sat at a desk with three very funny men; it really was a nonstop laugh, the others in question being Sub O's Dennis Halliwell and Biff Baker and Stn O Roy Caterer. I did all the usual stuff that they do, fire certificate visits, petroleum inspections and general fire safety advice. I would get into work, get my files for the day and go out and do as much as I could.

Over the past few months the Watch, together with some St Albans lads, had undertaken a project to prepare the old "Fighting 105" AEC for service in Africa. The seventeen-year-old appliance had been donated to Liberia via the World Volunteer Firefighters Association in a scheme designed to aid struggling African countries increase their firefighting capabilities.

On Friday 19th September we had a handing over ceremony at the station, for which I went back to take part.

Bruce Hogg, CFO of Norfolk Fire Brigade and representing the WVFA, accepted the keys and handed them over to Nathaniel Davies from the Liberian Embassy.

She left Liverpool docks on 2nd October.

I finished my time at the FP department and returned to Stevenage.

We had a very sad end to the year 1987.

The headline in the *Welwyn and Hatfield Express* for Thursday, November 5th read:

FIREMAN KILLED ON 999 CALL

On the morning of Saturday, 31st October, the ERT from Hatfield station had turned out to an RTA persons trapped near Royston with a crew of two.

At the roundabout in Baldock by the Tesco superstore, the appliance slewed out of control and crashed killing the driver, Fm Stuart Lough, after he was thrown out through the windscreen. With Stuart was Fm Barry Pomfret who suffered serious leg injuries and was taken to the intensive care unit at Lister Hospital.

A week later I lined up along Fore Street, Hertford, to pay my respects as our HP with Stuart's coffin passed on its way to St. Etheldreda's Church.

C Division DC, John Potipher, who was also the Brigade Chaplain, took the service and finished with "Stuart paid the ultimate price. He gave his life for others. Greater love hath no man than this."

It wouldn't be the last such service I would attend.

1988. AN EMERGENCY CALL TO THE RIVER RHINE.

At the beginning of the year John Story was promoted to ADO and left us. Mick Milton was temporarily promoted to the rank of Stn O.

Also around this time we had firemen join and leave and I really can't remember who came and went when.

At some point Fm "Taff" James arrived, Nick "Snoz" Hoeplemann came on temporary transfer from Blue Watch and Doug Pirie came for a year or so. Just after 0800 hrs of 10th April we got a call to a flooding in Stony Croft. Picking up the tip sheet Doug said, "That's funny I recognise that address… it's my mum's house."

Another real bonus to the Watch from Training School was Fm Pete Fotios, what a character. We were playing football in the bays and said we should have our names on our shirts so I chalked "Baldrick" on his back and it stuck!

Pete had been a fireman in the RAF Regiment and apparently when he joined them they got him to take a pump out and flood the runway because a sea plane was coming in for a crash landing!

On one of his first days with us Taff, who had been a Royal Marine, took the piss out of his marching and took him out for some practice. He got into his fire gear onto which we had sewn a third leg to his yellow leggings complete with boot. What a sight, Baldrick marching up and down the yard, middle leg swinging and Taff strutting after him… LEFT, LEFT, RIGHT, LEFT, LEFT, RIGHT, RIGHT, LEFT. Brilliant.

Two new pieces of equipment arrived, firstly a 15m inflatable path, developed in Sweden I think. It came rolled up and consisted of two inflatable sides and a wooden slatted path between. It was inflated using two BA cylinders and as it inflated it would unroll.

We took it to Fairlands Valley Park lake to practise with it on occasion but I can't ever remember using it operationally.

The exact opposite could be said about the next item.

We also received £12,000 worth of hydraulically operated, Lukas rescue equipment, consisting of a petrol driven generator, a cutting tool, a spreading tool and a jack.

On Thursday 11th February the station yard was a complete jumble of crashed cars and suffering casualties as we had our last training session before the equipment was put on the run.

A real advance in the art of extrication.

The Stevenage Comet of February 7th reported on a "blazing car" in Broadhall Way, a "blaze in a rubbish bin" at Longmeadow School, Oaks Cross, a company director who watched in horror "as a boiler burst into flames amongst ceiling-high bales of costly fabrics at her workshop" and a quick thinking resident and her friend who "restricted the damage when a chip pan caught alight at her home in Chancellors Road."

On the 11th April at 0014 hrs we went to a fire at a Council storage depot in Willows Link, Stevenage. We made pumps three but couldn't save beds, sofas, cookers and other furniture that were stored there destined for the elderly and needy.

ADO Rayner sent the stop message "A single storey building, approx.10m x 15m used as a furniture store, severely damaged by fire and collapse, two jets, two hosereels in use."

Less than two weeks later on 23rd two floors of the Towers, Stevenage in the town centre were evacuated as fire took hold in a fifth floor flat. The blaze started on a settee in the lounge, the smell waking the sleeping occupant who escaped and raised the alarm. Two BA crews used a jet to fight the fire but the flat was severely damaged.

On 15th May, Roydon, ADO Story and I took the steamer and manual pump to Duxford fire engine rally.

In Brigade Routine Order no. 2/88 issued on Monday 11th January there had appeared an invitation to visit the Rhineland Pfalz fire brigades as part of an exchange programme.

On 25th May I set out in the PCV for Dover, together with Sub O Jepson (Training School), L/Fm Hardy

(Rickmansworth), Fm Sage and Teare (St Albans) and Fm Gray (Borehamwood).

Jon Sage and myself were to be stationed at Koblenz fire station on the rivers Rhine and Mosel, and were accommodated with German firemen and their families. My host was Oberbrandmeister (OBM) Hans Kievernagel, a Sub O on Watch 2 and I was to shadow him during work and free time. Hans took me to see the Königsbacher brewery and play kegelball (a type of bowling), a tour of Koblenz, the Military Museum, the Horcheimer Kirmes a local festival, Ehrenbreitstein fortress and Stolzenfels castle and a boat trip on the Rhine to Braubach and the Marksburg castle. All good fun, Koblenz is a favourite city of mine.

The brigade has six front line appliances: -

Appliances	Fahrzeuge	Abbr
Command vehicle	Einsatzleitwagen	ELW
Water Tender 1	Löschgruppenfahrzeug 1	LF 1
Water Tender 2	Löschgruppenfahrzeug 2	LF 2
Turntable Ladder	Drehleiter	DL

For small incidents the attendance is the ELW and one of the LFs. In the event of a property fire or major incident all four appliances turn out, this is called the Löschzug.
There are two other vehicles crewed by two men for breaking in to property or clearing wasps' nests etc. or oil spillages.

Transit van	Gerätewagen-Haus	GW-H
Unimog gritter	Gerätewagen-Öl	GW-Ö

There were sixteen Headquarters and Control staff and eighty-seven operational firemen dealing with roughly 2000 calls a year. There were twenty-one other vehicles, including a coach, a tanker for sucking up spills, a rescue tender, sub-aqua unit, and two roll-on roll-off vehicles with nineteen different containers. There are two other containers for use with GW-Ö, 500kg of dry powder and one for forest fires. There are seven small rescue boats and a big fire boat.

On top of all that there are 450 volunteer firemen at fifteen fire stations around the city operating another twenty-eight vehicles and eight boats!

The big difference is that here in Germany every city, town and village operates its own fire brigade, mostly run by volunteers, only towns with a population of more than 90,000 people are required to have a professional brigade.

On Saturday, 28th May Hans took me down the Rhine to Ingelheim where I had been invited as guest of the Youth Fire Brigade. We met David Oudôt and went on a tour of historic Ingelheim with half of the Youth Firefighters and then back to the station to watch the other half demonstrating a lightweight pump/foam drill.

I gave them an interview for their National magazine and back to Koblenz at 2000 hrs.

On the 30th we went to Interschutz at Hanover, the largest fire exhibition in Europe.

Back home I am not forgotten. The 1st of June edition of the *Stevenage Comet* runs an article titled,

SID'S FIRE CALL – TO GERMANY!

On Thursday 2nd June I am back in Ingelheim, this time as a guest of the Mainz-Bingen Fire Brigade Association, a district with sixty-six volunteer brigades and over 2,500 firemen.

I met up with David for a tour of the local area and then we met Karl Heiser the Chief of the District and CFO of Heidesheim, Horst Weitzel, CFO Ingelheim, Karl-Heinz Knittel, CFO Guntersblum and Hans Neumann of Weinolsheim for a tour of the district. We stopped a few times, once at a village called Stadecken-Elsheim that had two pumping appliances and a transit van rapid attack vehicle for 25 calls a year!

Finally, we ended up at Oberdiebach at a restaurant called Dorfschänke, the owner... Manfred Fahl, the retired CFO of the village.

I agreed in principle to lecture on BA procedures when I returned on holiday in September.

Karl Heiser presented me with a Silver Fire Brigade Needle (lapel badge) awarded for services to the Mainz-Bingen District.

Friday 3rd June.

At 1521 hrs a call came in for "Rescue Boat 3, to Mosel Oberhalb Schleuse, oil spillage."

The call is to an oil spill on the river Moselle almost opposite the fire station. A crew of four was mobilised OBM R. Schmitt, Brandmeister (BM) (L/Fm) R. Nagelschmidt, Fm Sage and myself.

We collect an oil-absorbing float and drive down to the fire boat mooring. The rescue boat 3 was launched from the fire boat and we were in attendance at 1531 hrs.

We met the ELW on the opposite bank with Brand Inspector (BI) (Stn O) R. Kluth and a crew of three. The oil slick was 50m x 5m along the bank.

A line was tied to each end of the float and I took one end ashore while the other was tied off to the boat. The float was then towed/walked up and down until the oil was absorbed.

We made up the float and on the way back to the fire boat Rudi Nagelschmidt treated us to some high speed driving and tight turns, throwing us all over the place.

Time returned 1700 hrs

Jon Sage and Me with the oil-absorbing float on the
River Moselle.

Picture: Rhein Zeitung

(Later, I saw this picture on the notice board at St Albans Fire Station
with the heading 'German diet doesn't agree with English firemen.')

We had only been back a couple of minutes when, at 1704 hrs, there was a call for the GW-H.

I quickly swapped my kit over and turned out with BM's W. Schoor and G. Alderath to a wasps nest in Schillerstraße, Oberwerth, Koblenz.

We were there at 1716 hrs.

The nest, about the size of a fist, was in an attic at the top of a three storey block of flats. I went up into the attic with BM Alderath who used a highly technical piece of equipment, a plastic carrier bag, which he put under the nest, and with a quick sideways movement knocked the nest from the rafter and into the bag which was tied at the top.

Once outside, the nest was dispatched with a size ten boot and deposited into the nearest bin.

Back at the station at 1735 hrs.

0730 hrs the following morning and we are off duty.

Today is the South West Fire Brigades football tournament. All of us UK firemen meet up for the day.

The Koblenz results are:
>
> Lost 3-0 against Stuttgart
>
> Won 3-2 against Kaiserslauten
>
> Drew 0-0 against Karlsruhe
>
> Lost 1-4 against Freiburg

FINAL: MAINZ 0 v 1 KARLSRUHE

Koblenz finished 7th, although I don't remember how many teams were competing.

On Sunday 5th June we were back on duty and had four calls.

Firstly, with GW-H, to a person locked out.

Then, while we are out clearing up after yesterday's football tournament, at 0832 hrs...

1-46-1, "LF 1 ordered to a bungalow on fire, Laubach 84, Koblenz."

LF 1 mobile, Hauptbrandmeister (Sub O +) H. Krause in charge, driver OBM K. Klein, BM W. Schwarz, BM R. Nagelschmidt and myself in the back.

ELW mobile, BI R. Kluth in charge, driver OBM R. Schmitt and BM B. Herter.

Both appliances in attendance at 0837 hrs.

Smoke was issuing from the front door and window with the ceiling, door frame and window frame alight.

The fire was extinguished using a hosereel jet from the LF 1 and the door and window frame was removed and the ceiling cut away using a large axe.

Mobile returning 0900 hrs.

This fire had previously been attended by the off going Watch at 0712 hrs, who had treated the occupier for smoke inhalation.

2245 hrs a call for the LF 1 and ELW to attend a television fire at Zwickerstaße 6, Karthouse, Koblenz.

The address was not easy to find, these were blocks of flats and block number nine followed block number five! Just like being back in Stevenage!

Anyway the television had overheated and there was no fire situation and the TV was removed to the balcony.

Time left incident – 2312 hrs.

Monday 6th, just before going off duty at 0727 hrs a call for the Löschzug to attend an AFA at Oberfinanzdirektion, Rudolf-Virchow Straße, Rauental, Koblenz.

We got there at 0730 hrs and found that workmen using an angle grinder had created enough dust to set off the alarm.

We left at 0740 hrs.

Back to the station and off duty. On Tuesday 7th June the local newspaper, *Rhein-Zeitung* reported on our trip to Koblenz with the headline:

ZWEI ENGLISCHE KOLLEGEN ZU GAST BEI DER
KOBLENZER FEUERWEHR
(TWO ENGLISH COLLEAGUES ARE GUESTS OF
THE KOBLENZ FIRE BRIGADE)

All in all, I attended eleven incidents during our time in Koblenz.

We left for home in the PCV on Friday, 10th June at 9 o'clock and broke down outside the town of Ghent in Belgium at two o'clock in the afternoon.

We get a temporary repair and leave Ghent at half past four, arriving at Calais and sailing for Dover at half past eight.

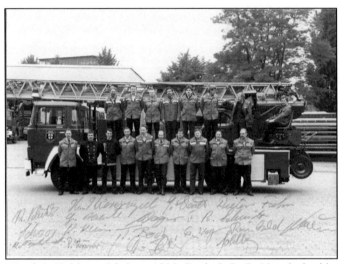

Watch 2, Koblenz, 8th June 1988: Back, L-R: R. Nagelschmidt,
P. Krämer, D. Fahr, G. Alderath, J. Scheid, R. Schmitt,
R. Neumann, B. Herter.
Front, L-R: R. Kluth, Me, J. Sage, H. Kievernagel, W. Schwarz, M.
Sutor, K. Klein, W. Schoor, H. Wagner, T. Bock.

Back in Codicote at eleven o'clock at night

Back at work at Stevenage on Tuesday 21st June around 2100
hrs, a nurse had a miraculous escape after also struggling to
turn the steering wheel (remember Potters Bar?)

As she turned left into Coreys Mill Lane she put her arm
through the steering wheel to set the trip meter! Unable to
remove her arm in time the car continued to turn left, crashed
through railings and plunged four metres onto a cycle track,
landing on its roof.

She managed to get out of her car and walk across the road
to the Lister Hospital for treatment.

We just had to deal with the petrol spillage. Priceless!

Other incidents recorded during June and July 1988 were a
spate of children in trouble.

Firstly a young lad in Jessop Road with his finger stuck in
a garden table, another child locked in a bedroom in Peartree

Way and then finally a run out to Whitesmead Road where a four year old boy had managed to trap his arm in the neck of a large bottle while trying to retrieve a sock!

At 0800 hrs on Friday 15th we were called to Watton-at-Stone railway station where one of the oil tank wagons of a goods train had jumped the rails and ripped up several lengths of track during a shunting manoeuvre. British Rail took charge and finally managed to reopen the line on Sunday morning.

I don't remember why now but our call signs changed around this time and the WrE changed from 230 to 232 and the WrL changed from 231 to 230.

On 21st August in York Road neighbours were returning home after visiting relatives and spotted smoke issuing from some ventilation holes above the patio doors.

1316 hrs, BEEP, BEEP, BEEP, "Both appliances to York Road, Stevenage, house fire."

1317 hrs 232, 230 mobile to incident Stn O Milton in charge.

1322 hrs 232 and 230 in attendance.

1324 hrs Informative from Stn O Milton "Ground floor well alight, one jet, one hosereel, four BA in use."

I am in BA working the jet into the property through the patio doors at the back of the house.

Everything is on fire and it is very hot.

The fire is soon under control and the Stn O sends the stop message at 1333 hrs "One end of terrace house approx. 9m x 6m, seventy per cent of ground floor severely damaged by fire, 1 jet, one hosereel, four BA, "D" Delta."

232 mobile returning at 1416 hrs and is ordered to another call on the way back.

230 mobile returning at 1434 hrs closed down at 1438 hrs.

The headline in the *Stevenage Gazette* for Wednesday, August 24th read:

PAPERBOY IS HOUSE FIRE HERO

and reported, "after checking that the fire brigade had been called and that no one was in the house next door, the brave youngster smashed a patio door to gain entry."

He said "Another boy was passing and helped me to break the double glazed window with bricks and we went inside to make sure that no one was inside."

The Stevenage Herald on Friday, 26th:

FIRE HITS HOUSE

Neighbours said, "they called the fire brigade but before the two tenders arrived youths tried to save goods in the three-storey house by smashing the double glazing and the blaze appeared to get worse."

Finally the *Comet* on the following Wednesday, the 31st:

FIRE WARNING TO YOUNGSTERS
LEAVE IT TO THE BRIGADE

ADO Alan Rayner said, "What started as a minor fire could have ended in tragedy... the children could have been overpowered by two or three breaths of fumes from blazing furniture. And it is possible their action exacerbated the blaze by letting oxygen into the double glazed house."

So there you go kids, here's my fire prevention message to you and your parents– "GET OUT, STAY OUT AND DIAL 999"

Back to Germany.

You may remember back in June I had agreed to lecture to the Mainz-Bingen Fire Brigades Association on BA procedures in the UK.

On Wednesday 14th June I arrived at Ingelheim-am-Rhein fire station to give the talk.

The audience consisted of fifty or so members of the Association including Karl Heiser, Karl-Heinz Knittel and the CFO of the Rheinland Pfalz Works Fire Brigades, Richard Booch. The lecture was structured into four stages, was simultaneously translated by David Oudôt and lasted for four hours with a break and practical demonstrations.

Ingelheim-Am-Rhein lecture: L-R: Karl Heiser, Me, Karl-Heinz Knittel and David Oudôt.
Picture: Allgemeine Zeitung

A good night and the talk was very well received by everyone.

The fire brigades in Germany at this time had little or no procedures in place to protect their BA crews and I like to think this got them moving a bit. I know that the Ingelheim Fire Brigade certainly brought in new measures based on my lecture and two years later at a fire in Mainz their lack of procedures came into focus again.

Both the local newspapers, the *Mainzer Rhein Zeitung* and the *Ingelheimer Zeitung* carried a detailed report on the lecture.

Back at Stevenage, at a quarter past ten at night on the 3rd November, the bells went down and we turned out to St Michaels School, Sandown Road, Stevenage.

I was driving the WrE and following me was Dave Rees driving the WrL. Pulling up alongside the school there was a lot of smoke on the other side of the building but all looked quiet where we were. Crews were committed to the building in BA with jets to try and find the seat of the fire.

The block contained chemistry rooms, classrooms and storage areas and was well alight. Pumps were made five and appliances were mobilised from Hertford and Hitchin to assist and DO Dave Wilson arrived to take charge.

The structure became unsafe and the BA crews were ordered to withdraw and not a moment too soon as shortly afterwards the roof collapsed and the oxygen fuelled the fire.

Dave and I were operating our pumps and managing the water supply from a hydrant over 300m away, when we heard the crash of the collapsing roof, this was followed by silence and then a whooshing sound. The next second all the windows in our side of the building blew out as the fire flashed over with a huge ball of flame shooting from the windows. Dave and I dived for cover but the WrL was caught in the blast, melting the paintwork and the blue lights on the roof.

Once the fire had vented itself through the roof it became easier to see and attack although it was another hour and a half before we started to get the upper hand, the fire being fought from outside the building.

Crews remained on site for another nine hours.

DO Wilson sent the stop message "a single storey derelict school building used as a science block, 40m x 25m, 100% of ground floor severely damaged by fire and collapse, 4 jets, 2 hosereels, 4 BA.

Me at the
St. Michaels School fire.
Picture: HFRS

St. Michaels School fire flashover.
Picture: HFRS

A duo of final snippets for the year 1988.

On Monday 19th December, we had a call to the A1(M) at Langley Sidings, Stevenage south.

A Ford Escort van being driven south, left the road and mounted a crash barrier where it came out of the ground and effectively launched the vehicle up and through a large road sign. The sign was mounted on a scaffolding frame and as the vehicle passed through, the roof was removed and the driver suffered severe head injuries.

We attended to remove the victim, who was pronounced dead at the scene, and to wait while the vehicle was recovered.

The station received a Christmas card from Norman Davis Freemantle, the Director of Fire Services in Liberia, West Africa.

Attached to the inside of the card was a photograph of the old Fighting 105 in attendance at a fire at the Ministry of Information in Monrovia, on 11th November 1988.

The last bit of information to filter back from Liberia was that she had been set on fire and burnt out during a demonstration.

1989. 02 4 GP.

We had a shit start to the year. On the evening of 14th January we got a call to a flooding at the Coreys Mill Beefeater Steak House, Coreys Mill Lane, Stevenage.

A few minutes earlier a routine maintenance job had gone wrong when a workman turned off the wrong pump causing raw sewage to flow out into the underground chamber housing the pumps.

When we arrived the sewage had flooded the chamber and was spilling out into the car park and to make matters worse it was starting to appear in the restaurant's kitchen and the staff were quickly trying to get the food boxes off the floor to higher ground.

We set some pumps into the chamber and started to move the sewage to some "waste" ground. Meanwhile the flood had started to creep out of the kitchen door and spread across the carpet into the dining room towards the oblivious diners.

It didn't take long to clear the chamber so that the contractors could turn off the pump and then it was just a case of clearing up and mopping out the kitchen. A specialist cleaning company turned up for this task.

The restaurant gave a free glass of wine to the guests for the inconvenience!

At the beginning of the year we got our new Stn O Ian Clinton who was previously on the Watch as a fireman. Also arriving were Fm John McGrinder and Andy Mansfield.

Going the other way was Spiros Hillier who transferred to Royston fire station. Apart from Johnny One Note, Barry was the last fireman to go who was on the Watch when I arrived ten years earlier.

Two little snippets about Spiros before we leave him. One night in the dormitory, in the early hours, there was a cry of "OI!"

It was so loud it woke us all up and as we cautiously checked on Spiros, he was sitting bolt upright in bed and continued...

"WHO'S GOT MY F*****G BOOTS!" and lay down again sound asleep.

On another occasion we were all sitting around the table having breakfast talking about the house fire during the night. I could see Barry looking around, clearly not understanding any of it. He had slept through the call and missed the whole thing. It wasn't the fact that he'd missed the call but that nobody had missed him during it!

On Wednesday 1st March just after 1900 hrs a huge blaze broke out at the Kuehne and Nagel warehouse on the Colonial Way Industrial Estate in Watford. It was one of the biggest fires ever to be seen in the town and was fought by over a hundred firemen using fifteen pumps from around the county and London.

We were called to attend with our hydraulic platform and what makes this fire special is that it was the first time that all three of Hertfordshire's HPs were working at a fire at the same time, and maybe not since.

The building was collapsing, all crews were withdrawn and the fire extinguished using the HPs and the rain on Thursday morning helped.

The warehouse was completely destroyed including books, furniture, woks and 2½ million light bulbs.

Around this time the first Ambulance paramedics started to arrive on station and we started to get a whole different approach to casualty care and handling.

White Watch, Stevenage, 1989/1990: Back, L-R: G. Williamson, J. Mcgrinder, P. Fotios, B. Hillier, D. Rees,
Sub O M. Milton.
Front, L-R: L/Fm J. Miles, Me, Stn O I. Clinton, R. Mitchell.

Friday 10th March it's Red Nose Day! Fun and frolics.

We got involved with a number of things, the boss at the Stevenage Valuation Office was unceremoniously dunked into one of our portable dams, and we took the opportunity to dunk Sub O Milton and DO Dave Wilson at the same time.

We hoisted a man into a bath onto the roof of the Royal Oak pub for a twenty-four hour stay and hosed down the

Headmaster of Longmeadow School whose pupils had tied him to a tree.

At half past midnight on Monday 13th March a drama was unfolding in Jowitt House, Sish Lane, Stevenage.

A granny leapt into action as fire threatened to engulf the three bedroomed, top floor flat. She was staying with her daughter for a visit.

She told the *Stevenage Herald*, (March, 17th), "I was just dropping off when I heard a bang and a noise like a tornado."

She went out into a smoke filled hall and woke up her daughter and son-in-law and between them they grabbed the four kids and fled the flat.

Both pumps from Stevenage were mobilised to the fire and on arrival we got our BA on and took a hosereel up the stairs to the third floor where we found the lounge to be well alight with thick, black, toxic smoke. We had been told to look out for the family's ten week old puppy, Zeuise, and during a search of the kitchen I found the dog cowering behind the fridge.

With the fire extinguished and the puppy rescued we made our way back down to the street and reunited Zeuise with the owners. They then told me that there was a guinea pig in one of the bedrooms so back on with my face mask and back into the smoky flat. I found the GP and came back out. The animal was a bit limp and very sooty! We used the oxygen (O_2) equipment to try and revive it and after a while it started to perk up and was given over to the seven-year-old daughter.

Of the two smoke alarms in the house, the one in the lounge had been removed during decorating and not replaced.

During the 80s our Watch had the job of updating the maps of the villages on our station ground.

This was a great job and I got into it with gusto. In the summer we would go out into the countryside for the afternoon and painstakingly plot all the main features. The road names, farms, larger houses, pubs and churches as well as the locations of hydrants, rivers, ponds and other open water supplies.

We spent many an hour sitting in the sunshine with an ice cream.

I remember we were in the one of the villages checking house names in a posh road with big properties. I came across a house with a long drive and neither name or number visible so went to check with the owner. No reply from the front door so I went round the back. As I got to the corner of the house I had a peek round into the back garden.

And there, a semi-naked woman was sweeping the patio around a big swimming pool. I watched for a bit and then did the only decent thing; I went back to the pump and got the rest of the boys!

And so it was, that with four little heads poking around the corner the sweeper looked up and spotted us.

Quick as a flash One Note leapt from cover and said, "Good afternoon madam, we are from the Hertfordshire fire brigade and we are out and about updating our maps and wonder if..." seeing the funny side she threw a string of expletives in our direction and we beat a hasty retreat. Never did get the address, I thought it best to enquire next door.

We had a scorching summer culminating on Tuesday 8th and Wednesday 9th of August.

For the previous week or so we would get into work on days and receive a list of fires to attend and off we went, working our way through the list sometimes ending the shift miles from Stevenage and passing other crews going in other directions.

Two big fires on the Tuesday broke out in quick succession.

The first started on Council property just off the B158, Lower Hatfield Road at Essendon. About 200 tons of brushwood caught fire and we attended initially with Welwyn Garden City. A water relay was set up from the nearby River Lea but we were unable to stop the fire from spreading through undergrowth and into a field of standing corn. At the height of the blaze the police had to close the surrounding roads as the smoke blew across the area. Seven pumps were needed to control the fire and with the help of the farmer creating a fire break with his combine harvester we started to get the upper hand. The fire continued to smoulder for ten hours. As our pump left this incident we were ordered to attend Bayfordbury House, Bayford where we were faced with forty acres (sixteen hectares) of standing corn alight. Thirty-four firemen using hosereels, beaters and a water shuttle brought the fire under control.

Finally we were directed to Bramfield Road, Datchworth to tackle a huge fire on Forestry Commission land. Thirty acres (twelve hectares) of straw were alight which rapidly spread to adjoining land. In all, nearly a hundred acres (forty hectares) were on fire taking twenty fire engines to bring it under control.

What a day, but worse was to come tomorrow.

Wednesday, 9th, and it started off slowly with a couple of small grass fires during the morning.

Back to the station for tea break about 1100 hrs but as we sat down to cheese rolls the bells went down again.

Initially one pump was mobilised to Moat farm, Bramfield Road, Datchworth but the large amount of smoke was looking ominous. As we pulled into the field the size of the incident became apparent. Old Welwyn's pump had arrived just ahead of us and their officer in charge ran over shouting, "It's OK I've made pumps two!" Our officer in charge, John Miles, looked at him, nodded, and immediately sent "make pumps eight."

The farmer who lost hundreds of pounds worth of harvested straw told the *Stevenage Herald*, "We spotted the fire and phoned the fire brigade. It spread so quickly because of the wind and we had to get out of the way very quickly."

The fire spread to involve a second farm and into woodland, at its height it covered a two-mile area and ten pumps were called to the scene.

This was the only time I have seen a whole wood alight with one hundred per cent of the trees on fire, I mean the trunks, branches and canopy all on fire. It resembled the fires you see on the television in America or Australia. I walked for miles all afternoon, at one point even having to use BA in the woods and strangely, coming across ADO John Felstead with a beater looking totally lost.

Stn O Ian Clinton told the *Herald*, "This is the biggest field fire this year. The wind was blowing so strongly the fire spread to another farm and into the woods."

We got back to station around 1900 hrs in the evening but the fire burned late into the night, the last crew leaving just after 2200 hrs

The following day, Thursday 10th, it started to rain and the *Hertfordshire Mercury*, issue for the 11th, reported.

"Yesterday's rain came as a welcome relief to the Hertfordshire Fire and Rescue Service, which had been stretched to the limit in fighting fires in the county's tinder dry fields."

The first week in November the local newspapers carried the headlines: -

'MIRACLE' DISASTER AVERTED AS PETROL TANKER CRASHES

Welwyn and Hatfield Times, Wednesday November 1st

HEROES AT WORK

Welwyn & Hatfield Citizen, Wednesday November 1st

M-WAY PILE UP COULD HAVE BEEN A 'FIREBALL' OF DISASTER

Welwyn Hatfield Review, Thursday November 2nd

On Friday 27th October shortly after 1400 hrs, the northbound carriageway of the A1 (M), just before the Welwyn slip road, ground to a halt following an RTA between a Vauxhall Astra towing a caravan and a BP petrol tanker. The caravan overturned and the tanker crashed into the central barrier and ended up on its side.

The fully laden tanker, carrying 4,000 gallons (15,000 litres) of leaded and 3,000 gallons (11,000 litres) of unleaded petrol began to leak fuel across the carriageway.

Six appliances from Stevenage, Hatfield, Welwyn Garden City, Welwyn and Wheathampstead as well as the divisional foam stock and equipment were mobilised to the incident.

The tanker driver and the family in the car were treated for minor injuries and conveyed to the QE II hospital in Welwyn Garden City.

Tanker crash on the A1(M).
Picture: HFRS

Once we had sufficient foam on site we began to cover the area with high expansion foam, the motorway as well as the tanker.

BP dispatched advisors from their terminal at Buncefield in Hemel Hempstead and from Essex and Kent, and once the risk of explosion had passed two other tankers were sent to decant the remaining fuel from the crashed tanker. The southbound carriageway was closed for this operation.

We managed to stop the fuel from entering any water course and the Water Board attended to prevent the fuel from contaminating the supply.

The southbound carriageway remained closed until late on Friday night, while the northbound one didn't re-open until Sunday.

The Welwyn and Hatfield Citizen had a quote from DC Andrew Russell, "We were very, very lucky the petrol did not ignite. The crews all did very well. It was hairy for a moment and we were worried but the police, fire and rescue service, ambulance and BP all liaised extremely efficiently."

However, the *Welwyn and Hatfield Review* managed to get the scoop, "One spark could have turned it into a fireball in a split second," said Leading Fireman Malcolm Currie!

OK, let's mention a bit about training.

After Training School we had constant on-going training, retraining and updates.

We would of course train on-station. Most shifts would see us out in the yard drilling with the everyday equipment we used regularly, ladders, pumps, RTA etc.

Not as often we would practise with things like foam equipment and the shear legs.

On top of that, every two years we would have to attend a two day BA refresher course to catch up with new procedures and train in the hot cans.

Even though I couldn't get a L/Fm's job I was sent on a Junior Officers Course, that didn't help either!

1990. CRAZY THINGS THAT TURN YOU ON.

The watch seemed to become a bit of a transit camp over the next few years with people coming and going and a couple staying with us.

Among those I can remember are Fm Daryl 'Spud' Stroud who went off to London Fire Brigade and got promoted through the ranks, Lee Jacobs left us for Blue Watch, Bob Adamson got promoted, Andy Mansfield who transferred to Baldock and the stayers, two blokes I really liked Paul 'Mad Dog' Riley who joined us from Blue Watch and Tom 'Sludge or TC' Andrews who came from somewhere that I don't remember, and don't push me on the 'TC!'

Unfortunately, Dave Rees went off to Hatfield and then, subsequently, to join Spiros at Royston.

We had been out to a fire in the Old Town, some old derelict tower thing if I remember rightly. It was around four in the morning and we were packing up the gear.

On the way home I was dozing in the back of the appliance when, as we were passing by Stapleford Tyres I fancied I saw a bit of smoke issuing from the roof. No I was imagining it, back to dozing.

Back at the station, off to the dormitory and hopefully a few hours sleep.

Ten minutes later and the bells went down and the lights came on and guess what it said on the printout... Stapleford Tyres, Old Town, Stevenage.

Smoke was coming from the roof and Andy Mansfield and I donned our BA and picked up the jet that had been laid out for us. The door was forced and we entered the building, light smoke so we started to look for the seat of the fire. We kicked down another door and pressed on; another door was kicked in, still working our jet through the rooms. No sign of the fire and our way is blocked by yet another door. Two size tens and we were through... outside again, about ten feet from where we had entered!

The first big fire of the year broke out at the Stevenage Bowl, Danestrete at 1413 hrs in the morning on 3rd February.

Both pumps turned out with Stn O Clinton in charge who, on arrival sent "make pumps 4."

Control mobilised two additional appliances from Hitchin.

I was in BA with Andy Mansfield again and we made our entry at the front of the building with a jet. The fire was at the far end of the bowling lanes in the machinery. The building was heavily smoke-logged and got steadily hotter as we penetrated further. We also had a thermal imaging camera to help us to locate the fire.

We were relieved by a second BA crew who took over our jet and we left the building to report to the Stn O on the progress being made inside.

It took two hours to bring the blaze under control, when we could ventilate and tidy up.

Me and Ian Clinton at the Stevenage Bowl fire.
Picture: HFRS

Stn O Clinton sent the stop message around six in the morning "a building, approx. 50m x 50m, used as a bowling alley – undergoing refurbishment – 6 bowling lane return machines severely damaged by fire, twenty-five per cent of building severely damaged by heat, remainder of building severely damaged by smoke, 2 jets, 1 hosereel, 12 BA and thermal imaging camera in use, "D" Delta.

The thermal imaging camera was a new piece of equipment which showed heat and enabled us to locate fire hot spots or alternatively the body heat of casualties.

I think I am right in saying, on 1st April, 1990, we became the Hertfordshire Fire and Rescue Service as it was thought to describe our role better, as if it actually mattered, even today lay people still refer to the fire brigade. I also seem to recall hearing that it cost over £12,000 just to change the letter headings etc. money well spent!

Saturday, 31st March, the early hours of the morning and the landlord of the St Nicholas Pub in Canterbury Way, and his wife and dog, are awakened by the fire alarm sounding.

He said, "The alarm system woke us up at 0200 hrs and we just got out. The whole place was blazing and the fire doors just held it back.

Back at the fire station…"

BEEP, BEEP, BEEP… "Both appliances to St. Nicholas public house, Canterbury Way, Stevenage, fire."

230 and 232 mobile to incident at 0207 hrs, Stn O Clinton in charge.

I am driving the WrL with a crew of five.

We are in attendance at 0211 hrs and the Stn O immediately sends "make pumps 4."

The whole of the ground floor bar area is well alight and we have two BA teams with jets making an entry into the rear of the pub.

320 and 321 mobile to incident with a total crew of nine.

It is slow progress, a further attack on the fire at first floor level, via a short extension ladder to a flat roof, is made by a third BA crew with a jet.

The stop message is sent at 0254 hrs, "A building of one and two floors approx. 15m x 15m, used as a public house, ground floor and twenty-five per cent of first floor severely damaged by fire, remainder damaged by heat and smoke, three jets, one hosereel, eight BA in use."

St. Nicholas Pub fire.
Picture: HFRS

After hours of damping down and making the building safe, we finally got back to the station at 0611 hrs.

The previous evening a rowdy customer had been thrown out of the pub and one theory was that it was a revenge attack.

To make matters worse, after the fire, looters broke into the burnt out bar and stole bottles of spirits and cash from a fruit machine totalling over £700!

Over the weekend of the 27th-28th June we are off to the Royal Norfolk Show and an appointment with Royalty!

Roydon, his uncle and I are off to display the steam fire engine at the Norfolk Showground just outside Norwich.

We had been invited by the Norfolk Fire Brigade, as there was to be a fire theme this year with a parade of fire engines on the Sunday.

We were taking the Divisional lorry to tow the steamer and once there it was to be converted into our accommodation using some scaffolding poles and a salvage sheet. After we set up and the steam engine was put on display, we had time to look around the show. There was so much going on including military bands, aircraft, livestock, horse drawn vehicles and craft and produce stalls.

During the afternoon I was with the steam engine when a rustic looking lady came up to me and said, "'allo cock, how big are your whippletrees?"

That's a bit forward I thought some local Norfolk name for a body part perhaps! After a bit more conversation it transpired that this lady was going to be supplying and driving the two horses that would pull the steamer in the parade tomorrow and a whippletree is part of the harness that will connect the engine to the horse. So crisis over, she seemed to be pleased with the size of my whippletrees and went off happy.

That night we were guests of the army who had a big marquee with a bar. Their challenge for the night was to get a girl to pose naked, wearing only one of their bearskins!

The following morning we prepared for the parade. Our steam engine was hitched up to two absolutely stunning Suffolk Punch shire horses and with Elmo, me and our lady driver resplendent in Victorian fireman's uniform we set off for the parade arena and our drive past the guest of honour HRH Anne, the Princess Royal.

We followed a hand drawn manual pump and a horse drawn manual fire engine and entered the arena to the strains of *Chariots of Fire.* Following us was a parade of vintage appliances bringing the display up to date.

We did a couple of circuits of the arena passing in front of the Royal Box to constant applause and cheering.
Our Suffolks took us back to our display stand and we waited for our moment of Royal fame. A little while later, following her security men, the Princess Royal paid us a visit and we chatted for a short time, she was very interested in the steamer and us.

HRH The Princess Royal meets HFB The Roy and Sid.

A good weekend all round.

On Monday 2nd July, we had the first of many rescues from fire that happened this year.

We were out mobile when at 1720 hrs, our call-sign came on the radio.

"VI to Charlie 230, order your appliance to Ashwell Close, Graveley, kitchen fire."

I was driving the WrL with a crew of five.

The address was a bungalow and a light smoke was issuing from the front door. A BA crew with a hosereel entered the building and emerged again moments later carrying an elderly woman who was suffering from smoke inhalation.

The crew re-entered to extinguish the fire and an ambulance was requested for the lady. In the meantime we put her on oxygen and monitored her condition.

The lady was taken to hospital and the fire put out very quickly.

The stop message was sent at 1740 hrs,
"A terraced bungalow, approx. 10m x 5m, kitchen severely damaged by heat and smoke, remainder damaged by smoke, 1 elderly female suffering the effects of smoke inhalation and conveyed to hospital by Herts ambulance."

On Thursday 26th July, I had to carry out a different sort of rescue… my fire engine!

Baldock firefighters were the first in attendance just before 4 pm and we had been called to Ivel Grange Farm, North Road, Baldock on a "make pumps 7."

1606 hrs and we left the station, I was driving the WrE with a crew of four.

In attendance at 1618 hrs.

The other pumps were 310, 311, 320, 300, 301 and 230. Also attending was DO Alan Wallace and the control unit from Hatfield, with a total of forty firemen. Any fire over five pumps warranted the additional attendance of the control unit.

The fire had started in a barn and spread to the surrounding fields.

I pulled into a gate and entered the field, stopping just inside. I was on the edge of a field of standing corn, the crew went off with their beaters and I stayed by the pump. Next minute the wind changed direction and the fire front was heading back my way. The smoke became very thick and blowing back over the road. The crew ran past as the fire reached the pump, I jumped in and threw it into reverse, shooting backwards through the gate and into the road unable to see anything with my eyes streaming. I spun the wheel round to try and stay on the invisible road, and when the smoke cleared I was parked perfectly by the kerbside! Luckily the police had closed a number of roads around the fire and diverted traffic.

We were relieved by the night crew in the station van and we arrived back at home station at 1802 hrs. The stop message wasn't sent until 2026 hrs. and read, "1 hectare (2½ acres) of standing corn and 2 hectares (5 acres) of stubble destroyed by fire – barn, 20m x 20m, containing 50 tons of straw and 4 tons of hay well alight, water shuttle in use from hydrant 1 mile away."

Three days later we were back to rescuing people again.

At a three storey block of council flats a fire had broken out in a bedroom on the third floor.

A visitor staying in one of the flats dragged the burning mattress through the flat and out onto the landing, setting fire to the landing and effectively blocking the escape route of the third floor residents.

BEEP, BEEP, BEEP, "Both appliances to Yarmouth Road, Stevenage, persons reported."

0053 hrs, WrE and WrL mobile to incident.

I am driving the WrL with a crew of four total eight.

In attendance at 0057 hrs.

When we arrived there were ten or so residents, some in nightgowns, outside in the street.

Two BA crews with a jet moved up to the third floor where the landing was alight, there was a fire in the bedroom of one flat and two further flats were smoke-logged.

With the fire on the landing out, one crew went on to tackle the fire in the bedroom while the second crew started a search of the other two flats.

Forcing the door of one flat they found a sixty-nine- year-old man in his smoke filled flat. He was led to safety by the crew and handed over to the ambulance.

They then checked the other flat on the second floor, which was empty.

Meanwhile the fire in the other flat was brought under control using the jet.

The visitor who dragged the mattress out of his flat had suffered burns to his feet, and both casualties were treated at the Lister Hospital.

Stn O Clinton sent the stop at 0125 hrs, "a building of three floors used as residential flats, approx. 20m x 15m – 3rd floor flat damaged by fire and smoke – 3rd floor landing severely damaged by fire – 2 further flats on 3rd floor damaged by smoke, 1 male person led to safety by Service, 1 other male person with burns, conveyed to hospital by Herts Ambulance."

Once the fire was out and the scene made safe, the residents were allowed to return to their flats.

The Council turned up to secure the burnt out flat.

Back on station at 0218 hrs.

From 10th to 23rd August I was off back to Germany.

Back in 1989 I had written to the chief with a proposal to take a fire engine to Germany for combined drills.

After due consideration the idea was sanctioned and it was decided to incorporate it with our exchange trip to Germany this year.

So it was on Friday, 10th we set out with a PCV and a Dennis SS series appliance, WrL, (G318 WNM).

The other members of our crew were Stn O Pete Hazeldine from Brigade Headquarters and Bishops Stortford Sub O Frank Freestone. Temporary L/Fm Stuart Crichton, who had lost an ear in a road accident and had a tattoo of an ear at the top of his arm. If you spoke to him he would lift up his sleeve to reveal the tattoo and say, "Sorry, pardon me?" My old mate Fm Dave Rees, now at Hatfield and Bob Williams from "A" Division. Bob was an amateur boxer whose nickname was "Rembrandt" because he spent so much time on the canvas!

The first two days we would stay at Koblenz and go to the Rhine in Flames festival.

On the Saturday, after lunch, we had a mutual driving exchange. We took turns in driving a German appliance and they drove ours. They set off with an ashen faced Pete Hazeldine and completed the drive without incident. We were doing OK until Dave Rees got behind the wheel, took off a wing mirror, mounted the kerb and reduced our host to a gibbering wreck!

Our evening on the Rhine was spectacular indeed.

We boarded our cruise ship *Stolzenfels* at 6 o'clock in the evening and, joined by David and Ilse Oudôt and four town officials, we had dinner heading down river to Braubach as part of a huge armada of similar cruise boats.

At 10 o'clock they all turned round and headed back towards Koblenz. All the castles along the valley were lit up with red flares and each staged a firework display. Finally, back at Koblenz the biggest display took place from the fortress Ehrenbreitstein. Back on dry land we walked around the festival with thousands of others.

The following day we drove down to Mainz, where Pete and I were to be based for the next week or so. The other four were collected by representatives of the Ludwigshafen and Kaiserslauten fire brigades.

Mainz fire station is huge with over twenty various appliances including a brand new twenty-five ton, six wheeled crane and a fireboat. There is a second station in the suburb of Mainz-Lerchenberg, with three appliances and a further eleven volunteer stations in the suburbs throughout the city.

We can ride on any appliance that is mobilised, a clue to the severity of the call is in the call out message. After a gong, for a minor incident the message would be prefixed with *ACHTUNG*, meaning attention and for a larger incident *ACHTUNG, ACHTUNG* when the Löschzug would be mobilised, (for Löschzug see page 96).

MAIN STATION: MAINZ-INNENSTADT.		
SRW	Schnellrüstwagen.	Fast rescue tender.
LF24 1	Löschgruppenfahrzeug 24.	Water tender ladder.
TroTLF	Trockentanklöschfahrzeug.	Dry powder WrT.
DLK 1	Drehleiter mit korb.	Turntable ladder.
KLAF	Kleinalarmfahrzeug	Small incident tender.
GW–ÖL	Gerätewagen Öl.	Tender for oil spills.
GW–AS	GW atem/strahlenschutz	Tender BA/radiation.
RW 2	Rüstwagen 2.	Rescue tender.
FWK 25	Feuerwehrkran 25.	25 ton crane.
STATION 2: MAINZ-LERCHENBERG.		
LF16	Löschgruppenfahrzeug 16.	Water tender.
DLK 3	Drehleiter mit korb.	Turntable ladder.
KLAF	Kleinalarmfahrzeug.	Small incident tender.
LF24 2	Löschgruppenfahrzeug 24	Spare water tender.

Watch A are on duty.

> 1653 hrs. DONG, DONG, DONG "ACHTUNG, ACHTUNG, SRW and TroTLF to Mainz-Lerchenberg, Hindemithstraße 39, fire." I turn out on the TroTLF, H. Reitz in charge, crew of five. SRW, Herr Hofer in charge, crew of three.
> The fire is on Station 2 ground and our two appliances, together with their LF 16, O. Schneider in charge, crew of 6 and DLK 3, Herr Kaltenbach in charge, crew of two, make up the Löschzug.
> We were in attendance at 1711 hrs to find the crews from station 2 had already extinguished the fire using 2 BA and a hosereel. The fire was in a large rubbish container in the basement of a block of flats.
> Herr Hofer ordered the RW 2 to attend as it carried a smoke extractor unit.
> Pete arrived on the RW 2, L. Harf in charge, crew of three.
> I went back with Herr Hofer in the SRW. We stopped off at the site of the new fire station, still under construction.
> Back at station 1801 hrs.

The new station is being built at Mainz-Bretzenheim and when completed will become the main station, with a Löschzug being maintained at the current station and station two will close.

On Monday 13th Watch B came on duty and we had some training on the new crane and fireboat.

The crane has a thirty-ton lifting capacity and extends to a height of thirty metres. It can drive normally or, by engaging all six wheels, can move diagonally. It can go forward or reverse, controlled either from the crew cab or the crane operating cab.

The fireboat is powered by water jets that can be revolved 360° and thus can move in any direction. It has a 5,000 litre per minute monitor. Later in the day we went to check it.

We went for a short trip out onto the river Rhine and as we came back in, there was the crane with a number of firemen at drill on the harbourside. In true worldwide fire service fashion, they got a 5,000 l p/m soaking as we passed!

Over the next few days we are quite busy:

13th – Two calls to wasps' nests, smell of smoke and an AFA.

14th – Diesel spillage following RTA, car fire, flooding and another wasps nest.

15th – Tub of flowers on fire and an oil spillage on the road.

16th –AFA, wasps nest, petrol spillage following an RTA and gas leaking from a cylinder in a laboratory.

Which brings me onto Saturday 18th August. This will be a very interesting twenty-four hours.

Watch C come on duty at seven a.m.

DONG, DONG, DONG "ACHTUNG, KLAF to attend Windmühlenstraße, Mz-Oberstadt, special service."

1137 hrs mobile to incident, Herr Manz in charge crew of three.

Herr Manz tells me that the call is to a street signpost that has been knocked over!

1148 hrs in attendance.

A twelve foot (3.5m) metal pole with two street name plates attached has been bent almost flat. They broke the pole off and tried to undo the locking nut in the ground to re-erect it but were unable to so. The remaining part of the pole was hammered flat. The next problem was that the pole wouldn't go into the back of the appliance, it was too long. No problem – out came an angle grinder and generator and three feet was cut off, it fit's OK now.

Apparently at night and weekends when the City Council workers are not at work, incidents such as this become the duty of the fire brigade.

Incidentally, streets that run parallel to the Rhine have blue name plates, while those with red name plates run towards the river.

DONG, DONG, DONG "ACHTUNG, SRW & FWK to Mombacherstraße / parkhausneubau Hochstraße, RTA."

1754 hrs SRW mobile, BI Nuber in charge, crew of three.

FWK mobile, Herr Schieferstein in charge, crew of two.

1800 hrs in attendance.

This is the first operational turnout for the new crane and I join the SRW crew.

The incident is located on the flyover behind the main railway station where building work on a new car park was being carried out.

A Fiat Uno 146A being driven by a twenty-six-year-old, under the influence of alcohol, had crashed over some concrete blocks and reinforcing steel rods and ended up in a position where it was impossible to recover it normally.

The driver was taken to hospital by ambulance.

The crane was brought up alongside on a different part of the flyover and a flatbed recovery truck was positioned behind it.

The vehicle was attached to the crane by straps and was then swung over and secured on the truck.

1843 hrs, home station.

First Call for the Crane.

Seven p.m. dinner time.

Ten p.m. bed time.

The clock ticks over into Sunday, and a lot more rescues.

Sometime after 0200 hrs in the morning, three kilometres away, an unknown person is setting a fire in the basement of the married quarters at the United States Army Central Barracks.

At 0233 hrs fire control receives a telephone call from the US Fire Department.

DONG, DONG, DONG, "ACHTUNG, ACHTUNG, Löschzug to attend building number 6719, Fritz-Ohlhof-straße, Mz-Innenstadt, Fire."

0235 hrs, SRW mobile, OiC BI Nuber, crew of two.

0235 hrs, TroTLF mobile, OiC Herr Birkmeyer, crew of four.

0235 hrs, DLK 1 mobile, OiC Herr Lupp, crew of two.

0235 hrs, LF24 1 mobile, OiC Herr Fuchs, crew of five.

I am riding the LF24 1 and as we approached the incident smoke was drifting across the road.

An American pumper was in attendance.

The Löschzug was in attendance at 0240 hrs

On arrival at the front of the building, thick smoke was issuing from the door and windows on the ground, first, second and third floors of the central block of three. Four of the windows on the second and third floors had people trapped.

Bi Nuber requested the GW-AS and station two to attend.

0240 hrs, LF24 2 mobile, OiC Herr Trappel, crew 5.

0240 hrs, DLK 3 mobile, OiC Herr Schröder, crew of 2.

0243 hrs, GW-AS mobile, OiC Herr Pessara, crew 2.

Prior to our arrrival, in their efforts to escape the fire via the stairwell, five people became affected by smoke inhalation and one fell down the stairs and broke their arm, all being taken by ambulance to the military hospital in Wiesbsden.

A two-man BA crew entered the main door and proceeded down to the basement with a jet from the TroTLF. Simultaneously the DLK was pitched to the windows on the second and third floors and six adults, one child and a dog were rescued. My first involvement was to assist the casualties from the cage of the DLK.

0249 hrs, GW-AS in attendance.

0253 hrs, LF24 2 & DLK 3 in attendance.

Bi Nuber then came over to me and, almost apologetically, asked me if I would wear BA. I got a BA set from the TroTLF and reported for orders.

Our task was to ventilate the centre stairwell and check the flats for further trapped persons. I was teamed up with OBM Birkmeyer and we entered the building in thick, black smoke. With me hanging onto his tunic we proceded up to the first floor where he said "you search that flat and I'll search this one" and he was gone!

I searched the flat, nothing, and again on the second and third floors. I met up with the elusive Birkmeyer on the third floor and we made our way down to the basement, to the scene of the fire, which was pretty much out and a crew was getting a smoke extractor to work. We then made our way back to the ground floor and out into the fresh air.

We reported to BI Nuber who then asked us to ventilate and check the flats in the left hand block which was also smoke logged.

Same thing, I checked the left hand flats and Birkmeyer the right. On the third floor I found a man in one room and his wife and child in another. All three were put in one room by an open window so that in the event of the situation deteriorating the DLK need only one pitch to rescue all three. In the flat opposite two more people were instructed to stay by an open window.

On my way back out I came across two US servicemen and told them the location of the trapped persons and all five were brought to safety as the smoke cleared.

Found Birkmeyer and went to the GW-AS to change BA sets.

The final job was to go up on the DLK to enter a couple of flats to secure them from the inside.

The fire had occurred in a large basement lock-up cage containing furniture and household effects.

Nothing was moved prior to the arrival of the K10 Criminal Investigation Police.

We make up the equipment and head home.

0331 hrs, GW-AS home station.

0333 hrs, LF24 2 and DLK 3 home station.

0431 hrs, TroTLF, LF24 1 and DLK 1 home station.

0433 hrs, SRW home station.

Well that was different! Thirteen years of BA training in the UK went out of the window. You can see now the potential benefit of my lecture in Ingelheim two years previously.

The *"Mainzer Rhein-Zeitung"* and the *"Mainzer Zeitung"* of 20th August both reported on the weekend's incidents.

On 21st August we joined all the big-wigs, including our CFO Ted Faulkner, in the town of Landstuhl, for a presentation on the removal of the US army's chemical and nuclear weapons from Germany as the Iron Curtain collapses.

Over lunch the seeds are sown, again, for me to return in September to lecture on BA, this time in Luxemburg.

After an unbelievably boring tour of the Opel factory in Kaiserslautern, Pete and I head home via a town called Alzey with Herr Besand who introduces us to the CFO Hans-Gunther Hoffman for something to eat and a lot to drink. In the town square there is a bronze statue of a horse under which there is a wine tank, which, on certain festival days is filled and the wine served via a tap in the saddlebag.

A walk around the town, taking in the castle and the town walls and most of the bars and then back to the fire station for a presentation box of local wine.

Back to Reiner's house in Mainz for a beer and then out with his wife to visit a few of their favourite watering holes!

Back to the station around half twelve, much the worse for wear. Pete cut a dash with his jacket undone, tie askew, a German helmet on his head and cases of wine under his arm. Great night.

In all I attended twenty-one fire calls during my time in Mainz.

Watch A, Mainz, 20th August 1990, L to R: F.J. Pleger,
Norbert Hahn, Wilfried Jahres, Michael Blecker,
Hans Jörg Dauner, Frank Oppermann, Matthias Daarsch, Thomas Mock,
Andreas Pils, Pete Hazeldine, Henry Reitz,
K. Hans Hofer, Heinz Fiedler, Günter Löffler, Me, Josef Bacher,
Bernhard Muders, Lothar Harf.
Back Row: Our Dennis WrL, FWK, DLK 1.

Other activities included passing the six monthly fitness test, a tour of station 2 with Reiner Besand the OiC of the station, a visit to Frankfurt Airport fire station and the Merck factory fire brigade in Darmstadt with the third officer Herr Kahn, who also took us on a tour of Mainz including dinner in a bier keller.

A visit with our WrL to Viernheim, and to Bingen to discuss the forthcoming exercises.

At Bingen we were invited up into the hills behind the town for a traditional vine root barbeque with around fifty firemen and six or seven appliances. Much talking, singing, eating and drinking. The beer served via a cooler powered by a fire brigade generator.

Also a trip to Mannheim to visit my old school pen friend Norbert Maliske and wife Karin.

On Wednesday 22nd August we left Mainz and headed to the Mainz-Bingen area for the second part of our visit.

After a busy day touring the District of Mainz-Bingen we have an invite to a barbeque and social night at Wackernheim fire station.

Another great evening drinking, eating and singing.

Stum Bob, Rembrandt and myself gave a superb rendition of the Frank Sinatra classic *New York, New York* to rapturous applause.

Mr Faulkner, who had been watching our performance stood up and banged his fist on the desk, oh no a step too far I thought. Instead he led everyone to the appliance bays and got someone to drive the pumps out. Marshalling our German hosts he introduced them to the delights of the *Hokey Cokey!* Great fun.

Saturday 25th and it's the day of the exercise.

The first location is the Boehringer pharmaceutical factory in Ingelheim-am-Rhein where we are taking part in a chemical exercise.

A fire has broken out involving a chemical trailer and the contents are leaking out and on fire.

A company TroTLF has responded with foam and chemical suits.

Our appliance supplies two BA wearers and a cooling jet and two chemical suit wearers using foam.

The chemical is pumped into special containers.

Decontamination of firefighters at the Boeringer exercise.

Decontamination is carried out by us using our decontamination shower.

Lunch and then off to Bingen-am-Rhein for the second exercise.

This location was Bingen-am-Rhein town centre and the appearance of an English fire engine driving through the streets on the blues with sirens wailing caused quite a stir.

The incident involved a fire in the Bingen Cultural Centre with pupils from the Music School trapped on the second floor.

Our task was to rescue several of the pupils via a ladder and provide a BA crew with a hosereel into the building and a jet working from the head of the ladder. Water supplied from an LF 16 and using a previously engineered coupling enabled us to connect the German hose to our pump.

Also the DLK carried out rescues, LF 24 firefighting, RW ventilation, GW-AS for BA and ELW acting as incident control.

After the exercise the CFO of Bingen, Kurt Sperling and our CFO gave a little speech, we passed around a glass of wine the size of a two-gallon bucket and the German fireman's toast of "Gut Schlauch, Gut Schlauch, Gut Schlauch," which translates as "Good Hose?" The UK fire brigade mascot "Welephant" amused the crowds.

Back home to the UK and plenty more excitement to come before the year is out.

A couple of big incidents in September.

On Wednesday 5th at the old George King factory site in Argyle Way, Stevenage, a JCB digger being used by demolition workers fractured a four-inch medium pressure gas main.

Hundreds of nearby workers were evacuated and police sealed off an area between Gunnelswood Road, Six Hills Way and Fairlands Way.

We were called just after nine a.m. I was driving the WrL with a crew of four, also mobile was the WrE and Hitchin's WrL.

Gas Board engineers isolated the leak and fire crews dismantled debris from around the ruptured main using Lukas cutting gear. The pipe was repaired and three hours later the workers were given the all clear to return to work.

A stop message was sent at twelve fifteen p.m.

On the following Thursday, 13th, we were called to a flooding at the Town Square bus depot in Danestrete.

Mobile at 1029 hrs and in attendance at 1033 hrs. Driving the WrL again with a crew of five. Also attending is the WrE and, following a "make pumps 4" message, Hitchin's WrL and salvage tender and Old Welwyn's WrT.

The Stevenage Gazette of Friday 14th carried the headline –

and continued, "shoppers watched in astonishment as the geysers sent a massive ten-ton block of concrete measuring twenty-six feet by sixteen feet into the air while one jet of pressurised water after another ruptured the ground."

We used three major pumps, one lightweight pump and two WEDA pumps to try and control the flood.

Adjacent shops and basements were also flooded.

The Gazette went on, "Fire Chief Mick Hodgkins said: "We had four appliances and a salvage tender there for about an hour – it was really hectic. Water was shooting up all over the bus concourse and flooding the shelters. We had to pump away thousands of gallons until the water board managed to switch off supplies."

The stop was sent at 1125 hrs and we were back at station at 1148 hrs.

One final trip abroad.

From 27th to 30th September I am off to Luxemburg for another BA lecture. This time the CFO Ted Faulkner is coming and they have given me an assistant, Sub O Gordon McMillan from the Training Centre!

We are lecturing to the annual tripartite meeting of the fire brigades of Luxemburg, France and the Saarland and Rheinland Pfalz in Germany. The lecture will take place on the MV *Princesse Marie Astrid* while cruising the river Moselle.

Because the chief is coming we will be flying, departing Gatwick at 7.37 p.m. and arriving at Frankfurt at 8.40 p.m.

During the flight I ask him if I can buy him a drink, "Sure Sid" he says "I'll have two gin and tonics."

"Two, sir?"

"Yes, it's a short flight and they only come round once."

We are met by Wolfgang Dörsch, our driver and guide for the week. Wolfgang became a good family friend over the years and I spent many happy hours with my family at his house in Marienhausen drinking beer and eating sausages.

That night we went out to dinner with David Oudôt and Karl Heiser in Bacharach.

Saturday, 29th and its lecture day.

We drive to Gravenmacher on the Moselle.

The host is Henri Birscheidt, CFO of the Luxemburg fire brigades, and after the opening speeches, the lectures start in earnest.

Manfred Siebenhaar and Wolfgang Dörsch (foreground) and the Luxemburg BA training vehicle at Grevenmacher.

We follow Lt. Col. Dr Ferdinand Metzler, Inspector of Doctors, Luxemberg fire service whose subject was "Medical Fitness in Hazardous Atmospheres," and a monotonous speech from German fire officer, Dr Regenbogen (Dr Rainbow!)

The CFO introduced us and broke the microphone. Our lecture went from 1130 hrs to 1245 hrs and was well received, bearing in mind their lack of BA procedures.

A buffet lunch was followed by a lot of backslapping, exchanging of gifts, drinking and talking.

The highlight was the CFO having a clumsy moment and knocking a Luxemburg officer's kepi hat overboard, which floated off downstream!

At 3.30 p.m. we docked back in Gravenmacher and following a group photograph and a look at the mobile BA training vehicle, the real purpose of the tripartite meeting got under way.

We all pile into the Caves Bernard-Massard a local Champagne cellar for an hour or so of tasting.

Returning to Koblenz and straight to the Königsbacher brewery, more beers and a meal with Herr Eisinger, chief of the Rheinland Pfalz Training School, Manfred Siebenhaar of Mainz-Bingen, Wolfgang Dörsch, David Oudôt, CFO Faulkner and Gordon McMillan.

Back to the training school.

From quarter past ten to half past twelve at night, Mr Faulkner, Wolfgang, Gordon and I drink another two crates of beer by way of a night cap!

Gordon is up all night talking to the toilet!

Sunday, 30th and home.

Day shift, 6th October and at 1515 hrs the bells go down and the teleprinter tells us "230 and 232 to Hitchin Road, Stevenage, RTA persons trapped."

I am driving the WrL with a crew of five and with the WrE crew of five, we are mobile at 1523 hrs.

Enroute the WrE is diverted to a chip pan fire and control mobilise Hitchin's WrL with a crew of four to back us up, also mobile is Hatfield's ERT with a crew of two and an ADO.

Three cars have been in collision on a dual carriageway leaving a female passenger trapped in a red Vauxhall Nova and her driver husband injured. The female drivers of a white Porsche and a dark blue Metro City were also injured and had to be treated in hospital.

We had to use the Lukas cutting gear to free the woman and she was removed from the vehicle after about 25 minutes.

The stop went in at 3.47 pm and we were back on station at 3.55 pm.

On Monday 15th October we were called, at 1344 hrs, to a property in Hertford Road, Stevenage.

I always seem to be driving, this time the WrL with a crew of 4 and, together with the WrE, crew of 5 we are in attendance at 1347 hrs.

The building was well alight and the stop message sent at 1415 hrs sums it up:

"A detached, unoccupied bungalow approx. 15m x 5m, 75% of roof severely damaged by fire, 4 gas cylinders involved, 2 jets, 2 hosereels, 4 BA in use, "D" Delta."

Home station at 1534 hrs.

The owner of this property was trying to get planning permission which had been turned down.

Our fire investigation found that the fire had started under the stairs and in two more places upstairs in the roof space.

Another temporary promotion for me starting on 7th November. This is due to Stn O Clinton leaving us. Mick Milton will act up to Stn O and John Miles to Sub O.

One last rescue before the year ends.

A kitchen fire has broken out in a flat in Wellfield Court, Norwich Close, Stevenage.

I am in BA on the WrL, our WrE is off the run and we have a spare WrT in its place, total crews of eight.

Not much of a fire but a lot of smoke and an elderly lady found inside is led to safety by BA crews.

On 27th November I am riding in charge of the WrT (232) and we are called to one of our regular false alarms, British Aerospace in Argyle Way.

As the stop message is sent we are instructed to return to base to pick up the HP and proceed to another call.

We return on the blues, closing down at 0828 hrs.

At 0829 hrs we are mobile with the HP crew of two to Bowmans Mill, Ickleford, near Hitchin.

We are attending as part of a "make pumps four, HP required."

As well as Hitchin's two appliances, Baldock and Old Welwyn are also mobilised.

We arrive at 0843 hrs.

The fire is in a hopper in an elevated tower, containing around eight tons of flour, approximately two tons of which are damaged by fire. One hosereel and 8 BA are used to extinguish the fire.

We are back on station at 0941 hrs so two hours overtime!

To give you an idea of some of the more usual calls we used to get, here is a list the twenty-three incidents that I attended in December:

A garage fire, petrol leaking following an RTA, forty tons of baled straw alight in Weston (make pumps 4), relief for the previous fire, fire in a toilet, fire in a garden, kitchen fire, RTA persons trapped, wash down roadway following an RTA, child with his finger trapped in a car seat belt, person shut in lift, workshop on fire in Hitchin (make pumps 3), chimney fire, rubbish fire, flooding and eight false alarms.

At some point, and I don't remember exactly when, but about now, we got involved with a charity event organised for a cause that I don't remember!

However the interesting thing here is that it was supported by singing stars Marty and Kim Wilde.

Here we all are, in the bowling alley in Stevenage.

Standing L to R: Marty Wilde, Kim Wilde, Spud Stroud, John Miles
and Ronnie Barker (From Baldock). Kneeling L to R: Andy Mansfield,
Me, 'I can't remember' and Taff James.
Others: on the left in a white t-shirt, Joe Heeney (Blue Watch), on the
right in a blue Brigade sweatshirt, Terry Game (Blue Watch) and Frank
Gollogly in blue t-Shirt (Green Watch).

Now to the National newspapers!

Starring our very own Dave 'Budget' Magill and his wife
Avril.

On Tuesday, December 4th, 1990 *The Sun* carried the
headline:

CRAZY THINGS THAT TURN YOU ON

Our hotlines were scorching after we asked *Sun* readers: What
wacky things turn you on?
The article went on "Housewife Avril Magill's heart is set
alight with passion when her fireman husband comes in from

work – because she loves the smell of his uniform after a blaze."

Avril went on to say "I love the smell of burning wood so when David returns from work, black and filthy, I won't let him shower before we have a bit of hanky panky."

And continued "When I first met David he could hardly believe his luck… but it doesn't half mess up the sheets."

Finishing with "And after a fire he always jokes with his mates at Stevenage fire station by saying, "Avril's in for a good night tonight."

Fantastic and I think he was charged with "bringing the brigade in to disrepute."

Finally, given that he was a Sub Officer and didn't do much firefighting, I reckon Avril only had to wash the sheets two or three times a year!

Another sad end to the year.

A young girl has been visiting her Dad at his work in Stevenage and is driving home to Welwyn Garden City, and at around half past one in the afternoon, is travelling along Martins Way towards the Hitchin Road and the A1(M).

Travelling in the opposite direction is a Sunblest Bakeries lorry.

At the station we are just finishing our lunch break…

1343 hrs, BEEP, BEEP, BEEP, "Both appliances to Martins Way, Stevenage, RTA persons trapped."

I am in charge of the WrT with a crew of four, also mobile WrL, crew of four and Hatfield's ERT with a crew of two.

We are in attendance at 1347 hrs and find a Ford Fiesta in a head on collision with a lorry. The car has crossed the central reservation, over a lamp post knocked down in a previous accident and is severely damaged front and back. A young female is trapped inside and unresponsive.

The police have closed the road and an ambulance is in attendance.

We use Lukas to open both doors so we can get access to the casualty but the Ambulance crew can find no life signs.

> I remember holding her hand as we prepared to remove her from the vehicle.
>
> She was taken to Lister Hospital by Herts ambulance and declared to be dead from multiple injuries on arrival.
>
> Stop message sent at 1356 hrs.
>
> Home station at 1409 hrs.

The poor girl was only seventeen years old and would have celebrated her eighteenth birthday in three days time.

She had passed her driving test just three weeks before.

We were called back to the scene of the crash later in the afternoon to wash down the road once the vehicles had been recovered.

The Welwyn and Hatfield Times of Wednesday, May 8th, 1991 reported on the inquest.

A vehicle examiner stated that "the rear wheel locked because the hub retaining nuts had been over tightened when the new brake shoes had been fitted and the hub bearing seized."

Recording a verdict of accidental death the Coroner said: "This was a horrendous and tragic accident."

About now Ron Barlow arrived as our Station Commander. Previously the Stn O of Blue Watch, he was in overall charge of the station. Great bloke, I liked him a lot.

1991. CHICKEN PUTS DOG'S LIFE AT RISK.

It's February and it's freezing!

We have just taken over from Red Watch for a night shift on Wednesday 6th and almost immediately the WrL is called out to a house fire in Watton-at-Stone, a village halfway to Hertford. Hertford's WrL has also been ordered.

I am riding on WrE and so we continue to check the pump until...

At 1817 hrs the bells go down "order WrE to High Street, Watton-at-Stone, house fire, make pumps 3."

Mobile with Stn O Milton in charge with a crew of five.

We are in attendance at 1825 hrs after a careful drive in icy conditions.

The whole of the roof of the bungalow is alight and I am in the second BA team to enter with a jet.

It is so cold that the hose, pumps and even BA sets are freezing up. Water put onto the roof is freezing into icicles as it runs off the eaves.

A salvage tender is requested to attend, and as Hitchin's is off the run, control mobilise, 073 and 070, the salvage tender and WrL from Rickmansworth on the other side of the County!

Stn O Milton sends a stop message at 1858 hrs:

"A chalet type bungalow, approx. 8m x 6m, one hundred per cent of roof and fifty per cent of rooms and contents severely damaged by fire and heat, salvage work in progress."

Five days later, two adults and two children escaped from their four bedroomed house in Holly Copse, Stevenage when fire broke out in one of the bedrooms. 5 BA wearers extinguished the fire with a hosereel jet.

The set of four shifts starting on the 7th March proved to be busy, I am in charge of the WrE turning out to fifteen calls.

On Thursday, 7th we started at 0920 hrs with an AFA to John Lewis, Cavendish Road, Stevenage.

1409 hrs to an AFA at Acer Environmental, Wedgewood Court, Stevenage.

1436 hrs same thing.

1529 hrs another false alarm call to the Leisure Centre, Lytton Way,

And then, we are called to a bonfire out of control in London Road, Knebworth.

We are mobile at 1600 hrs with a crew of four.

Driving down London Road, the main street in the village, large amounts of thick black smoke can be seen behind the shops on the left. We turn into St Martin's Road and we can see two buildings on fire.

In attendance at 1616 hrs.

One jet is run out and the water supply is supplemented from a hydrant.

As I walk towards the fire, a man runs up to me and says, "It's alright mate everything's under control!"

I look at the smoke and the extent of the fire and reply, "It is now I'm here… mate!"

The man and his two colleagues tell me that they own the buildings and set fire to them on purpose. They ask me to let it burn out, which I consider, sending an informative message at 1624 hrs, "From L/Fm Payne, this is a derelict building, people are in attendance overseeing, crew standing by."

However in less than fifteen minutes, and much to the annoyance of the owners, I get the crew to play a jet on each of the buildings, and police closed the road due to the high volumes of smoke.

A further informative message went off at 1638 hrs, "From L/Fm Payne, crew delayed approx. thirty minutes, 2 jets in use."

We have had small, vandal related arson attacks here before, but on this occasion the "vandals" were the Church Buildings Committee, the Rector and two Churchwardens who, somewhat irresponsibly, took it on themselves to set fire to the two buildings.

At 1727 hrs I send, "Stop message from L/Fm Payne, 2 derelict buildings, 1st 5m x 16m, 2nd 8m x 8m, both 100% destroyed by fire, 2 jets in use."

Back on station at 1740 hrs.

Friday, 8th and at 1442 hrs we are ordered to standby at Hitchin fire station, crew of four.

Before we get there we are called on to a "make pumps 3" at Chalkdell Path, Hitchin, where we join both of Hitchin's pumps at a house fire.

Inside, all the rooms are piled high with clothes, books, magazines and newspapers. The first floor and the roof are severely damaged by fire with adjacent houses roof voids and 1st floors also damaged by smoke. The fire was brought under control using one jet, one hosereel and six BA.

At 5.35 pm we are called out again, this time to standby at Baldock fire station and the start of a very hectic few hours.

Just as we were driving up the slip road onto the A1(M) we are redirected.

"Charlie 232, order your appliance to Gage Close, Royston." What, that's miles away!

Apparently there has been a problem with the town's domestic gas supply and fires are breaking out all over the town.

We are in attendance at 1810 hrs.

Not much going on here other than the house stinks of gas.

We isolate the gas supply and ventilate the property.

Stop message sent at 1810 hrs.

At 1819 hrs we get our next call, "Charlie 232, order your appliance to Parthia Close, Royston, fire."

In attendance at 1820 hrs.

We had been called by the neighbours who had heard a smoke alarm and said, "I knew there was no one at home and so we rushed round and looked through the cat flap. Through the smoke we could see Anabel the cat lying on the floor."

Also in attendance was a pump from Sawston, (Cambridgeshire Fire and Rescue Service) with a crew of five.

A BA crew with a hosereel entered the house, where the gas fire has exploded and the lounge is on fire. The cat is rescued, the fire extinguished and the house ventilated.

Stop sent at 1836 hrs.

In attendance at Royston fire station at 1854 hrs.

It is chaos with so many fire engines in the town.

Given our next job, The Close, Royston, dogs involved.

Mobile at 1906 hrs.

In attendance at 1911 hrs.

The boiler in the kitchen had failed and gas was leaking into the house.

The gas supply was turned off and two dogs were found in a conservatory which was ventilated and they were left there.

The third dog, "Basenjy," was a different proposition. I found out afterwards that he was an African Hunting Dog and he was isolated in the lounge because he would fight with the other two!

We had to get him out of the gas-filled lounge but as we gently opened the door he came flying out, dodging our attempts to grab him and he was in the front garden.

A man was walking by with a little dog on a lead; one of the crew shouted at him to pick his dog up, too late, Basenjy had it by the throat and was shaking it wildly. Big Spud Stroud grabbed it by the neck until its eyes were bulging, carried it back into the house and threw it into the kitchen and slammed the door.

The house was ventilated and the stop sent at 1928 hrs.

Back to Royston station at 1936 hrs.

We were released and returned to Stevenage.

The Royston Crow of Friday, March 15th, quoted Royston Sub Officer Pete Lemon, "the first fire call was received at 1720 hrs – with a total of thirty-four answered in the first half hour."

The Service took fifty-seven calls altogether to fires and explosions in the town.

I remember enroute to our last call, we were approaching a roundabout with three exits. Approaching on the other three roads were three more fire engines, all going on various calls. We all went round like a carousel and drove off in different directions, with much rude gestering. Very amusing.

The Royston Crow went on to say "British Gas has admitted human error led to the surge of high pressure gas which caused numerous fires and explosions in Royston last Friday.

The network of high pressure gas which carries supplies between the various towns was connected directly to the network supplying houses in Royston.

The link resulted in a massive surge of high pressure gas entering the system in the town."

The headlines in *The Sun* of Saturday 9th March said:

FAMILIES IN GAS BLASTS NIGHTMARE

And went on "Hundreds of families fled their homes last night after dozens of gas blasts ripped through a town. More than a hundred firefighters ran from house to house to fight blazes."

One last thing, a memory of Pete Lemon. It was announced that we were to have our names put on our fire helmets.

Pete wrote to the Chief Fire Officer saying "If you think I'm going around wearing a yellow helmet with LEMON written on it you're mistaken!"

Saturday 9th, first night duty.

2003 hrs. Both appliances are called to The Glebe, Stevenage to a malicious false alarm.

2014 hrs. Both appliances mobile to Pankhurst Crescent, Stevenage to another malicious false alarm.

2057 hrs. Both appliances are sent to Shephall Way, Stevenage to a flat fire. An eleven-year-old girl, who was passing by, raised the alarm and then went back to the flat and managed to open the front door.

When we arrived we found her and two rats suffering from smoke inhalation. The fire started in the television set and was confined to the living room by four BA wearers and a hosereel jet.

Finally the last night shift, and on the morning of 11th March at 0836 hrs, both appliances attend The Hyde, Stevenage to a smoke-logged supermarket.

On Wednesday, 10th April we are called to a house fire at Hillmead, Stevenage.

It's just after seven in the evening and I am in charge of the WrE with a crew of four. 230 is out somewhere else.

We arrive at 1907 hrs. and are the first pump in attendance. I manage to kick down the door and send in two BA with a hosereel.

A second BA crew is deployed when the second pump arrives.

The kitchen is slightly damaged by fire, the rest of the house by smoke.

A chicken, cooking in the oven started the fire and a dog had to be rescued from an upstairs bedroom.

Stop at 1912 hrs and home station at 1922 hrs.

This period of temporary promotion ended on 30th April and I assume this is when our new Guvnor arrived.

He was Dave Stokes, a real career fireman. He joined Bedfordshire Fire Brigade as a Junior Fireman and left, probably kicking and screaming, after around forty years of service.

I liked Dave a lot. He always wanted to get involved in the firefighting and was always dirty afterwards. He could even get filthy at a false alarm!

I think Phil "the Snot Monster" Hadley also arrived about now. He was later promoted to L/Fm on Green Watch.

From 17th – 22nd June my old friend from Germany, Wolfgang Dörsch stayed with Patsy and me in Codicote.

On 21st June, he joined recruits on BA exercises at Blood Products Ltd. at Elstree and Luton Airport.

Our only fatality for the year took place on the roof of the Provident Mutual building in Wedgewood Way, Stevenage. On Wednesday, 19th June, a pair of roofers, a father and son, were repairing a flat roof when the father suffered a heart attack.

A company first aider was on site when we arrived with the ambulance, WrL and HP.

The HP was pitched to the roof and we prepared our stretcher to take the roofer to the ground. An ambulance paramedic was on the roof with us and was working on the casualty.

The stretcher with the casualty was put onto the platform on the front of the HP cage and the paramedic was attached by harness to the cage. He carried out CPR during the descent and the casualty was conveyed to Lister hospital where he was declared to be dead on arrival.

Three days later we had to cut a seriously injured driver free from his wrecked car after a collision with a lorry outside a house on Stevenage Road, Walkern.

I had been noticing over the years that there is an awful lot of rubbish spoken by firemen. So I decided to start a book of bollocks, which I called the "Gibber Book" and it went on until I left Stevenage in 2002.
When I retired, Tom Andrews asked his wife Jane to type it up for me, which she kindly did.
The front cover reads:

THE BOOK

Sid's attempt to save the English language from the fateful blabberings of his fellow man.
1991–2002.

Let me demonstrate with the first six entries:
Elmo Mitchell: "It's just a fly in the ocean."
Dave Stokes: "I was reversing backwards."
Elmo Mitchell: "The word's mum."
Spud Stroud: "I am going to take these apples home and make a rhubarb crumble."
Mad Dog Riley: "forty-nine, blimey that's nearly fifty."
Baldrick Fotios: "I've got a mate who's got these hands."
Get the idea?
Over the years we recorded thousands of entries and, without a doubt, the two top gibberers were Roydon Mitchell and Paul Riley.
I don't remember when, but these two lads restored and delivered a fire engine to Stevenage's twin town of Kadoma in Zimbabwe. They spent some time there training the African firemen and putting their brigade in order.

Their efforts were well received and they were soon getting letters along the lines of "thank you for the fire engine, can you please send me a washing machine etc."

Also, again I am not sure when, but Tom Andrews was involved with the town twinning, taking an engine to Chimkent in Kazakhstan.

On the 14th August, my German friend and colleague David Oudôt is joining us for the day.
He came on two calls with us, a car fire in Boxfield Green, Stevenage, where he extinguished the blaze using a hosereel, and an AFA to Bulwer Lytton House in Knebworth.

The Stevenage Comet of 21st August carried the headline:

GERMAN FIREMAN ON BUSMAN'S HOLIDAY!

Dinner night.
L to R: Hugo Wassermann, Patsy, me, Karl Heiser, Ted Faulkner, Ilse and David Oudôt and Hans Neumann.

Between the 16th and 18th August, a delegation from Mainz-Bingen arrives for a visit.

The Stevenage Gazette of 23rd had the headline:

FIRE HQ PLAN FOR SCHOOL SITE

This was the start of the process to take over the closed, Longfield School site and turn it into our Divisional headquarters, training school and fire control.

An amusing incident worth a mention.

On 2nd September we were called to the Lister Hospital. We got into the WrL and I started her up. Just as we started to pull out of the bays there was a banging on the roof and Baldrick's face appears, upside down, in the windscreen! He had been on the roof trying to stow some equipment and got caught out!
Hertfordshire Mercury for December 6th reads:

BLAZE RIPS THROUGH THATCHED ROOF AS FAMILY FLEE FOR THEIR LIVES: INFERNO AT PUB

The fire had broken out around three in the morning at the Three Tuns public house, Great Hormead, the landlord had jumped from a first floor window and his wife and two children had escaped via a ladder from a flat roof. All four were taken to hospital with smoke inhalation; the landlord had also suffered a head injury when he fell into the stream outside the pub!
We went on relief at 0924 hrs and didn't get back to Stevenage until 1512 hrs. Other appliances in attendance were 232 and 240 up to 1300 hrs and 300, 291 and 280 after that.
On 31st December 1991 the teleprinter comes to life, and prints out the following message:

- - - - - - REFERENCE INFORMATION FILE LISTING - - - - - -DATE 31.12.91 TIME 1537

PAGE NUMBER   2

LINE 1 :TO ALL STATIONS.
LINE 3 :I HAVE TODAY, TUESDAY 31 DECEMBER 1991, AT 1530HRS,
LINE 4 :HANDED OVER COMMAND OF THE HERTFORDSHIRE FIRE AND
LINE 5 :RESCUE SERVICE TO MY SUCCESSOR, ROBERT KING.
LINE 6 :THANK YOU ALL FOR HELPING ME TO DO MY JOB FOR THE LAST

55

LINE 7 :FOURTEEN AND A HALF YEARS - WE HAVE ALL SHARED IN HELPING
LINE 8 :THOSE IN TROUBLE - A NOBLE CAUSE.
LINE 9 :BEST WISHES FOR THE FUTURE AND GOD BLESS YOU ALL.
LINE 11 :SIGNED.
LINE 13 :E.S. FAULKNER.

- - - - - - - - - - - REFERENCE INFORMATION FILE LISTING- - - - - - - - - - -

A well respected Chief Fire Officer signs out for the last time.

We come on duty at 1800 hrs and at one minute to midnight the bells go down for the last time in 1991, and we are on our way to a skip on fire in Broadhall Way, Stevenage. Stn O Dave Stokes in charge with a crew of four, I am driving. We see in the New Year on route, booking in attendance at two minutes past midnight.

This was the last call received by the Hertfordshire Fire and Rescue Service for 1991.

I just can't resist a few more gibbers.

Silver Fox Miles: "I've got bare patches on my lawn. I've put bird seed down but the birds keep eating it.

Sue (the cook): "Would you like an egg omelette."

Baldrick Fotios: "Keep cutting the cake in half until we get nine bits."

Stokesy: "You don't want to leave your car in Newgate, you'll probably come back and find it up on wheels."

Mad Dog Riley: "Have you got a shovel on the end of your penis?" (Swiss Army pen knife?)

Spud Stroud: "He likes to light fires, he's a bit of an insomniac."

Ron Barlow: "The trial period of the Motorola Radio is finished, you will be issued Rolos in due course."

TC Andrews: "The G is silent, it sounds like an H."

Ron Barlow: "It's a new school, some of them are deaf, some of them are blind, some of them are deaf and blind and some of them are both."

Taff James: "It's like banging your head against a bush."

1992. SANTA!... SANTA!

At 0041 hrs we are called out again, this time to the first call to be received by the HFRS for 1992.

"Water Tender Ladder to Cholwell Road, Stevenage, smoke in house."

We are mobile, Stn O Stokes in charge, crew of four.

We were on scene at 0043 hrs and the fire, in the bedroom, was put out by 2 BA wearers with a hosereel.

The lady was suffering from smoke inhalation and I put her on oxygen and asked for an ambulance.

The couple had returned from a New Year's Eve party and told the *Stevenage Comet* (Wednesday, 8th):

"We heard Rusty (the dog) scratching at the door and my wife opened it. There was smoke in the hallway and Rusty ran up the stairs, I went up after the dog and saw flames in the bedroom. I picked up the dog and got the cats, and shut the doors, before calling the fire brigade."

Stop sent at 0053 hrs.

Home station at 0124 hrs.

8th January and we are called by the police, at a quarter past eight in the morning, to an incident at St. Andrews and St. Georges Church, St. Georges Way next to the fire station, where there is a Nativity scene damaged by fire! I hope the owner of the stable had fire insurance!

The outgoing CFO had a couple of retirement dos.

155

One took place at Hertford fire station where he was seated on an escape ladder and pulled around the station by the Service officers.

Now that Mr Faulkner had retired the life expectancy of the escape ladder was definitely limited. I think that we were the last brigade in the UK to operate escape carrying appliances. It was a very good, steady, versatile ladder but I can only remember using it in anger half a dozen times.

The second party was held at the Longfield site.

I had been asked by the Mainz-Bingen Association to present Mr Faulkner with a gift on their behalf, which I did. I gave a short speech on the German exchanges, "Do you remember, 1001 things to do with a German sausage, a 1002 if you eat the bloody thing!" etc, etc.

There were a great number of other presentations from various groups as well as individual gifts.

My favourite present was given by Albert Sharp of Royston. A hand-engraved mirror, depicting the Chief's favourite pastimes, the fire service, swimming and Germany. The mirror showed Mr Faulkner swimming down with a hosereel to a German U-Boat that was on fire, fantastic!

After the presentations there were a number of Crackerjack style games, songs and sketches.

There were some Germans there, on the exchange visit, who weren't impressed with DO Dave Wilson's Hitler impression.

The Stevenage Comet of Wednesday, 12th had two articles of interest.

The first headline read:

FIRE-FIGHTERS FEAR FOR THOSE VITAL LOST
SECONDS
THE SENIOR MANAGEMENT TEAM BRING IN
NEW SAFETY MEASURES.

The Comet went on, "Fire-fighters are worried that vital life-saving seconds could be lost because of new safety regulations. In the past fire crews throughout Hertfordshire have changed into tunics, leggings and helmets on the appliance as it's on its way to an emergency.

And if they were told that people could be trapped, then they would also put on breathing apparatus before arriving at the scene."

The management team say, "The following measures are to be implemented immediately: All crew members, excepting the driver, are to rig in fire gear (including helmet) before moving off to an emergency and seat belts are to be worn at all times when the appliance is moving."

We argued the toss for a while, but it was soon adopted. Secondly:

MAN IS ARRESTED ON ARSON CHARGE
£2m BLAZE DESTROYS WAREHOUSE

It's the early hours of Sunday, 9th February.

A miscreant driving a Furnell Transport, white transit van, is steering it directly at the up-and-over warehouse doors of the Furnell Transport warehouse on the Pin Green Industrial Estate.

0137 hrs, BEEP, BEEP, BEEP, "230 to Furnell Transport, Senate Place, Stevenage, van on fire."

0138 hrs, 230 mobile, Sub O Milton in charge, crew of five.

0145 hrs, 230 in attendance.

There is a van and it is on fire, however, it has crashed through the front doors of the warehouse and the building is on fire.

Sub O Milton sends "Assistance message, make pumps 3."

232 and 320 mobile.

I am in BA and we are starting to take a jet into the building when there is a big explosion, a gas cylinder of some description. Several more explosions as we fight the fire from just inside the warehouse.

"Make pumps 6."

201, 190, 310 and 189 mobile.

232 in attendance.

A second BA crew is committed to firefighting inside.

320 in attendance.

201, 310 in attendance.

A Senior Officer arrives to take charge.

190, 189 in attendance.

"Assistance message, HP required."

112 and 114 mobile to incident.

Three C Division officers, including Ron Barlow, who is in charge of BA, are in attendance.

Repeated blasts on an Acme Thunderer whistle is the signal to withdraw from the building.

The roof collapses in and the fire intensifies.

All firefighting is now from the outside.

112 and 114 in attendance.

I managed several changes of BA cylinder during the fire.

Finally at 0430 hrs, "Stop message, a single storey industrial building, subdivided into units, 100m x 20m, twenty five per cent severely damaged by fire, 3 jets, 2 hosereels, 1 HP monitor, 9 BA in use, "D" Delta."

The fire is out and we are back at home station at 0536 hrs.

The *Stevenage Comet* of 12th quoted Sub O Milton, "When we arrived there were flames at the front of the building and terrible thick, black smoke covered a large area outside. Two men wearing breathing apparatus were about to go in and investigate the fire when a propane cylinder, a little bit smaller than a dustbin, exploded. When they were inside three more cylinders exploded. We had six pumps and a hydraulic platform at the incident and during the course of the firefighting the roof, which was about ten metres high and made of corrugated tin, fell in but all personnel were out at the time."

A twenty-year-old man appeared before Stevenage magistrates on Monday charged with arson, burglary and possession of an article with intent to cause damage.

From March to the end of May we had a number of interesting jobs. Here are the stop messages:

On 1st March at 12.44 p.m. we were called to Heath Mount School, Watton-at-Stone, where a fire had broken out during a christening party. Stop message sent at 1.52 p.m.

"A building of 3 floors and basement used as a private boarding school, approx. 100m x 30m, plus a single storey out-building attached to main building, approx. 15m x 5m, severely damaged by fire, five per cent of main building damaged by fire, thirty per cent damaged by smoke, 1 jet, 2 hosereels, 8 BA, make pumps 6."

19th March at ten thirty p.m. at Torquay Crescent.

"Severe flooding in ground floor flat, efforts being made to shut off water supply, WEDA pump, water hoover in use."

Stop message sent at 11.26 p.m.

The occupier was so drunk he slept on his sofa throughout the incident and he was still there when we left.

The next day we were called at 9.14 p.m. to a "persons reported" fire at Gonville Crescent, Stevenage. The stop being sent at 9.35 p.m.

"A terraced house, 6m x 5m, sixty per cent of kitchen severely damaged by fire, remainder smoke-logged, all persons accounted for, 1 hosereel, 6 BA in use."

15th May at 6.44 p.m. we were called to the A1(M).

"Private motor car and horsebox in collision on motorway, first aid rendered by service to female with broken arm, injured horse in horsebox being treated by vet."

29th May at 9.10 a.m., Stevenage Road, Walkern.

"Two cars in collision on roadway, two persons trapped, injured and released by service."

There used to be a maltings at Baldock. I say used to be, as an arsonist is just about to create a new car park.

Just after 2200 hrs on Saturday, 30th May a fire is being started that will see another historic landmark burnt to the ground.

Baldock crews are the first on the scene, and send an assistance message, "make pumps 8."

BEEP, BEEP, BEEP, "230 and 232 to the Maltings, Royston Road, Baldock, fire, make pumps 8."

230 WrL and 232 a spare WrL mobile 2224 hrs, and in attendance at 2235 hrs. I am riding the WrL with a crew of 5.

Other appliances attending are 310, 311, 320, 321, 300 and 301, together with DO Pearson, DO Baker and ADO Day.

The roof is already well alight and generating huge amounts of smoke. The police have to close the A505 Baldock to Royston road and British Rail stopped the trains on the nearby Baldock to Ashwell railway line.

Assistance message, "HP required."

There is nothing we can do to save the building and because of the threat of collapse we fought the blaze with six jets from outside the building.

The Water Board was asked to increase the pressure to keep our jets supplied.

A large crowd from the nearby Clothall Common estate turned out to watch operations.

The stop message was sent at 0012 hrs.

"A range of derelict buildings, formerly used as a maltings, of 2 and 4 floors, approx. 40m x 80m, one hundred per cent of building severely damaged by fire and collapse, 6 jets in use, D Delta."

230 mobile returning and closing down at home station at 0158 hrs.

Me, Roydon Mitchell and Paul Riley on a jet at the Baldock Maltings fire.

Picture: HFRS

On 6th June Sludge Andrews had a phone call from his wife Jane. Apparently their washing machine has caught fire and she wants to know what to do. TC hits the turnout button and we are on our way to his house in Hyde Green.

28th June and it's time to head back to Germany. This time I am going to work at Trier, Germany's oldest city, founded by the Romans in 16 BC and situated on the river Moselle only 10 km from Luxemburg.

At Dover I realise I have forgotten my passport.

Arriving in Calais at ten fifteen a.m. we set off for Bröhtal service station in Germany, and are met by Wolfgang Dörsch who guides us to Koblenz training centre.

That evening David and Ilse Oudôt and Karl and Klara Heiser drive to Koblenz to take us out for a few beers. We are joined by Herr Morlock, chief of the Rheinland-Pfalz training school.

Sludge Andrews is going to come to Trier with me. Joe Heeney and Richard Mardell are going to Mainz, Steve Logan and John Golding are off to Ludwigshafen and Andy Clark is staying at the training school.

Our hosts are Karl-Heinz Palzer and Stefan Willems, who arrive the following morning to drive us to Trier.

That evening we are out to the Löwenbrau Brewery with Karl-Heinz, Stefan, Hans Hau (headquarters) and Jürgen Schrömges from Wiesbaden.

So many beers and it's only the first night – it's got all the makings of a great trip!

During the night I witness a medical phenomenon, Tom is not just a good snorer, he is one of the all-time greats – physically moving beds and wardrobes – remarkable.

On the morning of Tuesday the 30th we have a tour of Roman Trier and in the afternoon we pass the annual BA fitness tests.

Later that day we join in with the drills.

Stefan shows me how to use the LF's roof monitor. He thinks it is great fun to soak one of his colleagues hiding behind the parked cars. He doesn't however find it so amusing when, after the drill he realises he's left his own sun roof open!

As on previous trips, Trier has a great number of appliances, around thirty plus a couple of inflatable boats, trailers and roll on/roll off pods. Trier is also unique in Rheinland-Pfalz in that it operates the ambulance service.

The CFO is A. Albers-Hain and he has ninety-one uniformed staff.

As well as the professional brigade there are eleven volunteer stations with over 250 volunteer firemen.

In 1990 they attended 1310 calls.

TRIER-MAIN STATION			
ABBR.	FAHRZEUGE		APPLIANCE
ELW 1	Einsatzleitwagen	Löschzug.	Command vehicle
ELW 2	Einsatzleitwagen		CV for larger incidents.
LF 24	Löschgruppenfahrzeug		Water tender
DLK	Drehleiter mit korb		Turntable ladder
GTLF	Grosstanklöschfahrzeug		Water tender with large water tank
GW-AS	Geratewagen-atemschutz		Breathing apparatus tender
RTW	Rettungswagen		Ambulance
EUREN-VOLUNTEER STATION			
TLF 16	Tanklöschfahrzeug 16		Water tender
ELW	Einsatzleitwagen		Command vehicle

Wednesday, 1st June. Today we are visiting the fire station in Luxemburg City and the Airport brigade.

We arrive at nine o'clock in the morning and get to look around, including the air ambulance which is in the fire station yard.

L to R: Hans Hau, Herr Blasius, Luxemburg fireman, Tom, Me, Stefan
Wilems, Karl-Heinz Palzer, Jürgen Schrömges and an unknown
Luxemburg fireman posing with the 50m Turntable Ladder outside the
fire station in Luxemburg City.

They have a fifty metre TL! We get to go up to the cage at the
top via a lift which fits onto the ladders.

We have an hour at the airport fire station and get a ride
in their foam tenders.

Back to Trier, where Stefan takes us to his parents' house.
His father and brother run a vineyard and we are expected to
try the wines.

8.20 p.m. and we are back on station.

2053 hrs. "ALARM for GTLF to Südallee between
Hindenburgstraße and Saarstraße, rubbish fire."

I join OiC Herr Stolz and Stefan to make a crew of three.

Mobile to incident at 2055 hrs.

In attendance at 2057 hrs.

Big fire, I take a bucket of water and empty it into a
smouldering rubbish bin. A second bucket and the fire is out.

Returned at 2110 hrs.

Thursday, 2nd.

Karl-Heinz and Stefan take us out in a brigade VW Beetle to visit the volunteer station at Herresthal for a look round.

Back to Karl-Heinz's house for a beer and then up to the *Marien Column* high above the river Moselle with great views of the city.

We have lunch at the hospital.

Back at the VW, Karl-Heinz turns on the radio and the Löschzug is out at a fire and the CFO is asking for us to attend.

We drive back to the station where Hans Hau is waiting for us with the GW-AS which has also been requested.

The Löschzug was mobilised at 1306 hrs.

ELW 2-1 crew of two, OiC Herr Kirsch. LF 24 crew of five, OiC Herr Hoffmann. DLK crew of three, OiC Herr Wagner.

A second ELW 1-3 and the GTLF was mobile at 1308 hrs.

ELW 1-3 crew of one, GTLF crew of three.

A third ELW 1-1 mobile at 1312 hrs. crew of one, OiC Herr Schmitt.

The Löschzug was in attendance at 1313 hrs.

ELW 1-3 and GTLF in attendance at 1314 hrs.

ELW 1-1 in attendance at 1319 hrs.

1328 hrs, we are mobile to "Gottbillstraße, Trier-Zewen, fire in silo."

Hans Hau in charge, crew of Karl-Heinz Palzer, Tom and me.

1332 hrs. The Löschzug from Euren station was ordered.

Löschzug Euren, ELW 1-5, crew of one and TLF 16, crew of seven in attendance at 1336 hrs.

We are in attendance 1356 hrs.

The fire is in a sawdust-drying tower silo, part of a window frame manufacturing factory.

CFO Albers-Hain is in charge of the fire.

The DLK has been pitched to the top of the silo and two firemen in BA are putting water onto the fire via the monitor.

The DLK was supplied from the LF 24 via a hydrant.

Other firemen were on the tower platform.

Herr Hau, Tom and me climbed the tower with a hearth kit and checked out the trunking underneath the fire.

We then went up to the platform at the top of the silo. The DLK had gone back down to collect a ladder, lighting, branch, hose and small gear.

When all was ready two BA wearers entered the silo to extinguish the fire.

We followed shortly afterwards and started to cut away the internal metal skin of the silo to get at the hotspots.

Tom and I worked bloody hard in there for three quarters of an hour or so until all the cutting away was finished.

We were taken down by DLK and reported to Herr Blasius for some drinking water.

We helped with the make-up and were congratulated on our hard work by the CFO, which was nice.

Home on the LF 24, closing down at 1530 hrs.

Time to clean up before we go out for a beer.

Just before 2100 hrs… "ALARM, Löschzug to Schmiede-und-Presswerk, Hafenstraße, Trier-Hafen, AFA."

In attendance at 2109 hrs.

No fire situation.

Home station, 2141 hrs.

Friday, 3rd, July.

Today's edition of the local newspaper, the "*Trierischer Volksfreund*", reports on yesterday's silo fire, and we get a mention as being there in the thick of it.

However, it seems that we are not finished with the silos.

At 1140 hrs a call is received in the control room by telephone from a Herr Müller at Gottbillstraße.

Silo fire at Gottbillstraße, Trier. Thursday, 2nd July.

1142 hrs "ALARM, Löschzug to attend a fire at Gottbillstraße 31."

1143 hrs, ELW 2-1, mobile, OiC E. Willems, crew of 2.

ELW 1-2, mobile, OiC Herr Fisseni, crew of 1.

LF 24, mobile, OiC R. Gauer, crew of 6 (incl. me).

DLK mobile, OiC Herr Bergheim, crew of 3.

1148 hrs, Löschzug in attendance.

The fire is in the silo next to the one involved yesterday.

Two firemen in BA climbed the external ladder to the top door in the tower. I went up in the DLK with another fireman and taking a length of hose and a branch.

No sign of fire and the crew descend one floor.

The door at this level was opened and the fire was seen to be about five metres below. The door was closed and the internal sprinkler system was operated.

Suddenly, the hose connection under the DLK cage burst and we had to go down to make repairs.

The two BA men enter the silo to make sure the fire is out.

As I start to help with the make-up there is a problem in the tower.

The officer in charge, E. Willems' report states:

"During the dismantling of a floor plate in the filter chamber, OBM Gauer suffered from the effects of heat exhaustion."

Two firemen hurried aloft to help with the rescue and the DLK is pitched to bring him down.

I go to the pump to get the O2 kit and assist to get the casualty onto a stretcher and administer oxygen. He is taken to the Mutterhaus hospital.

The fire was out by 1220 hrs.

The operation was supported by the Zewen volunteers and the burnt sawdust was put into a waste container and taken to the Mertesdorf landfill site.

Home station at 1410 hrs.

I am off for the night with my friend Wolfgang Dörsch, his wife Monica and son Hans-Lothar, at their house in Marienhausen, north of Koblenz.

Wolfgang was a fireman in Wuppertal in the state of Nordrhein-Westfalen, and now works with the Rheinland-Pfalz fire training school in Koblenz.

On Saturday, 4th, Wolfgang drives me to Heidesheim.

We are to be guests of the Mainz-Bingen District and joined by the new CFO Bob King.

After dinner we head to Ingelheim-am-Rhein and watch their annual exercises. A factory fire involving ninety-eight firemen and then an RTA with a car in collision with a chemical tanker.

At four o'clock in the afternoon we leave to take part in the dedication ceremony of the new fire station at the town of Stadecken-Elsheim. A typically German function, lots of beer, speeches, presentations and back-slapping. Love it.

We stayed the night at the new fire station in Mainz.

Sunday, 5th and we are back at the fire station in Heidesheim for some more discussions on various fire service subjects given by Karl Heiser and Herr Morlock for the Germans and Andy Clark, Steve Logan and me for the UK.

Tom and I leave for Trier at three p.m. arriving there at four thirty p.m.

1759 hrs, "ALARM, RTW to A-602, Höhe Scweich, Longuich exit, RTA."

My first ever turnout in an ambulance.

RTW 1, mobile with Herr Groß in charge, crew of Herr Plorin and me.

It's raining and a long journey.

No sign of the incident so we start to head back towards Trier. The radio crackled into life, and we hear our callsign, 1-85-1, and control give us a better address.

On arrival the casualty is in a police car and he's bloody French! He has apparently been in an accident but there is no sign of his car.

We take him to the Mutterhaus hospital and are mobile returning at 1857 hrs.

At eight o'clock that evening Stefan takes us to a wine festival in the beautiful town of Saarburg, another good night.

On Monday 6th together with Chief Albers-Hain, Karl-Heinz and Stefan, we give an interview to the newspaper on our exploits in Trier. The article appeared in the edition of Wednesday, 8th.

At eight p.m. another old friend arrived. Alyose Jacoby, a Luxemburg fireman from the town of Greiveldange. I had met Alyose whilst drinking champagne in Grevenmacher following my lecture there in 1990. How nice of him to travel to Trier to see me.

Together with Stefan, Karl-Heinz, a Herr Ackermann, the DCFO, Jürgen Schrömges and Tom we had a splendid night eating and drinking at a local bier keller.

Another day out for us on the 7th July.

This time to the USAF base at Bitburg.

We arrived there at one fifteen p.m. and boarded a military bus which took us to the fire station to check in before a visit to the F15 flight simulator.

Then we were shown a hangar where four F15 fighters called *Zulu Birds* are kept fully armed and on permanent standby. We are briefed on the set-up by an Air Force Captain and at two forty-five p.m. they demonstrate an alert. A klaxon sounds and two pilots slide down a pole into the hangar, they board their aircraft and are airborne within five minutes. Impressive stuff!

A tour of the fire station by the fire chief, Master Colour Sergeant Jones is followed by a demonstration of the crash tenders and the USAF pumper crew.

After all this, a huge American-style barbeque, great hospitality.

Back on station at 7.50 p.m.

One of the officers tells me that due to ambulance commitments there are only five firemen left on station, including me and Tom, and please could we stay in case of another call coming in!

OK, bed time.

Wednesday, 8th.

Around 0540 hrs the alarm sounds, a call for the RTW and although I get to the bays I am too late and arrive just in time to see the ambulance pull out... back to bed.

0555 hrs, "ALARM, ELW and LF24 to Georg-Schmitt-Platz, junction of Lindenstraße and Zurmaiener Straße, Trier-Stadtmitte, RTA.

0556 hrs mobile. ELW 2-1, E. Willems in charge, crew of two. LF 24, W. Ahnen in charge, crew of five.

This is the same incident that the RTW went to fifteen minutes earlier.

In attendance at 0558 hrs.

There are two cars in collision, a Ford Escort and a Fiat Argenta 2000 and both drivers are being treated by the RTW crew.

A hosereel was laid out and the fire extinguished using a dry-powder fire extinguisher.

Mobile returning at 0613 hrs.

Trier Fire Brigade: Back L to R: Horst Butterbach, Jürgen Sievenich, Gerhard Morgen, Stefan Willems.
Front L to R: Jürgen Schrömges, Me, Alfred Becker, Siegfried Schmitt, Günter Porn, Gerd Feiler, Tom, Karl-Heinz Palzer, Heinz Peter Schmitt.

The scene on Lindenstraße.

We are leaving today. We say our goodbyes and leave Trier at 1500 hrs, arriving at Koblenz training school at 1630 hrs.

A bar and barbeque has been set up in the bays.

When we are all gathered, Herr Morlock starts the proceedings. Karl and Klara Heiser and David and Ilse Oudôt join us for another night of beer and sausages.

Incidentally, David brings my passport that Patsy has sent to him.

Thursday 9th and we set off home with Wolfgang in a German personnel carrier as ours is broken.

Wolfgang takes us as far as Calais and a Hertfordshire driver picks us up in Dover.

Passing through the UK Customs back in Dover was the only time that I had to show my passport!

Back at work at Stevenage on 15th July and a call to the Lister hospital.

We go regularly to the hospital, usually for false alarms, in 1992 I went with White Watch seventeen times. Every now and then we got an incident.

On this occasion we were called to a man threatening to jump from the 9th floor.

We attended at 1408 hrs. with the HP, WrL and Hitchin's WrL.

We stood by just in case as hospital staff managed to grab the man and pull him back inside.

We had another busy, hot summer with eleven hectares of standing barley and stubble alight at Caldwell Farm, Ickleford on 24th July. It was a "make pumps four" and we used four hosereels, beaters and a water shuttle. The following day we had an open-sided barn containing thirty tons of euro-baled straw on fire. This time we used a jet, two hosereels and the farmer with his tractor.

The Stevenage Comet of 19th August reported that we had received a new fire engine.

The vehicle, which I think was probably a Dennis Dagger, cost £91,000 and was one of five provided by the Hertfordshire County Council this year.

A new helmet, the Cromwell F500, started to be issued.

Our first duty day with the new pump was the 17th and we took it out on three calls during the day, two false alarms and an RTA.

On the 6th October I had been to a palaeontology course at Ware College, an interest of mine.

Driving back through Hertford along Gascoyne Way, a dual carriageway, I was being overtaken by a car in the offside lane and ahead, standing on the central reservation, was a man presumably trying to cross.

As the car overtaking passed me, the man stepped onto the carriageway. The car struck him and he was thrown over the roof and in my rear view mirror I could see him lying in the road.

I went back and gave him first aid but he was unconscious and fatally injured.

I had to attend the inquest held on 18th March 1993 at Hatfield to give evidence.

The Hertfordshire Mercury of March 26th 1993 told us that the thirty-four-year-old Hertford man, was four times over the legal alcohol limit for drivers.

His mother said that alcohol was her son's life; "He was quite often under the influence of it." She added that her "son was deaf in one ear and usually wore thick glasses, which he wasn't wearing at the time of the accident."

The coroner recorded a verdict of accidental death.

It's Christmas time!

On Tuesday, 22nd December, just after 1000 hrs we joined both of Baldock's appliances at the Oval Transport yard, Jack's Hill, Graveley where an industrial skip lorry had overturned. The driver was trapped by his legs in his cab and had suffered leg and chest injuries. He was released and conveyed to hospital by Herts ambulance service.

On Wednesday, 30th someone came into the station at half past twelve one afternoon and reported that a duck was trapped in the ice on the town lake in St George's Way.

We popped along and freed it using a ceiling hook and a line. One Note Miles sent a great informative message "From L/Fm Miles, a Mallard duck trapped in ice, Stn O Drakes not required." (Paul Drakes was one of our officers).

Christmas was always good fun at the station. We would have a kids party which usually went wrong. A couple of memorable Father Christmas disasters spring to mind.

Ambulanceman Dennis Edwards made a great Santa, the trouble was by the time of his appearance he was usually pissed.

One year we had rigged an electric wheelchair as a sleigh, beautifully crafted, with two long poles sticking out the front with all eight cardboard reindeer fixed to it. All the kids' presents were in sacks sitting in the middle.

To a big build up with all the kids chanting "*SANTA, SANTA,*" in came Dennis, guiding the sleigh through the doors. Then, he lost control, swerved across the mess deck, clipping the door and crashing into the snooker table. The reindeer fell off, the presents fell out and Santa rolled drunkenly onto the floor! Great festive entertainment!

On another occasion we had built a huge chimney against the windows leading out onto the flat roof. The idea was that Santa, (Dennis again), would be picked up from the drill tower by the HP and delivered onto the flat roof. He would then disappear from view, climb in through the window and appear as if coming down the chimney.

Great, all set. Santa appeared on the fourth floor of the tower, the kids cheered, he was picked up by the HP, the kids clapped, he was delivered onto the roof, the kids shouted. They all gathered in front of the fireplace expectantly, *"SANTA, SANTA!"* A pause... again, *"SANTA, SANTA!"* Another pause. Then we hear a knocking, it's coming from the chimney. We had forgotten to open the window and Dennis couldn't get in! One of us had to crawl into the chimney and let him in.

The kids, some laughed, some cried and some ran to mum!

MERRY CHRISTMAS!

Christmas was also the time for our annual pub crawl through the Old Town.

One occasion, some years earlier, I was going to stay at the station and got as pissed as a fart.

However when I got there I decided to drive home. I got in my car and set off. Just as I left a police car appeared behind me. I crossed the roundabout, did a quick left and parked up and turned off the lights. The police pulled in behind me, bugger.

"Can you get out of the car please sir."

I got out, just about able to stand up.

"Do you have any ID?"

I got out my wallet, opened it and dropped it. The contents all over the floor, I picked up my fire brigade warrant card. The copper looked at it, "Oh, one of them are you, had a good night have you? Where do you live?"

"Just here," I lied.

"OK, sir, goodnight, Merry Christmas."

OK, some end of year bollocks from the Book.

Snot Monster Hadley: "My arms were going like hummingbird legs."

Mad Dog Riley: "The Van Trop family singing I am seventeen going on sixteen."

Elmo Mitchell: "Where's the tea bag strainer?"

Me: "A film crew from Radio Bedfordshire."

176

Mad Dog Riley: "I nipped down to the newsagents to get some petrol."

Ron Barlow: "Shut up Taff or I'll ring your ears!"

Lee Jacobs: "That was in the time of Norman the Conqueror."

1993: RED-FACED CAT LOVER RESCUED.

Having just mentioned Dennis Edwards, I think I will start the year by mentioning some of the other ambulance staff.

Probably my favourite was Len "Leaper" Hope, a daft bugger if ever there was one. Perry Cotter, who always looked as being at death's door, but the last time I saw him looked better than ever. Other old faces include George Pinner, Ted Andrews, Mick Glazier (Patsy's crewmate), "Sideways" Gazeley, John "Slowly" Samuels, John Ridley and John Jones who nearly came to blows with snooker cues, during an altercation, with Poodle Ellis.

One afternoon the police arrived with senior ambulance staff to arrest Pete, who had been up to no good. And then there was Steve Hollis who was a bit of a wheeler dealer.

Joan Thomas was getting over friendly with her crewmate whose name escapes me. They used to have lunch with flowers on the table. Her husband John Thomas, who checked hydrants for us, arrived one afternoon wielding a hydrant bar with evil on his mind and had to be restrained by Mick Milton!

Operationally, a sad start to the year for someone. On 1st January at 1934 hrs, we were called by the ambulance to Blakeney Road to assist in the recovery of a body from behind a locked door.

And the animal world was also suffering, with a call to the pond in Towers Road on 24th January at 1537 hrs where a one-legged duck was being attacked. My notes don't tell me by what and I can't remember!

Another animal rescue on 3rd February caused much merriment.

Just before 0100 hrs in the morning the alarm sounded and the WrL with a crew of four was mobilised to St Andrews Drive, Stevenage.

Initially the call seemed pretty standard, a cat stuck up a tree.

When we arrived, sure enough, there was a cat sitting on a branch, about three metres off the ground. However, sitting next to it was the red-faced owner!

The North Herts Gazette of February 5th had the headline:

ROYDON IS THE CAT'S WHISKER!

And went on to report. "The man, who does not want to be named, had recently moved to the house and the cat, "Maddie," had not adjusted to her new surroundings and would not come down from the tree. Her owner used a step ladder and pulled himself up on the branch but then could not get down. After more than an hour the embarrassed man asked his wife to call the fire service."

After getting the man down, using a short extension ladder, Elmo managed to get hold of "Maddie" who wasn't impressed, and she attacked him!

Roydon told the reporter "It just went berserk and put up a real fight. She was spitting and scratching and bit me. I had to go to the Lister for a check-up."

Readers will be pleased to know that following her check-up, Maddie was declared fit and suffered no ill effect from biting Elmo!

Another amazing animal encounter took place on the evening of 13th March. At 2254 hrs we went out to a car fire in Knebworth Park. I was driving the WrL with a crew of four.

We booked in attendance at the Park at 2259 hrs and proceeded to drive up towards the house, with no sign of fire. As we got about half way up I could see a big herd of the resident Red deer over to the left and approaching the road. As we got closer, a huge stag strutted onto the road, looked at us and stopped. We had to give way as his harem of females crossed over behind him, not fazed at all, despite our flashing lights.

After all that, we found the fire and put it out using a dry powder and light water extinguisher and a bucket of water.

Around this time the station took delivery of a new vehicle.

A 1992, four-wheel drive, Land Rover Defender (J581 SNK), to be used in an off-road capacity. All drivers had been on an off-road driving course and the vehicle was duly being put on the run.

On the 7th April at 2034 hrs, I was driving the WrL with a crew of five when we were called to Chells Farm, Gresley Way, Stevenage, to trees on fire.

On arrival five minutes later, we found the fire a long way from the road, with access across the fields. Trees and hedgerows were involved and threatening to spread to a haystack.

The OiC sent an assistance message "Second appliance with land rover required."

This was the first operational call for the Land Rover.

Utilising the Land Rover and using all available hosereel tubing and six lengths of hose, we managed to get a hosereel jet to the fire!

The stop message was sent at 2139 hrs.

We didn't manage to get back to the station, however, as we were called straight to a false alarm at Shephall Way and then to a fire in a portocabin at Glaxo, Gunnelswood Road.

I was on standby at Hertford fire station, on 1st May, when at 2145 hrs, we went to approx. 60 railway sleepers on fire at Waterford. Make pumps two, D Delta, 2 hosereel jets in use.

A couple of new members of the Watch arrived, Tom "Bungle" Davies, who came from Training School and stayed on the Watch for a while before transferring to Borehamwood. Also Dave "Pondlife" Williams who eventually moved on to Green Watch.

All through April and May *The Gazette* was reporting on our threatened strike over another pay row. Once again the

Government was going to renege on the pay formula devised after the 1977 strike. A National Officer of the Fire Brigades Union said in the April 9th edition, "I imagine they are polishing up the Green Goddesses right now."

The 21st May copy had a quote from the Chairman of the County Council Environment Committee, who said "To put the entire nation at risk for a few measly pounds is unforgiveable."

Also in that edition there was a report that the Service was to get its own chaplains. With the retirement of ACO John Potipher, we were without a chaplain and among the first ten to be appointed was the Reverend Tony Ruffell at Stevenage.

Finally, in the same edition, it was reported that "A twenty-four-year-old man had appeared before magistrates accused of arson at his Stevenage home. He was remanded to police cells until Friday morning when he is due to appear in the dock at Hitchin Court."

This referred to an incident that had occurred four days earlier, on Monday 17th.

I was driving the pump escape with a crew of five, when, at 2008 hrs, both appliances were turned out to Newgate, Stevenage, total crews of ten.

In attendance at 2010 hrs, where a house was on fire.

Flames were coming out of the downstairs windows and smoke from the first floor windows.

Two BA teams took a hosereel each into the building and located the fire in the lounge.

The OiC sent the stop message at 2021 hrs. "An end of terrace house, approx. 9m x 4m, fifty per cent of living room damaged by fire, remainder heavily smoke-logged, "D" Delta.

We were there for another hour tidying up.

This was the third house that the occupier had set fire to!

We started to do more fitness sessions.

We had always done the six-monthly physical tests, which included carrying two lengths of rolled up 70mm hose, lifting a 10.5m (35 ft) ladder and carrying a colleague with a fireman's lift.

Now we added a grip test, a body fat test and probably a couple of other things.

Each Watch had an allocated fitness trainer, ours was Taff James.

So we started doing warm up and down exercises and general physical jerks.

I think it was Taff who organised for a couple of aerobics trainers to visit the station in the evening to take an hour's session with the lads. They christened them "Sweaty Box" and "Two Bodies." No idea why, nothing to do with me!

As this wasn't compulsory a few of us fitter men could sit it out at the bar with a pint and offer encouragement.

Talking of fitness, thinking back, I remember we had to go for a medical when I first joined back in 1978.

The doctor that the brigade used back then was a Dr. Jury, and I can recall the examination as being a bit of a joke.

I think if you managed to walk into the surgery unaided you were almost there, and if Doctor Jury could count two of everything down the sides and one down the centre you had pretty much cracked it.

During the year I had been suffering badly with my shoulders. I had tried pain-killers and had progressed under the consultant to cortisone injections. I had two, the second one not giving me any relief at all.

The final straw came at an incident on Sunday, 4th July. We had been called to a manure heap on fire at Walnut Tree Farm in the village of Luffenhall.

We went out at 9.16 p.m. I was driving the WrE with a crew of five, Mick Milton in charge.

The water supply was rubbish and we had to drive to and from the nearest hydrant, emptying the tank on to the fire and then going back to refill the tank with water.

On one visit to the hydrant as I pulled the tank valve open, I got a terrible pain through my right shoulder and realised it was time I needed a permanent cure.

Another one of the crew drove back and we closed down at 11.01 p.m.

And so off I went to Pinehill Hospital in Hitchin to see the consultant, Mr Dorrell and I was booked in for my operations in the next few weeks, BUPA always helps!

Also we now had an Occupational Health department and on 11th August, Jo Young, the fitness co-ordinator came to ride the pump for the day. During the day she managed to get into the Gibber Book with: "On the whole the Watch looks pretty fat!" (Fit).

From 26th – 29th August we had a visit from the Mainz-Bingen fire brigades and my old German mates from Trier.

On 27th I drove them all down to Guildford for a visit to John Dennis Coachbuilders and a tour of the factory with a test run in the latest appliance.

Strangely, after lunch back at Stevenage, I got a request to join the Germans at the Longfield headquarters, in my best uniform.

Blue Watch were on duty and both pumps went down with me.

As well as the Blue Watch, Service senior officers and Control staff were all there.

In a great kept secret, Karl Heiser presented me with the German Fire Brigades Association "Medal for International Co-operation."

Karl gave a short speech and pinned the medal on me and Hans Neumann passed him the framed certificate to accompany it.

This was in recognition of the work I had undertaken over the last five years to form the successful partnership between Hertfordshire and the Rheinland – Pfalz fire brigades.

L to R: Claus Schick, Karl Heiser, Me, Hans Bock and
Bob King. Picture: HFRS

On duty on 28th August with Karl-Heinz Palzer and Stefan
Willems

In the morning the ERT from Hatfield came over to
Stevenage to demonstrate the oxygen cutting equipment and
in the afternoon, Karl-Heinz and Stefan came on a call with
us to the Lytton Way Service Station where we had a small
fire in a petrol pump.

The Gazette of 3rd September reported on their visit:

"Two German firefighters met up with old chums when they arrived at Stevenage fire station. Stefan Willems and Karl-Heinz Palzer are over on an exchange visit and since arriving last week have been billeted at the station, going out with local firefighters, seeing the Fire Service College at Moreton-in-Marsh and enjoying a number of social events."

The 10th September edition reported on my medal presentation: -

Karl Heiser said, "Firefighter Payne's work has brought the spirit of the Hertfordshire Fire Service into Germany, and has helped to foster many new friendships."

Bob King said, "Sid had been a good ambassador and brought honour to the fire service with the presentation of the award."

And so on the 30th August, I was on standby at Baldock fire station for my last duty for just over seven months as I went off to get my shoulders sorted out.

At 2021 hrs we went to Hillbrow, Letchworth to a grass fire which was extinguished using a hosereel jet. Home station and bed just after 2000 hrs.

Off I went to Pinehill Hospital on a Friday, early in September for my admission.

When I got there I was told that my first operation would have to be postponed until the Monday. I could either go home and return after the weekend or, as my room was booked, I could stay.

Easy choice, I settled in. A room to myself for three nights, three good meals a day and some pretty nurses looking after me. To be honest it didn't take much thought!

And if you have a medical bent, I had a reduction of the left and right rotator cuffs!

Some more gems from the Gibber Book.

Snot Monster Hadley: "You're driving the one you didn't drove yesterday."

Bob Adamson: "My Mastermind subject would be the 16th century Reconnaissance."

Ron Barlow: "June is in May this year."

Me: "I couldn't keep my eyes awake."

Me: "This spindle is as tight as a duck's drum."

Stokesy: "At Agincourt the English bowmen rained apples down on the French."

Spud Stroud: "The air in the face mask is at a higher pressure than the ambient temperature outside."

Taff James: "She's got a face like the inside of a bricklayers nail bag."

Elmo Mitchell: "Can you prevent an accident prevention day?"

Bungle Davies: "Annual tests are to be carried out yearly."

Mad Dog Riley: "Where did Pondlife get his sausages? Is his father a baker?"

Mad Dog Riley: "I'll get the food for the next lot of between nightsies!"

DCO Kent: "I'd like to propose a test to the ghosts."

Elmo Mitchell: "I didn't even wink an eyelid."

1994. ON THE BEER FOR THE SCOUTS!

January. Off sick.

February. Still off sick, wearing a bit thin now.

March. Still off sick. Bored.

April. Bugger, got to go back to work!

Finally, my consultant and the Brigade doctor declared me fit for duty and I was back at work on 8th April.

This happened to coincide with Martin Oudôt spending the day with us, working on the Watch.

Martin is the son of David Oudôt, my friend and co-founder of the exchange visits who was on a family holiday here in the UK. I went with them down to Barnet to visit David's father there.

The Comet of April 13th recorded the visit:

MARTIN PICKS UP HOT TIPS

"Student Martin Oudôt took time out from a family holiday in England to follow in his father's footsteps and spend a day with the firefighters of Stevenage."

Martin said "In the two years I have been a fireman I have seen a lot of fires and car accidents. My father said I could learn a lot from working with the crew at Stevenage."

Can't imagine what!

The following week Patsy and I were in Germany for five days.

I don't remember where we went or why but during the trip where we joined Karl and Klara Heiser and David and Ilse Oudôt for dinner at a restaurant in Guntersblum.

On 29th May we attended Harrow Court in Silam Road to release ten people trapped in a lift with a maximum capacity of eight!

People stuck in lifts in the high rise flats, hotels and the hospital were a regular call for us.

This would usually involve a couple of firemen going up to the lift motor room at the top of the building, turning off the power, releasing the brake and lowering or raising the lift manually. We had a special "U" shaped key, called a spoon key with which we would then open the doors and release the trapped people.

More National news.
The headline in *The Independent* for 14th June 1994 read:

IRA BOMBS CLOSE RAILWAY STATIONS: COMMUTERS SUFFER RUSH-HOUR DISRUPTION

The paper reported that: "The IRA bombed the east coast rail line yesterday and forced the closure of two London railway stations for much of the afternoon rush hour.

The explosion on an embankment happened a few hundred metres north of Stevenage station in Hertfordshire and followed a coded warning."

The bells went down in the station and we turned out to the railway station in Lytton Way where we booked in attendance two minutes later.

I was driving the WrL with a crew of five.

The Stevenage Comet of the 15th said "Workers and residents in the Fairview Road, Essex Road and Julian's Road area of the Old Town were shaken by the blast just after 1530 hrs.

No one was injured but a hole was blown in a pylon carrying power cables over the track near Gunnelswood Road bridge."

The Independent went on: "In a statement the IRA told a Dublin radio station that it had planted three explosive devices on the tracks near Stevenage station.

Recognised coded warnings were received by British Rail shortly after 1400 hrs and services were immediately suspended as police combed the line and surrounding areas. But the explosion happened ninety minutes after the alert on an embankment north of the station."

The Comet concluded: "As officers from Scotland Yard's anti-terrorist branch and forensic experts began their investigation, British Transport police with sniffer dogs carried out an extensive search of the embankment."

Army bomb disposal officers were also called in to deal with a package discovered nearby.

We stood by while all this was going on but nothing further was found and we were released after two hours.

For a number of years I have been collecting fire helmets from around the world. Even now I have over 150 in the loft!

On the odd occasion I would display them although not often because of the problems of getting them all down from the loft etc.

On 17th July I made the effort and took them to the "999 Emergency Services Day", held at Stanborough Lakes in Welwyn Garden City.

On Friday morning, 22nd July, not long before we come on duty, the Blue Watch had been called to a hedge fire at the edge of a field in Knebworth.

It is now the afternoon of the same day and the schools are emptying for the day. Just off of Watton Road, Knebworth some children are up to no good.

BEEP, BEEP, BEEP, "230 and 232, to Watton Road, Knebworth, field on fire."

At 1616 hrs both appliances mobile, Station Officer Stokes in charge.

I am driving the WrE with a crew of four.

We are in attendance at 1624 hrs.

Assistance message from Stn O Stokes "make pumps 8."

This fire is a regular for us in the summer, it seems to catch fire every year. It is in the same fields as Biggles' disaster back in August 1986, remember the hydrant and hosereel fiasco?

Control mobilise two pumps from both Hitchin and Baldock and one each from Welwyn Garden City and Old Welwyn.

We were confronted initially with a field of straw and stubble on fire, but before we can surround it, the fire broke through hedgerows and involved the railway embankment.

There was so much smoke that four firemen had to use BA.

We worked mobile, that is driving along stopping to use our hosereel, then moving on and filling our tank when required.

The fire covered an area from Knebworth down to the Roebuck Posthouse pub in Stevenage, an area of a square kilometre or more ablaze.

The high wind and its constant change of direction made for difficult working conditions for us.

The stop was sent at 1715 hrs, "Approx. five hectares of combined straw and stubble, hedgerows and railway embankment severely damaged by fire, 8 hosereel jets, beaters and 4 BA in use."

> We left and got back to Stevenage at 1809 hrs and our Blue Watch spent another hour or so at the fire before it was all out.

The Comet of Wednesday 27th had the headline:

HUGE FIELD FIRE BLAMED ON SCHOOL KIDS

and told its readers that "More than forty firefighters were called to deal with one of the biggest field fires in North Herts so far this summer."

Stn O Stokes said "We received a lot of calls from people whose homes back onto the field as they were worried about the speed the fire was spreading." He went on, "because of the way the fire was racing across the field, several times we had to pull lads out from where they were using hoses and beaters."

Three weeks later another big field fire, this time at Manor Farm in Bygrave, near Baldock, broke out and required six fire engines to attend.

We were called eight minutes before going off duty and sped northwards checking the route with our maps.

Somewhere we took a wrong turning and now no matter how hard we tried we couldn't find the right road. We could see the blaze but seemed to circle it for ages.

Anyway, we got there eventually and joined pumps from Baldock, Royston and Hitchin, at least we could help with the make up!

For the first two weeks of August I was on annual leave, being back at work, starting on the second day shift, the 14th.

Throughout the rest of August and September I attended thirty-five incidents, twenty-seven of which were false alarms; the others being the six pump field fire at Manor Farm, two calls to persons stuck in a lift, a waste compacting unit next to the Tesco store in the town centre that smoke-logged the store and took two and half hours to extinguish, three rubbish fires and a flooding.

Incidentally, with the old chief gone the escape-carrying appliances finally had their day.

We received a new WrL, 230 becoming WrL 1 and 232 changing to WrL 2.

On 22nd August, our first call for the new engine took us to persons stuck in a lift at the Lister, with me driving and a crew of five.

On 10th October up in the Pin Green area of the town, an eighty-three-year-old man is returning home in his car. He turns into his driveway but doesn't stop there, he goes through the garage, crashing through the back wall, demolishing the garage.

BEEP, BEEP, BEEP, "230, 232 to attend Headingly Close, Stevenage, RTA."

1439 hrs, WrL 1 and WrL 2 mobile, Stn O Stokes in charge, crews totalling 10. ERT mobile with a crew of two.

In attendance at 1442 hrs.

The car had impacted the rear wall of the garage and the roof had collapsed onto the passenger compartment trapping the driver in his seat.

The first task was to sheer up the building to prevent further collapse. This was achieved, initially using our Porto Power and subsequently the acro props from the ERT.

We could now access the casualty, who was conscious but quite badly cut around the head.

The ambulance paramedics worked on him as we tried to clear the debris from around the car, which was stabilised using blocks and the ERT's Ramsey winch.

Once all was ready, we released the man using the Lukas equipment and he was conveyed to hospital by Herts Ambulance.

Stop message from Stn O Stokes "One motor vehicle in collision with rear wall of garage, 1 male person injured,

---

> trapped, released by service, efforts being made to
> shore up garage."
>
> We didn't get back to the station straight away as we
> were sent on another call.

A rubbish fire in Aston on 17th October caused a bit of hilarity.

I was driving the WrL 1 with Stn O Stokes in charge, crew of five.

It was a big pile of rubbish which we put out with a jet.

After we had made up the equipment I was sitting in the cab waiting to drive back as the rest of the crew jumped on board.

Sudden silence, we all looked at each other, sniffing, the smell was horrendous and we all leapt out as one man.

We were all crying with laughter and Stokesy came out with those immortal words *"Who's dog-shitted up!"*

On Monday, 24th October the last of the old timers left me, when John Silver Fox Miles retired after twenty-seven and a half years of service.

The Stevenage Comet of Wednesday, 19th said:

LONGEST-SERVING FIREMAN RETIRES

"John, who lives in Baldock with his wife Gill, joined the Hertfordshire Fire Brigade after being a Royal Marine for nine years during which he saw service in Aden.

He is the longest serving firefighter at Stevenage station where he has been based for all but three months of his service.

John said, "Things have changed a lot since I joined. It is much more technical and the emphasis is now placed on prevention. They are a superb bunch of blokes at Stevenage and I will miss them."

I liked John and can't let him go without giving you a few parting anecdotes:

We were out doing some work on our maps in Graveley and One Note was driving.

We were heading north towards Baldock when we got a call back in Stevenage and One Note had to turn round.

Approaching a petrol station on the left, John said, "I can turn round there," even though the site was closed and had a bit of tape across the entrance. So John turned in, through the tape and swung in a big circle and exited the garage. As we turned right and set off down the road, I looked over at the petrol station and there stood a bemused builder with his trowel in his hand, looking at the four wheel ruts through his newly laid concrete forecourt!

We had been called to a fire in Old Knebworth and were trying to find the address. To be fair the radio reception wasn't great but we all heard the address as "The Runs." John queried it several times "can you confirm the address? Over."

Control "This is "the Runs", Old Knebworth, over."

After several attempts, John sent the message, "From L/Fm Miles can you confirm this address, the Runs, as in the Shits, over?"

Finally, we were at a house fire and as pump operator, I was standing behind the pump when John ran past heading away from the fire, a second or two later a woman in a nightdress followed, chasing after him with a bread knife!

Cheers, John!

I didn't see him for a long time after that, he and his wife moved down to Salisbury and then to Lincolnshire.

Years later I heard that he wasn't well and I went up to see him and thankfully we got to chew the cud before he died a few weeks later.

In November we had a couple of rescues.

On 6th, at Rockingham Way, Stevenage, a fire in the living room resulted in one female and three children being taken to hospital with smoke inhalation.

A week later on the 13th, a kitchen fire at Torquay Crescent was attended by both appliances and we found an elderly man and a woman in the house, both suffering from smoke inhalation.

On 29th a car fire in Faraday Road, Stevenage had us rushing up to the Chells area with Paul Riley at the wheel.

The car was well alight and melted onto the road. As we started to fight the fire using BA and two hosereel jets the appliance started to pass us by before Mad Dog could jump up into the cab and apply the handbrake!

Back in 1992, a mate of mine from Codicote had an accident. Barry Bishop, a window cleaner, had fallen from his ladder and been rushed to the Lister Hospital in Stevenage.

I was on shift a couple of days later and asked Stokesy if we could pop down to see him.

I was shocked to hear from the Sister there, that Barry had died during the night. I couldn't believe it.

Anyway, Barry was the Scout Leader in the village and his loss meant no Scout Troop.

For a while I had been contemplating helping out, as my boys were heading towards joining age. So after some thought I applied to the Welwyn Garden City Scouts to become the new Leader. I was accepted and ran the Troop for twelve years.

The Codicote Scout Group had been raising money for a new scout hut and it seemed like a good idea to help out.

I went down to see Dave Smith, the Sub O at Old Welwyn with a plan for a pub crawl to collect money for the scout hut and the Fire Brigades National Benevolent Fund.

The crew down there were well known for liking a pint and so didn't take much persuading. I liked the boys at Old Welwyn and had many a good night out with them, at Christmas for example. In fact as I am writing this I can recall a good beer up at the Wellington one Christmas, where Pat Priestman and one of her fellow stripogram girls joined us and both spent the whole night topless!

I have to say though that the firemen at Old Welwyn weren't best liked by the crews at Stevenage or Welwyn Garden City.

On 11th, a Sunday, seven or eight of the Old Welwyn lads, John Whitbread of Codicote Scouts, Dave Stokes and I met up at Old Welwyn's fire station.

Stokesy had volunteered to drive a service PCV to transport us between pubs.

First off we drove up to Codicote. One fireman dressed up as Welephant, the fire brigade mascot, two wearing BA and the others rattling buckets, we visited the Bell, the Goat and the Globe. With everyone in the Christmas spirit the money started to drop into our buckets.

Back into the PCV and down to Welwyn where we visited the White Horse, the Rose and Crown, the Wellington, the Tavern, the White Hart, the Steamer, the Red Lion and the Waggoner's. The buckets were full (and so were we!)

Back L to R: Mark Smith, Keith Stammers, Me, Welephant, John Whitbread, Martin Long and Dave Smith.
Front, L to R: Brian Gill and Michael Stammers outside Old Welwyn Fire Station.

It was late afternoon by the time me and Stokesy got back to Codicote to count the takings.
Well, we made a start before one of us said "Fancy a pint?"

So off we went to the Globe, God knows what time we got back, too much beer. Patsy put us both to bed and we finished the count in the morning!

I don't remember the exact amount we collected but it was well into the hundreds of pounds.

Thanks to Dave Stokes, Dave Smith and his Welwyn boys, John Whitbread, Welephant and the pub goers of Codicote and Old Welwyn.

In a similar vein, I remember some years before, the garden shed needed taking down.

Dave Rees came round to help me.

We made a good start by removing all the stuff from inside and then took out all the screws and nuts and bolts holding it together before one of us said, "Fancy a pint?"

So off we went to the Globe, God knows what time we got back, too much beer.

Back out in the garden we moved in to finish the job in hand. Inside the shed we made a plan, looked at each other, nodded and in perfect time kicked out the side walls! Down came the shed with us underneath, much laughing before one of us said, "Fancy a pint?"

So off we went to the Globe, God knows what time we got back, too much beer. Patsy put us both to bed and we finished the job in the morning!

A few more new faces arrived towards the end of the year. Bernie Bush replaced John Miles as L/Fm. Ben Read, who I knew at Potters Bar and liked and Danny O'Neill. Danny I christened *"Pull-Through"* on account of him being so thin, left us to join Suffolk Fire Service some time later.

Some end of year gibber:

Mad Dog Riley: "My tea was too weak after you put half a pint of mug in it."

Pondlife Williams: "I'm not going to forget what you said, what was it again?"

Elmo Mitchell: "There's a Dandy Long Legs."

Ron Barlow: "From a layman's point of terms."

One Note Miles: "We drove back like a dose of clappers."

Mad Dog Riley: "Where I was standing I had a right good seat."

Mad Dog Riley: "That's like a red rule to a bag!"

Silver Fox Miles: "You are as fit as a feather."

Stokesy (choosing a menu): "I'll have rolls C and dinner C. No, wait, the other way round."

Spud Stroud: "We rescued a duck and its chicklings."

Mad Dog Riley: "This jacket is tight on the ankles."

Mad Dog Riley: (Trying to rescue a cat). "Here, come on, cheep, cheep... no, I mean puss, puss!"

Mad Dog Riley: "In the ABC of resuscitation the C stands for P."

Jim Dudley (Blue Watch): "I'd rather wear these bare hands than those gloves!"

Elmo Mitchell: "I'm as happy as a sand pit."

Elmo Mitchell: "He seems to get older as time goes by."

1995. HIGH RISE RESCUES.

Two big fires, not on our ground, resulted in some sleepless nights.

We were called as a relief crew. That is to say that we took over from other crews who had completed their four hour or so stint at the incident.

On 17th February, Control phoned us, requesting our attendance. We had to be at Moles Farm, Ware, at ten p.m.

I was driving WrL 2 with a crew of five and we joined 251 at the fire ground, also with a crew of five.

We used two jets to protect the barns and allowed the 5,500 bales (300 tons) of baled straw to burn out.

We got back to station at two thirty a.m.

Next we were sent to Watford on 5th March as part of a three pump relief for a ten pump fire.

The fire had broken out at 2310 hrs at the Lynx Express Depot in Balmoral Road and at its height there were ten fire engines and one hydraulic platform in attendance.

Our very own Phil Hadley was on standby at Watford and during firefighting operations he received some minor burns!

WrL 1 and the HP with a crew of five set out at 0155 hrs, incidentally, the same time as the stop message was sent from the fire ground. We arrived in Watford at 0220 hrs and together with Hertford WrL and Potters Bar WrL got to work. I got through two BA cylinders whilst working in the cage of the HP.

The fire involved twenty-two articulated trailer units, three tractor units and an adjacent, single storey factory.

Back at Stevenage at 0707 hrs, not worth going to bed!

On Tuesday, 14th March we rescued four cats from a house fire at William Place, Stevenage and a month later on Tuesday, 11th April at Kestrel Close, Stevenage, a man with burns and a girl with smoke inhalation were rescued from a house.

On the afternoon 5th May we had just returned to station after a call to the Roebuck Inn. My pump, 230, was at one end of the yard and 232 was at the other restocking with hose. Pull-through, who was part of 232 crew, was returning a radio to our pump when the bells went down again. Pullers ran back down the yard to his pump, which pulled out before he could reach it. He turned about and headed back towards us. Just as he was within range, we left amid much jollity and Pull-through shouting abuse at the departing pump.

The call was to the Gates of India Restaurant, the Glebe, Chells Way, Stevenage to a tandoori oven on fire, is that unusual?

On 8th May, a fire on top of the town's water tower turned to be a beacon celebrating the 50th anniversary of VE Day.

(8th May 1945, Victory in Europe Day).

The Watch at Drill in April, L to R: Danny O'neill, Ben Read, Me, Phil Hadley, Paul Riley, Tom Andrews, Dave Williams and Roydon Mitchell.

We were on duty on Saturday, 13th May for the Station Open Day.

A lot to sort out and no time for distractions such as fires.

Just after coming on duty at 9.12 p.m. we were called out to Glaxo's to a false alarm.

Just as the Day was getting under way at 1.45 p.m. both pumps went out to a gardener's shed on fire at the recreation ground in Knebworth. The shed was destroyed in the fire.

Finally, at 3.09 p.m., a false alarm call dragged us away from the festivities to the Museum in St Georges Way.

Anyway, all that aside, the day went really well. Mad Dog, Elmo and me had prepared the old Merryweather manual pump for a demonstration of its firefighting prowess.

With a volunteer crew from the public, it performed really well, extinguishing a huge blaze.

Also there was W1, a 1937 Leyland pump escape preserved by firemen at Hertford station which can be seen on the right of the picture below.

Elmo Mitchell, Mad Dog Riley and Me ready for action.

On the 29th May we were ordered to the A1 (M) to a horsebox on fire. We were initially sent to junctions 6 – 7, Welwyn to Stevenage South. Then it changed to junctions 9 – 8, Letchworth to Stevenage North and finally off we went to the stretch between junctions 9 – 10, Letchworth to Stotfold!

Never did find the horsebox, it was probably well into Bedfordshire by then, and a round trip of twenty-five miles for us!

Our first high-rise rescue took place on Monday, 17th July at the BMH Construction site, Pacatian Way, Stevenage.

A bricklayer is working at roof level on a new build house. As he stepped onto a scaffolding plank, it gave way and he fell onto the floor of the first floor.

Suffering head and shoulder injuries his colleagues called 999 for an ambulance.

The Ambulance crew assessed the situation and realised that removal in the normal way was impossible and they, in turn, requested assistance from us;

BEEP, BEEP, BEEP, "230, 232, 234 to attend Pacatian Way, Stevenage, assist ambulance."

0946 hrs, WrL 1, WrL 2 and HP mobile to incident, Stn O Stokes in charge.

ERT mobile.

0950 hrs, in attendance.

We head up to the first floor to make a plan. Our best option seems to be to take the casualty, on a stretcher, out of the window, and down to ground level using the HP.

Using two sections of short extension ladder lashed to the scaffolding, we made some runners to slide the stretcher out of the window.

I volunteered to travel under the HP cage with the casualty on the stretcher.

On the ground I put on the harness and hooked myself to the D ring under the cage and was lifted to the scene of operations.

With the stretcher temporarily tied to the scaffolding, it was slid out over the ladders and clipped onto the D ring. The HP operator then lowered us to the ground where the casualty was handed over to the ambulance service.

The stop message was sent by ADO Barlow at 1034 hrs.

We were back at the station at 1054 hrs.

Having a swinging time! at Pacatian Way.

Eight days later I turned out on the HP again. I was driving with a crew of three.

Strangely, according to my record it went without a supporting pump from Stevenage or Harpenden at the incident.

We mobilised at 1418 hrs to Fairclough Homes building site, Milton Road, Harpenden, arriving there at 1644 hrs.

The incident involved a male construction worker who had collapsed on the second floor of scaffolding.

He was brought down in a stretcher on the front platform of the cage and taken to hospital by ambulance.

Stop sent at 1507 hrs and back on station at 1540 hrs

July and August were again very busy for us with field fires around the county.

19th July, stubble and embankment alight in Walkern.

24th July, wasteland, derelict cars and buildings on fire in Potters Heath.

25th July, hedgerows in Stevenage.

25th July, seventy-five hectares of standing crop and woodland on fire in Knebworth, make pumps 7.

27th July, thirty tons of baled straw and a Dutch barn destroyed in Digswell.

17th August, two hectares of woodland and two hectares of grass alight in Stapleford, make pumps 3.

18th August, field fire in Titmore Green.

18th August, field fire in Stevenage, make pumps 3.

And then on 25th August a huge fire at Smallford Lane, Smallford. We were mobilised at 1353 hrs, WrL 2, crew of four.

In attendance at 2.07 p.m.

There we found forty hectares (nearly 100 acres) of stubble and baled straw alight and the Officer in Charge sends an assistance message, "make pumps 12."

Crews from Hatfield, Welwyn Garden City, St Albans, Garston, Wheathampstead, Old Welwyn, Hertford and Hemel Hempstead, as well as an ACO, C Division DC and an ADO from B Division attended, a total of fifty-six firemen, using hosereels and beaters to tackle the blaze.

At the same time appliances from Hertfordshire were assisting at a twenty pump fire in Buckinghamshire and in-County there were four pump fires in Stevenage, Waterford and in A Division!

There were only five pumps left available in the whole County.

At 3.23 p.m., we were called off of this incident and sent to standby at Hertford fire station and subsequently mobilised to Kentish Lane in Brookmans Park where there were roadside hedgerows and woodland on fire. We were joined here by a crew from Hertford Retained and extinguished the fire using three hosereels.

Finally got back to Stevenage at 7.25 p.m.

In the middle of all this, we had a big fire at Stevenage College in Monkswood Way. At 8 pm on Thursday evening, 27th July we are mobilised. 1959 hrs.

BEEP, BEEP, BEEP, "230 and 232 to Stevenage College, Monkswood Way, Stevenage, fire."

2000 hrs, 232 mobile, L/Fm Payne in charge, crew of 5.

2001 hrs, 230 mobile, Sub O Bush in charge, crew of 5.

2002 hrs, 230 and 232 in attendance.

A single storey building next to the main block is on fire, with smoke and flames coming from the roof. Two BA crews, one with a jet and one with a hosereel are committed to the fire.

2010 hrs, "informative message from Sub O Bush at same address, college classroom, approx. 5m x 8m, approx. twenty-five per cent of classroom and roof well alight make pumps 3."

2012 hrs, 320 mobile, L/Ff Costello in charge, crew of 6.

2013 hrs, Charlie 7, ADO Barlow mobile to incident.

2017 hrs, Charlie 7 in attendance.

2020 hrs, 320 in attendance.

A third BA crew with a hosereel is sent into the building.

2027 hrs, "salvage tender required."

2033 hrs, 321 mobile, Sub O Huthwaite in charge.

2034 hrs, 323, mobile, L/Ff Sullivan in charge.

2045 hrs, 321 and 323 in attendance.

Over the next couple of hours the fire is gradually knocked down and the crews are employed cutting away and damping down the hotspots and preventing water damage and salvaging equipment.

2110 hrs, "stop message from ADO Barlow for same address, a range of college buildings of one and three storeys on a one-and-a-half-acre site, twenty-five per cent of a ground floor classroom severely damaged by fire, heat and smoke and cutting away, remainder of ground floor damaged by smoke, 1 jet, 2 hosereel jets, 6 BA in use."

At 2237 hrs, the lorry is requested from the station with the smoke extractor

Golf 10 mobile, Sub O Milton in charge, crew of 2.

My pump leaves the job and is back at station at 2245 hrs.

Last appliance left at 0009 hrs.

One afternoon I was sitting on the mess deck, reading the paper, minding my own business.

A bloke comes in dressed in a white coat with a white trilby hat and a clipboard.

He says "Hallo, I'm from the Food Hygiene and Safety Department come to check your kitchen."

"OK, it's over there," says I.

"Have you noticed anything I should know about," he continued.

"Well, we used to have rats but something ate them."

I thought it was amusing but he, being of that ilk, had absolutely no sense of humour, and stormed out of the room.

Next minute the tannoy crackled, "Fireman Payne to the Station Officer's office."

Another bollocking, although this was a tongue in cheek bollocking, with a stern, white-coated idiot looking smug standing next to the Guv.

On Friday, 13th October I was on standby at Bishops Stortford fire station.

At 1559 hrs, we were called to an RTA on the A120 at Little Hadham.

We arrived on scene at 1602 hrs to find two cars in collision with two adult males injured. We treated them using our oxygen equipment and first aid kit, as we awaited the arrival of the ambulance. The retained, Charlie 281, were also on the call.

Stop sent at 1624 hrs. Home station at 1656 hrs.

RTA, A120 at Little Hadham.

On 7th December an emergency was developing at the Lister Hospital.

An electrical mains failure had caused the water supply to the dialysis machines to fail. With twenty-two patients undergoing dialysis treatment it was a matter of urgency to restore the supply.

The usual attendance to the hospital was mobilised at 1446 hrs, both Stevenage pumps and Hitchin's appliance and on this occasion because of the incident ADO Stokes was also tasked.

We filled the water tank and maintained it until the electricity supply came back on.

Stop message sent at 1734 hrs and home station at 1802 hrs.

Finally for 1995, two days before Christmas, a Range Rover has been stolen from Walkern and was being driven away at speed towards Stevenage.

A Stevenage man is driving his Rover 1600 Lsi along Gresley Way towards Walkern.

BEEP, BEEP, BEEP, "230, 232 to attend Gresley Way, Stevenage, RTA persons trapped."

185 also mobilised.

230 mobile at 1528 hrs, crew of 5.

232 mobile at 1528 hrs, crew of 4, (including me).

185 mobile at 1529 hrs, crew of 2

In attendance at 1531 hrs.

Two vehicles have been in a head on collision – the Range Rover has a big set of bull bars which have been substantially damaged. However the Rover has been severely crushed by the impact.

The driver is well trapped with the engine compartment pushed into the driver's area. He is in a bad way with some serious injuries, particularly to his legs. Both his femurs (thigh bones) have been broken and pushed out from the back of his pelvis. He is losing a lot of blood and fluids and the paramedics are working hard to stabilise him although they have trouble getting a drip into his hand.

Meanwhile we use a pedal cutter and two sets of Lucas cutting equipment to open up the vehicle.

After forty-five minutes he is finally released from the car and taken to hospital by ambulance.

The Gazette of 29th December reported that: -

"After the accident at 3.15 p.m. a fourteen-year-old from Aylesbury ran from the driver's seat towards Aston but was arrested shortly afterwards by police."

On 31st December the Watch was joined by Temporary Stn O John Mills and he arrived for a busy shift.

At 12.04 p.m. we went to a car fire on the A1(M) followed by a fire in Kimbolton Crescent where lighted toilet paper had been pushed through the letter box. At 4.03 p.m. we used the hearthkit to release a woman and child who were locked in a room at Ripon Road.

To finish the day, two false alarms, the first to Dale Villa, Park Lane, Knebworth and then straight off to Silkin Court, Campkin Mead, Stevenage, finally getting back to the station at 1718 hrs.

Time to wash the fire engine before the change of shift.

Want some more firemen talking crap? Okay…

Mad Dog Riley: "Apple pie! Yeah Pat brought some onions in."

Sludge Andrews: "You pat my back and I'll pat yours."

Me: "My wife was snoring her cock off."

Mad Dog Riley: "I bet that's only the tip of the ice cube."

Bernie Bush: "I couldn't shit through a whole Shakespeare play."

Mad Dog Riley: "We don't want a common currency, French for those Frog bastards, Deutschmarks for those German bastards and English for us Pounds."

Mad Dog Riley: "I come just below the budgie in the pecking order."

Mad Dog Riley: "It's a terrible thing that testicled cancer especially in men!"

Chankers Chapman: "I've got a six-inch roller, well it was four inches but I cut it down."

Elmo Mitchell: "We'll all have to grow false beards."

Taff James: "You need to get thirty-eight streaks of bacon."

1996. A VERY SAD YEAR.

Back on duty on New Year's Day for the start of another busy year.

Just over a week into the year we gave first aid to a woman with burns, following a bedroom fire at her home in Trumper Road, Stevenage. I was driving WrL 1 and the fire was tackled by 2 BA using a hosereel jet.

A month later on 5th February we had the first of several multi-vehicle pile-ups this year.

At 0823 hrs we were mobilised to junctions 6 to 7 of the A1(M), Welwyn to Stevenage South.

Also in attendance were Old Welwyn and Welwyn Garden City.

The stop message was sent at 0845 hrs, "eight motor vehicles in collision on carriageway, no persons trapped, assisting police."

We used three "spill kits" to clean up the oil and petrol spillages on the road and cleared away vehicle debris.

The accident caused long tailbacks, with only the hard shoulder open for around an hour and a half. A second accident on the opposite carriageway added to the chaos.

Spill kits had recently been issued to every pump and consisted of absorbent pads, booms, Fullers earth and "Dammit" putty for sealing drains.

On Monday, 26th February both pumps were mobilised to the village of Benington, where a fire had broken out in a grade II listed building.

Pound Cottage in Town Lane is on fire and it is a possible persons reported.

I was in charge of 232 with a crew of 4, we arrived at 1333 hrs and deployed two BA crews with hosereels and the thermal imaging camera to fight the fire and search the building.

The ground floor was severely damaged in the fire with the upstairs damaged by heat and smoke but nobody was found.

We got back to the fire station at 1645 hrs.

What's going on! There's a bloody Frenchman on the station!

Didier Mouzon, a firefighter from Marseilles is visiting us during his holiday to the UK in March. He tells *The Mercury*, in a French accent, "firefighting is very different in France; I could just as easily be driving an ambulance or be a coastguard."

At 4.18 p.m. on 15th May, the bells went down and immediately afterwards went down again! Both appliances were mobilised to fires at different addresses.

I went with the WrL 1 to Longmeadow shops in Oaks Cross and the WrL 2 was sent to Oakfields.

However, we both met up again as the fire was one and the same. Some bushes on fire!

A few days later the cleaner at the station, whose name was Yvonne I think, came up to me and said she had just been stung on the arm by a wasp and that she may have an allergic reaction to it. It was quite red and a bit blotchy.

I popped up to see the Station Officer and we decided to take her down to the Lister hospital. As the station Land Rover was out, I got the divisional lorry and we set off.

Not long into the drive she showed me her arm which had swollen up alarmingly! It looked like someone had blown up a red Marigold rubber glove.

It was now a matter of some urgency as she could go into anaphylactic shock so we drove the rest of the way on the blues and two tones!

She got her adrenaline and all turned out well.

On the 9th of June I was off to the hospital again, five of us on 230 were ordered to Ward 9b Lister Hospital to assist hospital staff.

Up on the ward we were confronted with a thirty stone female patient who had collapsed on the floor in a toilet. We lifted her back to bed.

Strangely as I am writing this, today's headline in the local paper here, the *Dorset Echo*, has the front page headline:

PEOPLE BECOMING 'TOO FAT TO RESCUE' SAY UNDER STRAIN FIREFIGHTERS

On the 25th June, another multi-car pile-up resulted in the worst time of my service.

This incident remains the only one that is guaranteed to make me cry so I won't dwell on it.

230 was called to junctions 9 to 8, A1(M), Letchworth to Stevenage North, where five cars were involved in a collision.

Also attending were 310, 311, 320 and 185.

One person was trapped and we used two sets of Lucas to free her.

Sadly, our casualty was Kim Bygrave, wife of our colleague Max who was previously stationed with me on the White Watch at Stevenage before he was promoted.

We had a nice social group, Max and Kim, Patsy and me, Barry and Mave Hillier and Dave and Tracey Rees, we would meet up, sometimes in Codicote or Letchworth or Royston.

This was the only time before or since that I went to talk to Jim Smith, at that time the vicar at Codicote.

Later that evening Dave Stokes (the OiC at the incident) turned up at my house and we went down the Globe.

Kim died on the 27th. So sorry I couldn't do more.

On 19th August, I was in charge of WrL 2 when we were called to extinguish a small fire involving a fence. We used a garden hose to put it out. Not much of a job I'll grant you, and the only reason I mention it is that WrL 2 callsign has been changed from 232 to 231.

The station open day fell on our shift again this year and we had a great idea for a spectacular show.

Elmo, Mad Dog and myself planned to demonstrate the dangers of using camping gas.

We managed to get hold of an old caravan and cut a hole in the back, big enough for us to get out and filled it with a lot of petrol. We had a camping gas stove by the wheel and a small, petrol soaked rag hidden in the wheel arch.

With a running commentary from the loud speaker, the demonstration got under way.

In front of a large, expectant crowd and at the start of the display, Paul and I were acting drunk with a can of beer each and several more strewn around. I am making a great show of trying to light a gas stove, unsuccessfully, as Roy staggers back carrying more beers.

At the last moment I surreptitiously ignite the rag in the wheel arch and the three of us disappear into the caravan.

We leave through the hole in the back and once outside Roy throws a lighted rag on a stick back into the caravan.

There is an enormous explosion and the caravan erupts in a ball of fire.

The crowd stand aghast, jaws drop and children start crying as a ball of fire heads skyward.

The sound of two tone horns can be heard and the fire engine screeches into the yard, the crew get to work putting out the fire (incidentally, one of the best we have had for weeks!)

Meanwhile Elmo, Mad Dog and I change into some ragged and torn clothes and black ourselves up.

Once the fire is out, we come back through the caravan and out of what is left of the door, initially to a stunned silence, then to rapturous applause and the amazement of the audience.

A great performance all round.

It's 22nd August, just after eight thirty in the morning. A builder is off to work.

As he approaches the roundabout at the junction of Broadhall Way and Broadwater Crescent he loses control of his van. He crashes through the railings surrounding the roundabout, demolishes two road signs and down the embankment. The broken leaf springs dig into the grass and stop the vehicle dead in its tracks, catapulting the driver out through the windscreen and onto the cycle path.

We were called to assist the ambulance and police recover the casualty back up to the road.

Even though he had taken his last drink the night before (so he claimed) when the police breathalysed him he was still three times over the safe alcohol limit.

At the end of September my old mate Ron Barlow retired as Stevenage Station Commander after thirty years' service.

He didn't retire completely however, as he went on to join the Commercial Training department, teaching outside companies.

The Comet newspaper carried the headline…

RON BOWS OUT IN A BLAZE OF GLORY

It also had an anecdote which is worth a mention.

Apparently Ron was working in the London rag trade as a dress cutter when his boss said he thought the bottom was about to fall out of the market. (Good job he wasn't working with ladies' underwear!) He advised him to get a safe and steady job with the London Fire Brigade.

The standard at the time was that recruits had to have a thirty-six-inch chest with a two inch expansion. Ron measured up (so he tells us) and applied to join. However, according to the man who checked his chest he didn't come close.

Off went Ron to do a bit of body building and four months later he was up to forty inches.
However when he was again measured again he still didn't make the grade.

Just at that moment an officer put his head around the door and said "Charlie, you've got the tape round the wrong way. I've told you about that before."

"The guy did it properly and I was in," said Ron.

I remember at a Union meeting at Stevenage, Ron made a proposal, arguing the point in his usual way, shouting and red-faced and then voted against it!

In his "thank you" card to the Watch he said "Thank you for being part of my life over the years. Where would I be without Sid Payne reminding me of Barlow's Bollocks." He finished with "Be happy, be lucky!! Ron B."

A few end of year incidents:

30th September. I was in charge when we took the lorry with the shear legs to a horse stuck in the Stanstead Mill Stream of the River Lea at Cappell Lane, Stanstead Abbots. We teamed up with Ware retained with Sub O Morrison in charge and Hatfield's ERT with L/Fm Gray.

Tony Morrison was a Station Commander at Welwyn Garden City when I transferred there some years later.

Malcolm Sawdy was in overall charge, and the horse was freed after an hours pushing and pulling.

17th October. A running call to three cars in collision at the junction of Broadhall Way and Monkswood Way. It was 1753 hrs, just before the change of Watch and Red Watch with both pumps were out. A passing motorist came into the station to report the crash. Bernie Bush and I decided to turn out in the Land Rover to the call. We made a job of the incident and a minute later we were rendering first aid on scene. 230 attended with the Red Watch crew.

15th November.We rescued two people from a window cleaners cradle stuck at 5th floor level at Glaxo's, Gunnelswood Road.

Our HP was off the run and so 111 and 114 were sent from St Albans. The window cleaners were rescued after an hour or so using the HP, a nine metre ladder and a short extension ladder.

18th November. Both appliances plus Old Welwyn and Hatfield's ERT were called to six vehicles in collision on the A1 Motorway between junctions 7 to 8, Stevenage South to North.

No personswere trapped, more absorbent granules in use.

26th November. Paul Riley and me in BA tackled a bedroom fire at Chauncy House, Chauncy Road in Stevenage. The fire was started by a candle and extinguished with a hosereel jet.

Gibber Book time!

Elmo Mitchell: "I can't wear my shorts; I've got a bit of a dodgy ankle."

Mad Dog Riley: "A Hock nock bick nock." (A Hobnob biscuit).

Me: "That's put a fly amongst the pigeons."

Ron Barlow: "And I'm unanimous in that!"

Pullthrough: (Singing) "Sailors for trail or rent."

Ron Barlow: "Keep your ear to the grindstone."

Frank Gollogly: "I heard that out of the corner of my ear."

Elmo Mitchell: "He couldn't hear, he'd lost his deaf."

Snot Monster Hadley: "Stranger things have happened with a bird in the hand."

Elmo Mitchell: "If you lose your American Express card, they can get you a stolen one."

1997. A WORD OF ADVICE, NEVER SHELTER IN A TREE DURING A THUNDERSTORM.

Things were changing, both in personnel and within the service.

With Ron Barlow retiring, it left a vacancy for a Station Commander at Stevenage and the man to fill it was Dave Stokes who was promoted to the post. This in turn left a vacancy on the Watch. We had several temporary Station Officers including Ian Mackenzie, Simon Brown and John Mills, before Iayn Thomas took on the permanent position.

Also joining us around now were Sub O Dave, "Dirty Harry" Callaghan, L/Ff Chris York and Ff Steve "Trigger" Manual.

Service-wise, the bars were closing, Health and Safety was kicking in and we had civilian staff taking over existing posts and creating new ones i.e. Equal Opportunities and Discrimination. Poor Pat Priestman was dropped like a hot potato by senior officers, just not politically correct any more.

Everything on Station used to be done by the junior officers, the paperwork etc. for which we seemed to manage okay. Then secretaries were allocated to stations and you couldn't get to your desk until they went home.

I recall an Equal Opportunities woman visited us on station to put us all straight on a few things, which actually meant a totally blinkered view of everything with no room for personal opinion. Or humour of course.

She split us up into groups of three or four to discuss matters of extreme importance. There were a number of questions to which each group presented their revelations.

For example, *how could we involve the disabled?* We suggested a retired pirate with hooks instead of hands would be perfectly suited to carry the buckets.

Should we have disabled access to the fire station in the form of ramps? Whilst we agreed in principal we thought that we would leave ourselves open to invasion by Daleks.

What would you do if a homosexual came onto the Watch. Well this one was easy, we would want "soap on a rope" for the shower!

Any way she sat there stony-faced throughout, no sense of humour, just like the rat-man of a few years earlier.

Health and Safety was also changing the way we did things.

We used to pitch ladders over the roofs, bridging gaps between buildings or sliding down hosepipes. I remember Taff jumping out of the fourth floor of the tower and running down the wall face first using a line, commando style or Biggles climbing up the outside of the tower just using the grouting and gaps between the bricks.

We once built a frame using ladders with nozzles tied to the corners and with high-pressure water pumped through hoses, we could sit on it and hover two or three metres off the ground. Ahh, happy days.

And of course women were starting to appear and so we became firefighters instead of firemen so that there was no distinction. Although strangely if needed they would become "women firefighters."

Finally, we were going computerised and most of us had to be sent on a Basic Computer Skills Course.

Mick Dyer, who I think was a Sub O over A Division somewhere, had the job of sorting it all out. Amusingly if you phoned him up he would answer the phone with "Dyer 'ere." (Get it?)

It took us ages to master it. On my basic course I put the mouse on the floor and started to push on it with my foot, asking the teacher "why my pedal wasn't working?"

All the training records were put on to the system, I think Max Bygrave had something to do with that, and then what used to take five minutes now took fifteen! That's progress for you.

Anyway, another cold December, with a thaw over the New Year, leading to… you guessed it, frozen pipes bursting!

Our first shift of the year began on 2nd January, a Thursday. I am riding in the back of 230 with a crew of four.

Hoping for a quiet shift, we put the kettle on and sort out the catering for the day.

Over in the Red Lion public House in Woolmer Green, the Landlord has opened up for the lunchtime trade and is banking up the fire against the cold outside.

A passer-by comes in to point out the sparks coming from the chimney.

He gets on the phone and dials 999.

1251 hrs, BEEP, BEEP, BEEP… "230 to attend the Red Lion pub, London Road, Woolmer Green, chimney fire."

1253 hrs, mobile and in attendance at 1258 hrs.

Flames can be seen coming from the chimney up on the roof, and we are going to start with the chimney gear at the hearth in the bar. We connect the chimney rods and move them slowly up the chimney applying the water as we go. No change with the fire, the rods aren't getting it.

Next plan, to attack it from the roof. We pitch a short extension ladder to the roof and run the roof ladder up to the ridge.

A hosereel jet is taken aloft and water applied down the chimney. I am at the hearth and eventually the water comes down cool.

Stop message is sent at 1343 hrs and we start to make-up.

At 1401 hrs the radio comes to life, "order your appliance to Smilin' Sam's, Leisure Park, Stevenage, AFA."

We are in attendance at 1405 hrs along with 231. 320 is also mobilised but are not required as the stop is sent at 1408 hrs.

Back home at 1412 hrs for lunch.

1529 hrs, BEEP, BEEP, BEEP… "230 to attend Wildwood Lane, Stevenage, flooding."

Water, water everywhere etc. "make pumps 2, wet vac required."

231 is mobilised with the wet vac, a hoover that can suck up water.

216

We start to remove the water and salvage the occupiers' belongings, when at 1545 hrs a call comes over the radio for us, "230 to Kimbolton Road, Stevenage, flooding."

Off we go again, leaving 231 to send the stop at 1602 hrs, and to finish clearing up.

We are in attendance at 1550 hrs, to find another flood coming down through the ceiling. The OiC requests the attendance of 231 with the wet vac, and at 1606 hrs, "order your appliance to Ansell Court, Stevenage, flooding." And we are off again.

231 attend the last job and send the stop at 1621 hrs.

We don't get very far before we are re-routed to another incident, "order your appliance to outside Sainsbury's, Hitchin Road, Stevenage, RTA persons trapped."

231 are sent to Ansell Court and send the stop at 1636 hrs. We are in attendance at 1615 hrs to find a vehicle in collision with a road sign and a male person trapped and injured.

Also at the job are 320 and 185.

The driver's door is popped open using the Lukas hydraulic cutting and spreading equipment and the casualty removed on a spinal board. With the driver released from his car, and conveyed to the Lister by Herts Ambulance, the stop was sent at 1635 hrs.

We are not finished yet and with 231 still tied up at Ansell Court, "order your appliance to Plash Drive, Stevenage, flooding."

We are mobile at 1648 hrs and in attendance at 1654 hrs.

Same again, water cascading through the ceiling and affecting electrics, we sent the assistance message "salvage tender required."

Control mobilise 321 and 323.

The stop message sent at 1757 hrs, and we finally got back to the station at 1800 hrs.

From the end of January through to the beginning of March I got to wear BA at incidents on five occasions.

On 19th January at a car fire in Hitchin Road; on 28th January we extinguished a fire in the loft of a house in Wisden Road, Stevenage and on 5th February another car fire, started maliciously, in Long Leaves, Stevenage. A third car burnt out in Fairlands Way, Stevenage on the evening of 1st March and finally at 2126 hrs, me and Elmo tackled a bedroom fire, persons reported, in Langthorne Avenue, Stevenage.

My reason for mentioning these fires is that, the incident on 5th February saw the introduction of another new piece of equipment.

Stations had been issued with a new, lightweight, BA cylinder. The back plate of the BA set was plastic/carbon fibre, (which had replaced the earlier metal), and now with the new cylinder, working in difficult, hot and cramped conditions became a little bit easier.

A word on the BA set itself.

Apart from the cylinder, back plate, harness and facemask, each set had: -

A torch.

A personal line; which enabled you to connect to another fireman or a guide line, and to search up to 6m/20ft away from the line.

A Distress Signal Unit. Once armed, the DSU would operate, giving out a loud alarm, if the BA wearer didn't move for a short period of time, thus alerting colleagues to his emergency.

Attached to the DSU is a Tally. At the beginning of the shift the BA wearer would check his BA set and write his name and pressure in the cylinder onto the tally.

At an incident he would remove the tally and put it into the BA Board, thus it would be apparent that he had entered the fire.

The appliance driver or number five was responsible for the BA Board on small incidents and a more dedicated BA Control Officer was responsible at larger jobs.

Using the Board the BACO would know what time the wearers were due to be back out from the incident, amongst other things.

There was also a 60m/200ft guideline to enable us to penetrate a building and return safely to fresh air.

One last thing, every pump had a Rider's Board, which would be completed at the start of the shift with the names of each crew member.

During the evening of Sunday, 9th March, fog closed in over the town causing horrendous driving conditions.

It got thicker as the night wore on and by midnight we couldn't see the roundabout in front of the station.

Just before midnight the bells went down and both appliances were mobile to Martins Way, Stevenage to an RTA persons trapped.

I was driving 231, WrL 2, with a crew of four. 230 had a crew of five and 185 a crew of two.

In attendance six minutes later.

No persons trapped, we assist the police and return.

So I went to bed, lovely.

The following morning and the Monday rush hour traffic was building, with the motorway becoming busy.

Back at the station, the Sprog was bringing the tea round.

0709 hrs, BEEP, BEEP, BEEP, "both appliances to A1(M), junctions 8 – 7, RTA persons trapped."

I pull out of the station into a blanket of fog, if anything worse than the previous evening!

Also mobile are 185, crew of 2, 201 with a crew of 5 and an ADO, Charlie 5.

In attendance at 0717 hrs to find a green, Peugeot 306 in collision with a tree.

Also involved is a white, Ford Scorpio.

The driver of the Peugeot is well trapped and looks very dead. His airbag has deployed. Using Lukas we remove the driver's door and cut through the offside A and B posts to open up a working space to access the casualty.

The driver has sustained severe injuries, particularly to his legs. He is declared to be "code 1" and removed from the vehicle and taken to the Lister Hospital by Herts Ambulance.

> It is thought that his airbag fired when he collided with the other car and that he had no protection from it when he crossed the hard shoulder and hit the tree.

"Code 1" is emergency service jargon for "deceased."
The Comet of Thursday, March 13th, told us:

DEATH CRASH CAUSES CHAOS

There was widespread traffic chaos on Monday when part of the A1(M) had to be closed during the morning rush hour after a fatal crash.

It happened in foggy conditions on the southbound carriageway between the two Stevenage junctions. For more than two hours thousands of motorists tried to find alternative routes.

It led to massive hold-ups in Baldock, Letchworth, Hitchin, Stevenage and further afield until mid-morning on Monday."

We had always had a good relationship with our Ambulance colleagues. On 11th June just after lunch we got a call, which always has me chuckling!

A car had hit a lamppost and overturned on Knebworth Hill, London, Road. Knebworth The woman driver was trapped upside down still strapped in her seat belt.

We arrived on scene and Ambulanceman Gary "Spindle" Sanderson and me crawled into the car to support and treat the casualty. After we had been in there for about twenty minutes, while the crews were cutting access, the woman started to get agitated "Is everyone OK? Please tell me no one else is hurt, I'm so sorry, is everyone alright!" A bit of a break then she started again, "Please tell me no one is hurt, please!"

Spindle looked over at me and said, "Well to be honest, I'm getting a bit of a back ache!"

After everything had been sorted out, we were surveying the scene, an upturned car and a lamppost bent double. Bungle, nodding knowingly, turned to us and said, "Do you know I wouldn't be surprised if the car had hit that lamppost!"

It's 13th July and outside a storm is raging.

At 1406 hrs we were called out to Bury Farm, Bury Lane in the village of Datchworth, to a tree on fire following a lightning strike.

I am in the back of the WrL 1 with a crew of five and we arrive at the farm at 2.13 p.m.

The tree is fairly small, standing on its own in a hedgerow and smoke is rising from the top of the trunk at about three metres, where the branches start to fork off.

We pitch a short extension ladder up to the fire and I climb up with a hosereel. The top of the trunk has been split open by the lightning strike, is much blackened and smoking. As I reach the top of the ladder, a strange sight greets me.

Sitting there is a Little Owl, with not a feather to its name, just two huge eyes in a pink skin looking up at me and if it could talk it would be saying "What the bloody hell happened just then?"

I pick it up and pass it down to one of the others, who, amid 'owls of laughter, wraps it in a cloth to keep it warm. I put out the smouldering fire and the stop is sent at 2.23 p.m. We make up the hosereel, stop on the way to top up the tank with water and head to the vets at the Roebuck shops.

The vet takes the owl but I never went back to see how it fared.

Back on station at 3.21 p.m.

By the way what do you get if you cross a rooster with an owl? A cock that stays up all night!

Throughout the rest of the year I get plenty of acting-up and temporary promotion.

It is just before four o'clock in the morning on Friday 19th September, and over in Letchworth, thieves have broken in to the Simmonds Coaches compound in Norton Way North.

They take an orange, thirty-two-seater, Van Hool coach and ram the locked gates to make their escape.

The coach is next seen at seven thirty a.m. being reversed into the car park at Hampson Park, Webb Rise, Stevenage.

Several men run off as flames were seen coming from the inside of the vehicle.

At the fire station the alarm sounds and WrL 1 with a crew of four turns out at 7.33 a.m. to a dustcart on fire!

On scene at 7.37 a.m. we are confronted with a coach well alight.

TC and me rig in BA and knock down the flames with a jet before entering the vehicle to put out the fire. It takes a while to extinguish and it is twenty-two minutes before the stop message is sent. We make up and are back on station at 8.14 a.m. in time for breakfast.

The irreplaceable coach was worth £50,000, one of only two right hand drive models ever built.

Remember, remember the 5th of November.
Two out of control bonfires in Canterbury Way resulted in us being attacked by kids with bangers as we put a damper on their celebrations.

One final incident to mention before the year is out.

I am riding in charge of 231 with a crew of four on New Year's Eve, when we get a call to Danesbury Park Caravan Site in Danesbury Park Lane, Welwyn.

In attendance at 2049 hrs, together with Welwyn and Welwyn Garden City.

The stop message sent at 2124 hrs and read, "a mobile home, 5m x 15m, severely damaged by fire and collapse, cylinders involved, no persons involved, 6 BA, 2 HRJ."

Another year of drivel.

Mad Dog Riley: "Don't let them take that shit, that's our shit, that shit."

Elmo Mitchell: "They saved the finale 'til last."

Ben Read: "After three throw it... NOW."

Pull-through O'Neill: "Her tits were so far apart they pointed to all four corners of the room."

Mad Dog Riley: "We had a bloke on my course called Yogi Bear, of course that wasn't his real name."

Elmo Mitchell: "You can correct me if I'm right."

Mad Dog Riley: "I'm going to have a shower, towel out – willy off."

Mad Dog Riley: "That's it, I'm ready for bed now... I've cleaned my piss and had a teeth."

Iayn Thomas: "I heard it with my own eyes."

Bungle Davies: "I've got a scrapbook, it's a bit pathetic, I've got one scrap and no book."

Sludge Andrews: "We'll have dinner, then pudding for desert."

Mad Dog Riley: "I want my bacon done really well, I want it incriminated."

Sludge Andrews: "Two sheep in a field, one went 'quack' the other went 'moo' – one was learning a foreign language."

Dirty Harry Callaghan: (After Ben's medical). "Did he stick his finger up your cervix?"

1998. CATCH ME IF YOU CAN!

Another year and I've still got Irritable Owl Syndrome!

This year is also a milestone for me. I have been a fireman for twenty years! Where has all that time gone?

As with so many other years, this one starts on a sad note.

A twenty-three-year-old woman is driving home to Cottered, near Stevenage, after visiting her father in Welwyn.

It's just after eight p.m. on Sunday 1st February.

Usually she would drive through the country roads, but due to the icy conditions she took the motorway.

Between Corey's Mill (Stevenage North) and Letchworth she loses control of her Peugeot car, collides with the central reservation, spins back into the carriageway and, side on across the road, was struck in the off-side by a Jaguar XJR.

2014 hrs, BEEP, BEEP, BEEP, "230 and 231 to A1(M), junctions 8-9, RTA, persons trapped."

2015 hrs, 230 mobile, crew of five, Stn O Thomas in charge.

Also mobile are 231 crew of four, 310 crew of five, 185 crew of two and ADO "Bravo 3".

In attendance at 2020 hrs.

Two crews are got to work with Lukas on the Peugeot where the woman is alive and unconscious but trapped.

A third crew attends the driver of the Jaguar, who is conscious but suffering from whiplash, chest and head pain and broken bones in his hand. His airbag has deployed which probably saved him from more serious injury. He is treated with oxygen and first aid.

Lighting is set up to help in the extrication of the female driver. The car is opened up to allow the paramedics to treat her. Sadly, she is certified dead at the scene by a doctor who has stopped to help.

A third driver involved, a German from Munich, is not seriously injured.

All the casualties are taken to the Lister by Herts Ambulance.

The stop message is sent at 2101 hrs, "two motor cars in collision on motorway, one female adult code one by doctor on site, all casualties conveyed to hospital by Herts ambulance, Lukas, HRJ, lighting, MARS O2 in use."

2122 hrs, home station, closing down.

Station Officer Iayn Thomas told *The Gazette*, "The fire and ambulance crews worked well together and we were able to get the woman out quite quickly."

Some more changes in personnel for the year.

Rob Horsfield transferred in from somewhere, I don't remember where from. Phil "The Gimp" Harris and Che "Turtle" Baker arrived and a bit later in the year Kevin "Jock" Morgan joined us. Jock was actually Welsh but we already had a Taff! At the end of the year or early next Chris York got a job back in A Division and he was replaced as the L/Ff by Steve Kendall.

The 18th February and the late night drunks keep us busy.

At 0157 hrs we are called out to Sish Lane in Stevenage to a car fire. I am in the back of 230 with a crew of five.

The car has been set on fire and I am in the BA team that fights the blaze with a hosereel. Despite our efforts, the car is gutted.

The stop is sent at 0217 hrs.

There is a fiery glow down the road and smoke is rising in the glare of the streetlights. We are tasked by Control to a second fire, this time the ne'er-do-wells have torched a residential garage.

I change my BA cylinder and we take a hosereel to tackle the second blaze. Full of rubbish and other things it takes us a long time to get the fire out completely.

Finally back on station 0337 hrs.

The BA cylinders are charged up and the sets cleaned.

Quick cuppa and bed.

Over the next few months we had a number of varied incidents.

On 11th March we had a call to a boy trapped in a pile of cut tree trunks at the Forestry Commission in Ashtree Woods.

This proved to be a difficult rescue as moving one tree had an effect on all the others. A giant game of "pick-up-sticks!"

At Sloan Court, Archer Road, on 6th April, we arrived to find an elderly lady on her first floor balcony, holding onto a UPVC door, both in danger of falling over the balustrade. She was rescued and the door made safe.

Six days later we attended Fairlands Park to standby while the Royal Logistics Corps, Bomb Disposal Team, carried out a controlled detonation on a two inch mortar round, left over from WW2. The bomb was dug up by a gardener in Angle Ways.

And so it went on, a baby trapped in a car, a cat trapped on a roof and a six-year-old lad with his head trapped in railings at school!

We assist the ambulance with a woman with a broken neck in Knebworth, person shut in lift, a squirrel trapped in a roof, a girl locked in and people locked out and in Lonsdale Road we used a 464 ladder to rescue a child struck up a tree.

The Governor Iayn Thomas had a great idea. He would send us out for the day to ride with our colleagues in other services.

I had a day out with the Ambulance Service and on another occasion I had a great day with the Motorway Police, rushing up and down the A1(M) and M25.

I don't remember what the others did but I seem to recall Elmo had a day at the Lister and watched a knee or hip replacement operation.

Iayn did draw the line however, at my request for a day with the RNLI.

On Friday, 17th July, around four fifteen p.m., the bells went down and 230 was called out to a garage fire at Thurlow Road, Stevenage.

I am in the back of 231 and so we stand down.

1624 hrs. BEEP, BEEP, BEEP, "order 231 to Thurlow Road, Stevenage, house fire, make pumps 2."

In attendance at 1628 hrs, and our other crew are running around like headless chickens! It's a serious fire.

We have a detached house with a garage attached to it.

The garage is well alight with a car inside, the fire is spreading through into the house and on top of that there is a line of fuel on fire running from the garage down the road.

The first BA crew is trying to extinguish the fire in the garage. They have tried a dry powder fire extinguisher and now have got an FB5X foam branch to work. I am in BA again and we try to pass the first crew to fight the fire where the garage joins the house.

Outside, another member of the crew is trying to stem the flow of fuel using a spill kit.

The fire is out after forty-five minutes, with the stop going back at 1733 hrs.

> In all we used 1 dry powder extinguisher, 1 jet, 1 hosereel jet, 1 FB5X, 4 BA and a spill kit.

We used another new piece of equipment for the first time on 9th August at a grass fire in Turpins Rise Stevenage.

It was a portable knapsack, carrying around twenty litres of water with a pump action nozzle. This was a great innovation. Previously we would have to carry buckets or run out a lot of hosereel or hose. Also the knapsack sprayer used the water sparingly, making it go further.

12th August at nine p.m. and we are tasked by Control to send WrL 2 to relieve crews at a big fire on Potters Bar's ground.

The fire broke out at 10.06 a.m. at the Welcome Break Services at Bignalls Corner at the junction of the A1(M) and the M25.

At its height there were twelve pumps in action.

We were there with 010.

At that time in the village where I lived we had a Gardening Club that met in the Globe. I took a fire blackened pasty and a very wilted tomato plant from the fire and entered them in the Friday night judging. I won a first with both exhibits!

21st September. Just after 0900 hrs in the evening, and 231 gets an unusual call, which came via the RSPCA. "Eagle Owl escaped from house, now on roof."

We are mobile with a crew of four and in attendance at nine fifteen.

Sure enough, sitting on the chimney pot in Ellis Avenue, Stevenage is a bloody great owl!

The question is how to catch it.

We are on a hiding to nothing, but we have to be seen to be doing something.

We slip the 464 ladder and pitch it up to the chimney stack. One of the firemen starts the climb, knowing full well what will happen. As he nears the top of the ladder the owl re-locates to the chimney of the house next door.

We re-pitch the ladder and start the procedure again.

The owl takes flight, and I remember it was a full moon and the owl flew off towards it and made a great lunar silhouette.

And that was the last we saw of it.

I have arranged for my son, Gary, to have a job-shadowing day at the fire station as part of his work experience from school.

Red Watch were to be our hosts for the day.

We spent the morning BA training in the smoke house.

After tea and rolls Gary and I went down to Longfield in the Landrover to visit the Control room, where the girls kindly showed Gary around.

While we were there, a call came in for Stevenage and we watched as Control mobilised 230.

Gary and I ran out to the Landrover and we were mobile to Furzedown, Stevenage, van fire at 12.32 p.m.

229

We were in attendance at 12.34 p.m. and Red Watch were tackling a van with its engine compartment on fire, using 2 BA and a hosereel jet.

The stop went off at 12.40 p.m. and Gary took a turn on the hosereel.

Back to the station for lunch break.

At 2.20 p.m, the bells went down and this time Gary turned out on the WrL 2 making the crew up to six. I followed in the Landrover, also mobile was 230 with a crew of five.

The call was to the Library at Lister Hospital.

In attendance at 2.25 p.m. The fire alarm system had operated, a false alarm. Stop message sent at 2.26 p.m.

Back at the station we have a play with the HP and a game of volleyball before going off duty at six p.m. Incidentally, look at the photograph of Gary and me on the right.

The helmet I am wearing, I had on trial; it was an American one made by Cairns of New Jersey.

It had a label inside that read:

WARNING – FIREFIGHTING IS INHERENTLY
DANGEROUS.

The Mercury of 11th December had the headline:

TOY OWNERS GIVE LOVED-ONES A "DEATH SLIDE"
IN FUND-RAISING CHALLENGE:
TEDDIES RISK ALL FOR CHARITY!

We had arranged to raise a bit of money for a couple of worthy charities, Hearing Dogs for the Deaf and the Gareth Hillier Fund.

Gareth, the son of our own Spiros Hillier, had unfortunately suffered a spinal injury earlier in the year.

"Furry friends belonging to children and grown-up's tackled a 'death slide' challenge from the top of the clock tower in Town Square."

Those who didn't want to subject their teddies to such a terrifying ordeal could enter a balloon race.

The Mercury went on, "one person who did think the death slide was safe enough for his favourite cuddly toy was Stevenage fire station officer Iayn Thomas. His bear Harold, even donned flying goggles!"

Chris York told *The Mercury* "We think we've raised about £540. Most of that came from the balloon race."

A busy time over the festive period. Some of the more interesting being:

Thursday, Christmas Eve.

A call at 1617 hrs took us to a car fire at the ESSO petrol station in Lytton Way, Stevenage.

We pulled on to the forecourt to find a car smoking next to the petrol pumps.

Bizarrely, the garage was functioning as if nothing was happening!

We pushed the vehicle to a safe place, extinguished the fire and left.

Friday, Christmas Day.

I am on standby at Hertford fire station.

We finish dinner and settle down for the usual Christmas television.

At 2138 hrs the alarm sounds, and the teleprinter tells us, "240 to attend outside St. Albans Sand and Gravel, Westmill Road, Ware, RTA persons trapped."

Also mobile are 251, 185 and Charlie 8.

We arrive on scene at 2149 hrs to find a Ford Escort car which has left the road, gone through a chain link fence and collided with a tree.

The roof has caved in after the collision and the male driver is trapped in his seat.

We use three sets of Lukas cutting gear to open up the car to allow the paramedics to treat the casualty and he is removed after an hour on a spinal board.

He is taken to hospital by ambulance and the stop goes back at 2253 hrs.

It turns out that the driver is just nineteen, straight out of prison and has no licence, tax or insurance!

Saturday, Boxing Day.

It's 1910 hrs, and two cars have pulled over onto the hard shoulder of the slip road at junction 9, Letchworth, of the A1(M).

The occupants get out to say their farewells after a Christmas visit! Can you believe it?

One car then leaves up the slip road to Letchworth. The sixty-five-year-old driver of the other car pulls out into traffic on the motorway and collides with two other vehicles.

Back at the station, the bells go down and at 1920 hrs, both pumps turn out. I am in the back of WrL 1 with a crew of five.

Up the A1(M) in Weston Road, Baldock, 310 responds and from somewhere, the DC of A Division is mobile.

Baldock are already in attendance, when we pull up at 1927 hrs.

Three cars are involved with six persons injured and two trapped.

We get to work with the Lukas, with the last casualty being freed twenty-seven minutes later. All the casualties are taken to the Lister Hospital.

Back on station at 2025 hrs.

At 2350 hrs, we are called to secure the roof of a roadside gas installation building of 3m x 3m.

The roof has become dangerous in the high winds, ripping across the County and is likely to endanger an adjacent house.

Thursday, New Year's Eve.

Finally for 1998, we were off to Plinston Hall in Letchworth where we had been requested by 310 to investigate a smell of petrol.

I am driving 231, crew of four, mobile at 0927 hrs.

We arrived with the explosimeter and thermal imaging camera at 0918 hrs.

Home station at 0943 hrs.

Let me peruse The Book for some 1998 gibber.

Iayn Thomas: "You saw it and twigged. It was only by twig that you saw it!"

Elmo Mitchell: "I can't remember how many I've forgotten."

Yorkie York: "Then the shit hit might the fan."

TC Andrews: "He's a typical northerner, I like what I see and see what I bloody well like."

Mad Dog Riley: "They're as blind as bats them moles."

Bungle Davies: "In the Arctic Pole, it's the year all the year round."

Mad Dog Riley: "The thick plottens."

Elmo Mitchell: "They're like a row of terraced houses with gaps between each one!"

1999. ANOTHER MEDAL.

New Year's Day and the first call of the year is a car fire at Dyes Lane.

On 10th January we had a call to the Royal Mail, London Road, Stevenage.

Both pumps were mobilised to a postman with his arm trapped between two delivery vans.

He was released using two air mats slid in between the vans and inflating slightly to allow us to remove him.

One afternoon we are sitting up on the mess deck when a policewoman comes in, and the conversation went something like this:

Riley: "Hallo, we haven't seen you around recently."

Policewoman: "No, I've been off for a while."

Riley: "Would you like a coffee?"

Policewoman: "Yes please."

Me: "Where have you been then?"

Policewoman: "I've just had a baby!"

Riley (from the kitchen): "**Black or white!**"

February 24th, Medal Presentation Day.

On 7th April the previous year I had qualified for a twenty-year Long Service and Good Conduct Medal.

We arrived for the evening, Me, Mum and Dad, Patsy, Gary and Matthew and my German friend Martin Oudôt who was visiting.

Also receiving their medals, from course 2/78 were Dave Greaves, Phil Gray and Geoff Puddy.

As well as these three stalwarts was Craig Herbert, who was a fireman on Red Watch, Stevenage when I went there. He was now a DO and later this year his son, Alan, would join us.

We all cut a dash in undress uniform with a little hook to hang the medal on. We marched out and lined up in front of the assembled guests and came to attention as the Lord Lieutenant of Hertfordshire, Sir Simon Bowes-Lyon, pinned on our medals.

Bowes-Lyon is the family name of the Queen Mother, and Sir Simon was having difficulty controlling his weapon. On one occasion his sword slid out of its scabbard and on another got between CFO King's legs!

After the ceremony we had a buffet, photographs and a chance to chat.

A good and I must say, proud night for me.

Picture HFRS

This year was a fairly quiet one, with no rescues from fires or vehicles and I only got to wear BA on five occasions.

The first half of the year saw a few property fires.

The first of any note broke out on 31st March at Sutcliffe Close, Stevenage.

I am riding BA and we were mobile at 2021 hrs, and in attendance at 2025 hrs.

The stop went in at 2045 hrs; and read:
"End of terraced house of multi-occupancy, approx. 6m x 8m, consisting of two floors, ten per cent of ground floor severely damaged by fire, remainder of ground and first floor damaged by fire, heat and smoke, 4 BA, HRJ, TIC and PPV in use.
The Herald of Wednesday, 7th April had the headline:

RESIDENTS ESCAPE HOME FIRE

And went on... "a twenty-two-year-old man was arrested for a breach of the peace as firefighters dealt with a blaze at a housing association complex."

1st of April we were called at 2221 hrs to a house fire, persons reported, at Webb Rise, Stevenage.

I am driving 230, OiC Iayn Thomas with a crew of five. Also mobile are 231, crew of five.

In attendance at 2225 hrs.

The guv requests a salvage tender and Control mobilise 321 and 323 with total crew of eight.

At 2252 hrs the stop read:

"A terraced house of three floors, approx. 4m x 6m, eighty per cent of 1st and 2nd floor damaged by fire and smoke, all persons accounted for, 1 fireman with burns to left arm conveyed to hospital by ambulance, 1 jet, 2 HRJ, 4BA, TIC."

The Stevenage Mercury of 9th April reported on the call:

CHILD SETS FIRE TO FAMILY HOME

"A Stevenage family were left homeless after a blaze, started by a child playing with matches, destroyed their home. The lady of the house, her three children, two dogs and three cats escaped unhurt as flames engulfed the three-storey house. Her partner, who had gone out to get a takeaway, tried to tackle the fire when he returned home. 'But when he went upstairs the flames had spread across the ceiling,' she said.

The family lost a hamster and a guinea pig in the blaze."

5.43 a.m! On 2nd April, we join Hertford's appliance at Florence Road, Hitchin for a two pump relief for a six pump thatched cottage fire.

It's around two o'clock in the morning, on Friday, 9th April.

In the Old Town a miscreant is snooping around the back of the shops in Warren Court, behind 114 High Street.

A fire starts in a wooden bin store and quickly spreads up to the eaves of the roof and catches there as well.

At the station I am sound asleep.

The lights come on and, BEEP, BEEP, BEEP, "230 and 231 to attend the rear of 114b High Street, Stevenage, fire."

I am in BA in the back of the WrL 2 with a crew of five.

WrL 1 mobile with a crew of five.

In attendance, and an assistance message is sent "make pumps 6."

Appliances from Baldock, Hitchin and Old Welwyn are mobilised to the incident.

The roof is well alight and all the electrical and gas intakes are involved.

We pitch a 10.5 m ladder to the roof and I go up in BA with a hosereel to start to put water onto the fire. Another crew do the same a bit further along from us.

Below us the gas main melted and exploded and had to be knocked down with a jet and isolated.

The fire had spread through the roof space and into other offices in the block.

It took us a couple of hours to get the blaze under control and cut away the smouldering roof timbers, before the guv was happy. I got through two BA cylinders during the fire. We start salvage work, working from the top of the ladders with axes, others working from inside the roof space and, as it gets light, we fetch our HP to inspect the roof for hot spots.

The stop message reads: "An "L" shaped, 2 storey, multi-occupancy building of shops and offices, part of a parade of shops. 40m x 20m of roof severely damaged by fire and heat, 1st and ground floors damaged by heat, smoke and water, salvage work in progress, gas and electricity supplies affected, 8 BA, Jet, 5 x HRJ, TIC,4 X 105, "D" Delta.

On Wednesday April 14th, *The Stevenage Herald* has the dramatic headline: -

FIREMEN IN GAS INFERNO ESCAPE FROM BLAST

"Firefighters thirty feet above the ground were lucky to escape unhurt after a gas main melted sending flames roaring into the air. It happened as they fought a blaze in Stevenage High Street in the early hours of Friday morning."

'The fire is certainly of doubtful origin' said Stevenage Station Officer Iayn Thomas.

And the *Stevenage Mercury* told us: "A fire which destroyed the roof of an office building in Stevenage causing £100,000 worth of damage may have been started deliberately.

No one was hurt in the fire, but residents who live above nearby shops were evacuated and one business, has had to relocate because there is no roof on its office."

Firemen arriving this year; Andy Springett and Alan Herbert, both the sons of serving firemen. Andy's dad was "Tiny" Springett, a Sub Officer serving at Hitchin station, and eight feet tall if he was an inch. Nice bloke Tiny.

Mick James came over from Blue Watch (I think) and finally Tim Deegan joined us in September from Baldock (I think)!

Back on station, the summer passed fairly uneventfully.

We had the usual fields alight in July and August and I had some more acting-up.

I read with interest in the *Daily Mail* of Friday, September 17th that: "Firemen were condemned yesterday as racist, sexist and homophobic by a Government report." (Interestingly we are firemen again and not firefighters). It then goes on to say: "Women, gays and those from ethnic minorities are victimised in almost every fire station." (What rubbish.) "The Service would need to recruit 2,900 people from ethnic minority groups to reflect the six per cent of the population."

Personally, I don't really have an axe to grind either way, but when you get hundreds of applicants for just a few jobs… so long as the best people for the job get recruited and we don't have to reduce our standards to accommodate them, then I'm happy and all for it?

Anyway, times were changing; the Brigade now had to actively recruit "women firefighters!"

Two days later on 19th September *The Mail on Sunday* had an article by Norman Tebbitt with the headline:

I KNOW WHO I'D TRUST TO PULL ME OUT OF THE FIRE

Norman Tebbitt you may recall was rescued from the IRA bombing at the Grand Hotel in Brighton in 1984.

He said: "In this lunatic, politically correct world, to do a tough job well and to satisfy the public is not enough to avoid a barrage of snide criticism, sneers and jeers and threats from a Government Department notorious for its failings."

"For goodness sake, not many public services are doing their jobs as well as the Fire Service. Because society is changing for the worse why should the Fire Service have to follow suit.

"The Minister says that it should be representative of the community it serves. Balderdash, when I was trying to control a fire at my house I did not ask the firemen why they didn't have a disabled, lesbian, single mother with them."

Anyway, I thought I'd put those articles in as they reflect the mood of the time.

OK so it's the 29th September. We had a false alarm call to the Pinewoods Old Peoples Home in Shephall Lane. So what I hear you say.

Well, this was the first call for our new Dennis Sabre XL fire engine which had arrived to replace our old WrL 1 (230).

On 3rd December just before the change of shift a call comes in for the Lister Tennis Club, North Road, Stevenage and the night crew, Blue Watch, turn out with 230.

They make pumps 2 and at 0912 hrs, I turn out with 231, crew of four, into a raging gale.

The tennis courts are covered by a huge air dome and it has broken loose in the wind.

Nine of us hang on to it like a bloody great kite! It is eventually brought under control and secured with lines.

It's the early hours of Sunday, 5th December.

0142 hrs, BEEP, BEEP, BEEP, "231 to attend EFM Ltd, Tewin Road, Welwyn Garden City, factory fire, make pumps 6, HP required."

I am driving, with a crew of four.

In attendance at 0152 hrs.

Also in attendance are 190, 201, 240, 241 and 211.

114 and 111 (HP) and 189 and 180 (CU).

Plus the officers H6, B8 and C7.

This is a serious fire and as we arrive you can hear the noise of the roof starting to collapse.

Jets are being run out and played onto the blaze.
Explosions can be heard from inside the factory as the tyres of a refrigerated lorry and two other flatbed lorries blow up. There is a roar as the roof falls in, endangering our BA crews working in and around the building.

The St Albans HP arrives and gets to work. And 189 becomes the control point.

The fire is thought to be of doubtful origin and the OiC requests the attendance of the Buckinghamshire Fire Investigation Dog Team and as it gets light Titan and his handler arrive.

It takes us around four hours to get the blaze out.

The stop message went at 0357 hrs, "a range of single storey terraced factory units, approx. 100m x 50m, a unit 50m x 10m used for food preparation and storage, 100% severely damaged by fire, adjoining premises damaged by smoke and water, 6 jets, HP monitor, 20 BA, TIC in use, D Delta."

We are released and are back at Stevenage at 0515 hrs.

At 0621 hrs, the bells go down again for the same address, this time for the HP

We are in attendance at 0634 hrs.

We are part of a three pump relief with 091, 121, 011 with A10 in charge.

HP monitor in use, damping down and fire investigation in progress.

We are relieved sometime after 0900 hrs.

Welwyn and Hatfield Times reported on the fire in their Wednesday, December 8th edition.

FACTORY INFERNO:
EXPLOSIONS AND FLAMES WRECK SITE

"A raging inferno has destroyed a company's storage site in one of WGC's biggest ever blazes."

Dave Stokes, now WGC's station commander, said, 'When we arrived the building was already starting to collapse which posed an extra danger to us'.

Fire and police investigators were still at the site on Tuesday working to establish the cause of the fire, which is being treated as suspicious."

Titan, the Buckinghamshire Fire and Rescue Service Labrador, was sponsored by *Eagle Star*.

A little item at the end of the article read: "Herts Fire and Rescue Service are looking for corporate sponsors to help them get their own fire investigation Labrador."

We did get our own dog in 2001, his name was Browza and his handler was Paula Pond, who used to be part of the control staff. At incidents he had his own little boots and could detect a great number of different accelerants. All clever stuff!

One last incident worth recording.

13th December, at 0.22 a.m. A call to a house fire at Ashby Way, Stevenage.

I am driving 231 with a crew of four. 230 has a crew of five.

The stop was sent at 0.51 a.m. "Detached house of two floors, 8m x 7m, seventy per cent of lounge damaged by fire, heat and smoke, remainder of ground floor and 1st floor slightly damaged by smoke, HRJ, 4 BA, TIC and PPV in use."

The fire started when a Christmas candle set fire to a sofa. Felicitations of the festive season!

A selection of Gibber from 1999:

Bungle Davies: "Dave's got a bear like a sore head."
    Mad Dog Riley: "Can't you hear me, am I talking below the hearing aid?

Trigger Manual: "Does the Pope shit in the woods?

Mad Dog Riley: "Is this your cheese sandwich here cheese, egg, bacon… Is this your bacon sandwich here Dave?

Mad Dog Riley: (Question – "What time's tea?") "Bun at one, three at two, tea at three, doughnut at er doughnut time!"

Bungle Davies: "You can see my arse from behind."

Elmo Mitchell: "I've got two pianos at home, and I can't play either of them."

2000. A DOG UNDER A BOAT? WHERE?

After a lean year, last year, things get busy again with thirty-three property fires, involving three more rescues.

First off on 13th January, at Hadwell Close, Stevenage.

I am riding BA in the back of WrL 1 with a crew of five, and together with WrL 2 with a crew of five; we turn out at 7.46 p.m. In attendance two minutes later and a fire is visible on the first floor.

Four of us in BA, take a hosereel jet in through the front door. Two BA take it upstairs towards the first floor flat that is on fire, whilst the other two follow and start a search of the flat.

The smoke was cleared using the PPV fan.

At 8.09 p.m., the stop message was sent; "fire in first floor flat, 6m x 5m, thirty per cent of flat severely damaged by fire, heat and smoke, HRJ, 4BA, PPV and TIC in use."

28th January, and another fire breaks out in a property in Stevenage.

Just before three in the afternoon we are mobile to Canterbury Way.

"Terraced house, 8m x 8m, ten per cent of ground floor severely damaged by fire, heat and smoke, 1st floor slightly damaged by smoke, HRJ, 4 BA, TIC in use."

At Burwell Road, a mother and her young son escaped their smoke-filled house in a suspected racist attack: The second attack at the property in a couple of weeks.

I am driving 231, when at 2013 hrs we are mobilised to the house.

We are there for an hour and use a HRJ and 2BA to extinguish the fire, which was started by burning material pushed through the letter box.

Next up, an external bin store at Eastgate, Stevenage, is set on fire at four p.m, on 21st February.

231 was mobilised to a rubbish fire. I am in charge with a crew of four. In attendance at 4.14 p.m. to find a storage area, containing large rubbish paladins well alight.

I make pumps two.

The fire is tackled using 2 BA, a hosereel jet and a short extension ladder.

18th March, it's 0451 hrs, and the bells go down, the lights flicker on, BEEP, BEEP, BEEP, "order both appliances to Cuttys Lane, Stevenage, house fire, persons reported."

I am OiC of 231, crew of four and together with 230, crew of five we are mobile, arriving at 0455 hrs.

The whole of the flat is involved in fire and crews lay out a hosereel jet as another crew don their BA.

230 is the fire pump and is connected to a nearby hydrant. The BA crew proceed to the first floor flat and once inside find an injured man who is brought to fresh air where firemen start first aid as the ambulance arrives.

The stop is sent at 0514 hrs:

"A three storey block of flats, fire in 1st floor flat, 7m x 8m, one hundred per cent damaged by fire, smoke and heat, one male adult rescued by Service, first aid being rendered, conveyed to hospital by BHAPS, HRJ, 2BA, PPV in use."

We finally extinguish the fire, make up and get back to the station.

As can be seen by the stop message, the Hertfordshire Ambulance Service had, some years earlier, merged with the Bedfordshire Ambulance Service to form the Bedfordshire and Hertfordshire Ambulance and Paramedic Service (BHAPS).

That happened back in 1992 and in 1993 it became an NHS Trust.

In July 2006 BHAPS merged again, this time with the East Anglian Ambulance NHS Trust, itself a merger of Norfolk, Suffolk and Cambridgeshire Ambulance Services, and the Essex Ambulance NHS Trust, to form the East of England Ambulance Service NHS Trust.

Spindle Sanderson, my old mate from the RTA on Knebworth Hill back in 1997, went on to become the Face of the Ambulance Service, and was constantly on the television.

It's the middle of May and I am back off to Germany to try and kick start the exchange visits. The visits had stalled somewhat, due mostly to our side being cash-strapped.

I had arranged to go with Steve Manual, who I got on really well with. If he hadn't already by 1999, Steve joined me in running the Codicote Scout Troop, when his lad Jack was old enough. We had some great times with the Scouts, perhaps I will write a book about it!

Anyway, our subjects were; the inflatable rescue path and a new reciprocating saw used at RTAs.

I arranged with the rescue path suppliers to pick one up from them, I think it was Guildford way but not sure now.

Trigger and I drove through the Channel Tunnel, quickly through France and down to Mainz.

It had been arranged for us to stay in the new Mainz fire station very nice too.

We had one day with the Mainz-Bingen fire brigades.

Firstly, we spent a couple of hours at the fire station in Ingelheim, where Steve instructed on RTA procedures, including the saw and glass management.

Mainz Fire Station.

Steve at Ingleheim Fire Station.

Rescue path on the Rhine.

Hans, Me and Trig.

The German firemen then showed us their new fast-cut angle grinder. Lunch at the fire station then we were off, down to the River Rhine to demonstrate the rescue path.

I explain procedures and use, and the path was inflated and used on the water.

The German firefighters try it out.

Both of our lectures stimulated a lot of interest.

In fact I think I am correct if I say that the Mainz-Bingen Fire Brigade Association purchased several of the paths to deploy on the Rhine at Bingen and Ingelheim.

During the visit we also trained with the Mainz professional brigade on the Rhine. The brigade there maintains a Water Rescue Unit, and we undertook an exercise involving rescues using our path and their inflatable stretcher/sled. Dry suits supplied!

A good experience for us all.

I am sure the social aspect of the trip was great as well although I don't remember what we got up to.

One thing I did want to do was visit my old mate Hans Neumann who was suffering from a long term illness. Karl Heiser had taken me to visit him in the Mainz Hospital but again I don't remember when that was.

So it was off to Weinolsheim on 13th to meet up with him at his house in Lettengasse. We joined him, his wife Edith and daughter Gabi for afternoon coffee and cake. It was to be the last time we would get to meet.

Another great trip to Germany, and although I went back a few more times, it was really the end of the exchange visits.

But what a great ten years or so, we had so many good times.

Back in UK on the 6th June, and a fire in the lift motor room at the top of the Ibis Hotel in Danestrete has both crews rushing to the town centre.

We arrive there just before half past six in the evening, and two crews head up to the top of the building. Forty-five minutes later at a quarter past seven the stop is sent.

"Fire in lift motor room of multi-storey hotel, 2 BA, TIC, PPV, 2 x 9l FX, 2 x 5kg CO_2X, in use." Look it up!

A week later, on Wednesday, 14th June at 1852 hrs, both pumps head out of the station on route to a house fire at Broom Walk, Stevenage.

In attendance at 1857 hrs.

The occupier had set fire to his flat, on this, his fourth attempt to kill himself!

A BA crew found the casualty and he was brought out suffering from smoke inhalation. We put him on O_2 and he is further treated by the Ambulance paramedics and conveyed to hospital.

The stop message reads: "Fire in first floor flat, 5m x 4m, 1 male person led to safety from flat suffering from smoke inhalation, first aid rendered by Service, conveyed to hospital by BHAPS, HRJ, 2BA, TIC, PPV, MARS in use."

On 20th June we had a fire in the Standing Order public house and on 28th the Fisherman pub in Fishers Green caught fire.

During this period we also attended a woman locked in her garage, when the door blew shut. Luckily she had a mobile phone on her.

Another woman locked in her bathroom.

A small child with his leg trapped in a tree and an elderly man with his hand trapped in lift doors at his old people's home!

Around this time, maybe a bit earlier, maybe a bit later, we lost our uniform in favour of some non-descript clothing.

For me, this was the start of the decline in morale in the Service. We lost our identity.

We swapped our smart light blue shirts with epaulettes, black trousers, tie and peaked cap for a red open neck, short-sleeved shirt.

We went from being instantly recognisable, a fireman, a person anyone could approach for help, to a... well, to be honest, we could have been a Post Office worker, a BT engineer or any one of a number of other company employees, (no offence to them meant).

I recall someone writing to the Chief saying that, with the new kit having an open neck and short sleeves, could we have sun cream for the summer.

Shortly afterwards we got an issue of a red, wide-brimmed sun hat. Who said Bob King had no sense of humour!

Even worse, now I had nowhere to pin my medals!

In August, four German colleagues visited the Brigade. My friend Martin Oudôt together with Michael Weitzel, Alexander Helm and Carsten Wahl.

Sunday 20th, and I arranged to take them down to London to visit the Brigade there. Also coming along was "Sludge" Andrews.

We drove up to Lambeth fire station to be met by an LFB officer who was to be our guide for the day.

We were shown around the Control Room and the new Incident Command Unit. Our LFB host was fantastic, he explained everything, and nothing was too much trouble.

The Control Room was huge, no idea how many work stations and Control Operators, certainly a lot.

Having seen the Control Room, we were taken to the yard behind the station to see one of the latest appliances, a Brigade Command Unit, (R131 KGH).

The brigade had recently taken delivery of the vehicle, built on the chassis of a Volvo B10 city bus. It included a forward briefing and planning area and a rear compartment with four work stations, enabling operators to overlay information on to an ordinance survey map and access building plans and hydrant locations. The CU also had telescopic masts for radio and CCTV.

Around eleven o'clock we went across the road to the River Station on the Albert Embankment.

We were given a guided tour of the boat, *Fire Flash* by the crew and then they took us for a ride down river towards Tower Bridge. We saw the Houses of Parliament, London Eye, Tower of London and HMS Belfast, our own private river cruise.

As we were passing under Tower Bridge the boat got an operational call.

1139 hrs, "H22Z, to attend, Dog trapped under a boat, outside St Mary's Church, Vicarage Crescent, Battersea, SW11."

Also mobilised were H271, Battersea PL, H332, Wandsworth P, and E202, a Senior Officer from South Eastern Command.

The fireboat turned round, picked up speed, and we headed back up river with blue lights and two-tone horns.

Good stuff, the Germans were delighted.

H271 in attendance at 1137 hrs.

H332 in attendance at 1140 hrs.

The dog was recovered, drowned. The stop went back shortly after and we slowed down and headed back to Lambeth.

The German fireman on board Fire Flash.
Picture: Martin Oudôt

After lunch we had a visit to the LFB Museum at Southwark. The museum is housed in Winchester House, the home of Captain Eyre Massey Shaw, Superintendent of the Metropolitan Fire Brigade and all subsequent CFO's from 1878 – 1937.

All in all, a very interesting day, thanks to the London Fire Brigade for their help in arranging it.

Also during this visit the German firefighters attended the retirement of CFO Bob King.

He passed the reins of power onto Steve Seaber, who took over in January 2001.

Apart from the German exchange trips I never had much to do with CFO King. He actively encouraged the exchanges and I am grateful to him for that.

He came to Stevenage station with some semi-important guests as part of a tour of the Brigade.

At the time we were looking after the steam fire engine, and Mr King called me over. Looking very smug, he introduced me, "This is firefighter Payne, he is the expert on the steam engine." He then turned to me and looking even more smug, went on, "you know what an expert is, don't you Sid? An 'ex' is something that has expired and a 'spurt' is a drip under pressure."

Well, suitably put down, I walked away and let him show his guests the engine himself.

Although pissed off at the time, it is a great line and I have used it myself since.

Two days later, on Tuesday 22nd August and I am driving the WrL 2, with a crew of four.

We had been called out 10.05 a.m., to Rectory Lane, Stevenage where we had tackled a small grass fire and were now on our way back to the station.

Meanwhile, down in the Old Town, staff at the Bingol Kebab and Pizza Restaurant are preparing to open.

The chip fryer is turned on and left unattended for a few minutes…

1045 hrs, the radio comes to life, "VI – Charlie 232 order your appliance to Bingol Kebab, High Street, Stevenage, fire."

In attendance 1050 hrs.

Smoke and flames coming from the front of the shop.

A hosereel is got to work through the door as two crews get rigged in BA.

Once inside the building, crews find that the fire has spread to an upstairs flat and into the roof space.

Floorboards, and part of the ceiling are cut away.

The fire has spread into the shop next door.

Outside, a short extension ladder and roof ladder are pitched to fight the fire from above, using a hosereel.

The stop message was sent at 1153 hrs, "A terraced property, affecting 2 shops, 10m x 25m, thirty per cent of ground floor of kebab shop severely damaged by fire, ten per cent of first floor flat severely damaged, remainder damaged by smoke, ten per cent of adjoining fish and chip shop severely damaged by fire, smoke and cutting away, 3 x HRJ, 6BA, TIC, RF/L, SHT/EX in use."

Once the fire is out we start to tidy up, getting back to the station at 1233 hrs.

We thought the fire had started in the ducting connected to the deep fat fryer.

I can't help thinking that it was at this fire that ADO Dave Stokes turned up and got dirtier and blacker than anyone else. I also think he may have got a bit of a telling off for not standing back and directing operations, (I could be wrong).

According to my records, we then went out again at 1.45 p.m. to the Old Wood Yard for some wood bark on fire, again at 1.52 p.m. to another grass fire, then at 4.32 p.m. to a false alarm at the Leisure Centre and finally to a false alarm at the Wine Society at 5.42 p.m.

27th of September and it's son Matt's turn to work a job-sharing day.

Our hosts today are the Green Watch.

We arrive at nine o'clock hrs for the change of Watch and introductions.

Up to the mess deck for a cup of tea before the rigours of the day.

Out for drill with the Watch. The drill is to slip and pitch the 464 ladder to the fourth floor of the tower, one jet got to work on the third floor, hauled aloft.

Matt and one other climbed the ladder and pulled up the hose, which was then charged with water with Matt on the branch.

After the drill we had a look at the equipment on the pump.

Tea break.

Stevenage's HP was unavailable and so we took the Landrover to St. Albans where I had arranged to play with theirs.

Matt had some instruction from "Hobnob" and then we were off up to 30m for some great views of the City.

I think we may have had lunch at St. Albans, but not sure.

Thanks to the Green Watch, B11 for their help.

Not long back at Stevenage when…

BEEP, BEEP, BEEP, "both appliances to Lister Hospital, Coreys Mill Lane, Stevenage, AFA."

230 and 231 turned out, both with a crew of five.

Matt and I jumped into the Landrover and 237 turned out with a crew of two.

The alarm had gone off on one of the wards. Fireman Payne (Jnr) went up with the Officer in Charge and a BA crew to investigate the cause.

No fire situation, stop sent and back to base.

Matt on duty at Stevenage.

After tea we went back out to the yard for some BA training.

I hid a "body" in the smoke house and turned on the smoke machine.

Matt and me rigged in BA, and carried out a search of the building, located the dummy and brought it back out.

A good day. Thanks to the Greens.

At this time, Matt was also playing football for Knebworth Youth FC. If I was on duty for a Sunday home game we would take the pump over to the Knebworth Recreation Ground for an afternoon watching the football.

It's the 13th November and I am about to get some more temporary promotion, although from an unexpected quarter.

Both pumps have been mobilised to a fire at the rear of Shephall Way, Stevenage. I am in the back of WrL 2 as part of a four man crew. WrL 1 has a crew of five.

We are in attendance 7.51 p.m.

The fire was fought by a BA crew using a jet.

A passer-by, dead drunk, staggered up to us and promptly collapsed in a heap. We had to treat him with MARS O_2 and first aid.

The next to go down was our own L/Ff Steve Kendall. He turned his ankle over and that was the end of him for a few weeks. He went off sick and I was promoted in the field to L/Fm.

An ambulance arrived and took the drunk away and we took Steve down to Casualty at the Lister.

Sorry about your leg Steve, but thanks anyway!

My promotion lasted through to the middle of January 2001.

An hour later, I was leading the troops into action at a bonfire in Ellis Avenue.

In a similar vein, I think around now, we had a big exercise at The Node, just outside Codicote.

I don't recall now what the exercise was all about but during the fun, Elmo Mitchell, stood on a charged length of hose and down he went. Off sick, and I think that was his lot, retiring sick some time later.

We also lost the Station Officers from the Watches. So Iayn Thomas left us and Sub O Dave Callaghan took control of the Watch.

I am guessing that these two left about now because they both have no more entries in the Gibber Book!

A sure sign of their departure.

Three more property fires in the lead up to Christmas.

On 21st December we had seven calls.

In the late afternoon the fifth call of the day took us to Burymead, Stevenage.

I was in charge of 231 with a crew of five, 230 crew of five.

A kitchen fire was tackled by a BA crew with a hosereel.

The PPV cleared the smoke and we prepared to leave.

As we pulled away, 230 was dispatched to a skip on fire at Sainsbury's.

We returned to station.

Seven minutes later at 1747 hrs, the bells went down and we were mobile, a minute later to...

"231 to George Leighton Court, Brittain Way, Stevenage, fire, persons reported."

We are in attendance at 1751 hrs.

We have a fire in a first floor flat.

At 1754 hrs I send "informative message from L/Fm Payne at same address, small kitchen fire, 1 HRJ, 2BA."

Also at 1754 hrs, 230 are in attendance.

In the flat the fire is extinguished and a person found inside is rescued.

At 1755 hrs, "further informative, 1 female person suffering from smoke inhalation, ambulance required."

The stop message is sent "from Sub O Callaghan, first floor flat, 10m x 10m, five per cent of kitchen slightly damaged by fire, remainder damaged by smoke, 1 female person led to safety by Service, suffering from smoke inhalation, 1 MARS first aid, 1 HRJ, 2BA, PPV in use, awaiting arrival of ambulance, require attendance of the Council."

Back home at 1830 hrs

22nd December, 1913 hrs both pumps are mobile to the rear of Elms Ltd., Primett Road, Stevenage.

I am in the back of 230 with a crew of four. 231, crew of four.

On arrival we find a two storey derelict building on fire.

Dave Callaghan; "makes pumps 3."

Hitchin are mobilised with a crew of six, as is ADO Malcolm Sawdy.

I am one of four firemen in BA and the blaze is fought using two Jets and a 105 ladder.

Stop sent at 1954 hrs.

Home station at 2037 hrs.

Well that's another year gone by all too quickly.

Next year sees a big change in my life as a fireman and, I am happy to say, increases my pension.

Let us check the Book for a few pearls of wisdom.

Jock Morgan: "They hated him at Cheshunt."

(Dirty Harry): "They sent him to Coventry, didn't they?"

"They sent him everywhere!"

Mad Dog Riley: "The kidneys filter the shit out of the piss."

Mad Dog Riley: "You've been fishing, catch any gibbons?"

Me: "Have you heard the joke about Alzheimer's, I can't remember if I've told you or not."

Trigger Manual: "I would have said something, but I had to bite my head."

TC Andrews: "Can you zip this bag up if I hold it together? you be the Zipper and I'll be the Zippee!"

2001. JUST HOW WIDE IS A FIRE ENGINE?

At 3.22 p.m., on 15th February the bells go down and we are mobile to Drakes Drive, Stevenage, fire.

I am driving 230 with a crew of four.

I am doing okay, up Six Hills Way, left into Chells Way and on towards Drakes Drive, weaving in and out of the traffic. Approaching the shops and the Glebe Pub, I have a bus in front of me and a car coming in the opposite direction.

Plenty of room, sirens on, I pull out to pass, as the car draws level... BANG BANG... I take the offside wing mirrors off the bus and from a very smart Mercedes!

We are through and on to the fire.

In attendance at 3.33 p.m.

We have some rubbish in a lock-up garage on fire. One HRJ and two BA extinguish the blaze.

Stop sent at 3.38 p.m. and we are back on station at 3.58 p.m.

Well there certainly looked to be room for me to get through and we had no complaints from either driver.

On Wednesday, 11th April we attended an unusual call, a house fire that we had started ourselves!

As a joint enterprise between the Fire Service, Stevenage Borough Council and the Recreational Sprinkler Association, a house in Haycroft, in the Old Town had been fitted with a special sprinkler system.

The idea was to demonstrate the effectiveness of the sprinklers in a fire situation, with a view to installing the system in new-build houses in the town.

Fires were set around the house in various locations, and we stood back.

With smoke billowing from the house and an enthusiastic crowd outside; the test continued, with the sprinkler system operating and all but extinguishing the blaze.
Two men in BA finished the job.

On inspection, the demo was very successful. I don't know if the Council built any houses with the system fitted, I hope so.

It's Good Friday, 13th April.

Eight o'clock in the evening in Watton-at-Stone; a couple have left their Hazeldell home for a night out in the nearby George and Dragon pub.

Back in the kitchen, a spark from a domestic appliance ignites gas escaping from the hob. The fire catches and smoulders for two or three hours. The double glazed windows remain intact and all seems well from the outside.

The couple return at around 11.30 p.m. and try to get in...

2341 hrs, BEEP, BEEP, BEEP, "230 to attend, Hazeldell, Watton-at-Stone, house fire."

2343 hrs, 230 mobile, I am driving with a crew of five, Sub O Callaghan in charge.

Also mobile, 240 with a crew of five.

2352 hrs, in attendance.

We are confronted with a serious fire, fuelled by oxygen from the open front door.

The two owners are both suffering from smoke inhalation.

The fire has spread through the ceiling into an upstairs bedroom.

Six BA wearers are deployed to the house using two Jets and one hosereel.

The crews are also tasked to look for the family pet.

The floor of one upstairs bedroom is completely burnt away, making movement difficult for the crew.

One of the BA teams emerge with the dead cat.

The fire is sufficiently under control for ADO Stokes to send the stop message at 0037 hrs, "end of terrace house, 7m x 10m, of two floors, kitchen well alight, ground and first floor heavily smoke-logged, two people injured, two Jets, HRJ, 6 BA, TIC, PPV and salvage in use."

The house is a mess, with the gas, electricity and water services all affected, and it will be some time before it will be habitable again. The fire also caused smoke damage to the loft of the adjacent house

We are finally back at Stevenage at 0212 hrs.

We had a visit to a school up in Pin Green, I don't remember which one.

All the usual stuff, the kids climbed all over the fire engine, and had a squirt of the hosereels. We talked to them about fire safety and they tried on our fire kit.

During the visit I felt a tug on my trouser leg, I looked down and a young lad looked up at me and said, "Hey mister, I want to be a fireman when I grow up."

I looked at him and replied, "You can't do both son!"

At 10.20 p.m., on Monday, 30th April, we had a call to the Pizza Hut on the Roaring Meg Retail Park.

They were cleaning the kitchen and two aerosols managed to get onto the conveyor that takes the pizzas through the oven. In the ensuing explosions, two members of staff were injured.

We gave first aid before the two lads were taken off to the Lister.

We had another new member of the Watch, when fireman Paul "Daisy" Day joined us from Blue Watch (I think), I have trouble remembering when and where people came from.

In Silam Road, Stevenage, there were three high rise residential blocks, High Plash, Brent Court and Harrow Court.

Over the years we had been to numerous fires in all three.

Tonight was the turn of Brent Court.

On a Tuesday night, the 8th May, in Brent Court an elderly man is retiring to bed and bangs out his pipe, not noticing the burning tobacco that falls from it. The fire smoulders.

The fire alarms activate.

Just before a quarter to eleven, he is woken by a neighbour hammering on his front door.

2246 hrs, BEEP, BEEP, BEEP, "both appliances to attend Brent Court, Silam Road, Stevenage, fire, persons reported."

2247 hrs, 230, crew of five and 231, crew of four mobile to incident. I am driving WrL 1.

ADO Stokes mobile.

Ten other residents from the flats have left the building.

Myself and the other driver start to set into the dry riser; a BA team get rigged. Two others get a couple of lengths of hose and some other equipment and together with the L/Fm start the climb up the stairs. The crews connect to the dry riser on the floor below the fire and then run the hose line up the stairwell to the 8th. Once we get the word, the dry riser is charged with water and the BA team eight floors up start to tackle the fire.

The fire was contained to the flat.

ADO Stokes sent the stop at 2308 hrs.

The lounge suffers burning to the flooring and the flat is smoke-logged.

We make up our equipment and head home.

The Stevenage Mercury of May 11th told us:

"A seventy-five-year-old Stevenage man lost his life savings when a fire broke out in his high-rise flat.

As the smoke cleared the occupier realised that the money – more than £500 in cash – which was stored in the flat, had been destroyed in the blaze."

A neighbour said, "It was quite frightening, the hallway was thick with smoke, but the fire did not spread and I was able to stay in my flat."

"A spokesman for BHAPS said that the occupier – who may have suffered the effects of smoke inhalation – refused to go with paramedics to Lister Hospital for a check-up."

A Stevenage Borough Council spokesman said: 'There is some smoke damage to the flat. The resident was offered alternative accommodation, but chose to stay in his flat'."

There appeared in Routine Orders, a request for applications for promotion. Well, I thought, maybe one last try!

So I applied.

A few weeks later, with my application accepted, I had to attend Fire Brigade Headquarters for interview, feint heart and all that.

As I have previously mentioned, the panel consisted of a Station Officer, a Control Officer and the equal ops woman.

Anyway, I guess the Brigade was struggling to fill the posts because a few days later I got a phone call from the DC informing me that I had been successful, and I was to be given a L/Ff job at B19 Welwyn Garden City.

Only a couple of months left to serve at Stevenage fire station, which had been my home for the last twenty-one years.

We used to play a lot of Trivial Pursuit and other games on nights and holidays, here is the level of our knowledge taken from the Gibber Book:

Q: Who was the Mad Monk?

Elmo Mitchell: "Friar Tuck."

Q: Which boxer was known as "Gentleman Jim"?

Lee Jacobs: "Harry Corbett."

Q: What is a feline?

Lee Jacobs: "A felion is a lioness."

Q: Which mammal lives the longest?

Snot Monster Hadley: "Tortoise."

Q: What was banned from English fridges in 1984?

TC Andrews: "Eggs."

Q: Name the Seven Wonders of the World?

TC Andrews: "The Hanging Baskets of Babylon."

Q: Who discovered Penicillin?

Elmo Mitchell: "Alexander Fleming… it gives me the shits!"

Mad Dog Riley: "What, Flemings does."

Q: What plant was named after Leonard Fuchs, the Naturalist?

Trigger Manual: "What was the question?"

Mad Dog Riley: "What bloke was named after a geranium?"

Q: Which Pope had the first double-barrelled name?

TC Andrews: "John-Paul II."

Great stuff, I loved these gibbering half-wits.

We had time for one last big fire.

I was in charge of WrL 2 with a crew of four on the night shift of 9th June.

At 2246 hrs, both pumps turn out to "The Horns public house, Bramfield Road, Datchworth, fire."

We were in attendance at 2255 hrs.

A thatched building was well alight, Sub O Callaghan sends an assistance message, "make pumps six."

Also attending the fire are Old Welwyn, two pumps each from Welwyn Garden City and Hertford and the Control Unit from Hatfield. Also mobilised are Stn O Pennyfather (remember him? The pair of gloves from Potters Bar) and DO Clinton (remember him? A Fm on Whites, C23).

Ian Clinton sends the stop message at 2332 hrs. "A single storey thatched out-building used for storage, approx. 6m x 4m, severely damaged by fire, heat and smoke, smoke and heat damage to adjacent public house, 2 butane cylinders involved, 3 x Jets, 2 x HRJ, 2 x TIC.

My last duty was the night shift of Tuesday, 28th August.

As per usual on these occasions, I spent most of the night wet, as every corner I turned there was someone with a bucket of water!

At 9.08 p.m. the bells went down and the following message appeared on the printer, a set up – more buckets.

```
21:08:00 on 28-08-01
*********** Message Start *************


Turnout      : 230

Fire type    "GOOD LUCK SID!!!!!!"

Address      C23
             STEVENAGE

Map ref      TL2423
Incident     19059

A1 map       48
Caller       CONTROL



************* Message Ends *************
```

And as such, at 9.14 p.m., when the bells went down for real, I turned out, driving 231, soaking wet to a small Kitchen fire.

I didn't even get a good, last night's sleep.

Just before ten to five in the morning, we attended a car fire at Fairlands Valley Park, Six Hills Way. A hosereel extinguished the blaze.

I had a leaving do at the Red Lion, Woolmer Green. The lads gave me an inscribed tankard.

Thanks to all the people I met at Stevenage, for all the laughs, the water fights and the piss ups; I enjoyed it all.

I wish I had a pound for every time I've mopped the bays, changed the roller towel, warmed my bum on the radiator in the corridor or made a cheese sandwich.

Some final words of wisdom from the Stevenage Gibber Book.

Taff James: "Up the creek without a swanee."

Mad Dog Riley: "I didn't clap when he went up for his present, his bangle, his dangle his trophy!"

Mad Dog Riley: "I'd better have a coffee to keep myself awake, but I'll have a de-caffeinated one so I don't have to stay awake too long."

Mick James: "She was soaked right down to her bare nipples."

Alan Springett: "It's dark, let's call it a day."

Dirty Harry Callaghan: "Elmo's electric gates don't work properly; he's got them closing but not shutting."

Sludge Andrews: "You need to hold it at a further arm's length than that."

One Note Miles (visiting the Watch): "I'm a pensioner now, I get free eyesight."

3. WELWYN GARDEN CITY: 2001 – 2008.

2001. MORETON-IN-MARSH.

First day of duty, 2nd September. I'm an officer! Better than that I get to be a Sub Officer if I am in charge of the Watch!

Also, I have fallen on my feet again, joining another great Watch.

I knew a couple of them but mostly our paths had only crossed at incidents or on courses. Let me introduce them to you: -

Sub Officer Alan Morgan, who, you may recall was with me at Potters Bar. I was really pleased when I got Whites B19, I liked Alan a lot.

Firemen Mark "Sabes" Saban, Gary "Crofty" Baker-Croft, Darren "Daz" Ward, Martin "Rodders" Rodmell and Adrian "Moley" Kimber.

Yes, I agree with you, as nicknames go, not much thought has gone in, not very amusing.

They had been together for quite a long time and as the new boy, I would have to try and fit in with them.

It didn't take long to realise that we were going to get on just fine. They called each other "the Sids", after Sid the Sexist in Viz magazine, as I was a Sid they called me Barry!

So there we were, seven blokes all called Sid, Barry, Baz, Basil, Bars or Staff! Ha, what a nonsense.

Back in the middle of last year the format of the stop messages changed. The new message consisted of the prefix – Papa for property fires, Zulu for secondary fires, Sierra for special services or Romeo for false alarms. This was followed by a series of letters to further designate the call.

Eg. Papa 19 = Offices, 89 = CO_2 extinguisher, 95 = Good intent.

Papa 01 = Dwelling house, 86 = jet, 94 = possible arson.
Sierra 01 = RTA person trapped.
Code 1 = Person deceased.
Code 2 = Person hospitalised.
Code 3 = First aid rendered.
Code 4 = persons involved but not injured.

I really don't remember them now but I will try and use both bsystems.

1653 hrs. My first call as a proper officer. I am in charge as we turn out to Xerox, Vision House, Bessemer Road, WGC.

Mobile at 1654 hrs. I have a crew of four.

In attendance at 1656 hrs.

1703 hrs. 190: "Sub O Payne – slight smell of smoke in building – further search in progress."

1710 hrs. "Make pumps 2."

1716 hrs. 191 in attendance, Sub O Dean in charge, crew of six.

1731 hrs. 190: "Sub O Payne – same address – single storey building – used as research centre – 30m x 30m – smoke logged electrical intake area – efforts being made to locate source of fire – TIC in use."

1737 hrs. 190: "Fire located in electrical intake – 2BA in use."

1754 hrs. 190: "Stop message. 190: Papa 19 89 95."

1755 hrs. 190: "Both crews delayed approx. thirty minutes."

The fire was extinguished using 4 x CO_2 extinguishers.

There you go, the full account of my first call as a fully-fledged officer.

We are on duty on 11th September 2001.

We had been out on a false alarm in the morning, to Woodside House, Bridge Road, WGC.

Not much compared to what's about to happen 3,500 miles away in New York, USA.

After lunch, we head out to fit some residential smoke alarms.

At around two thirty in the afternoon, the phone in the cab rings, it's Moley (can't remember why he wasn't on the fire engine). He gives us the unbelievable news of the Twin Towers disaster.

At 1345 hrs (0845 hrs US time), American Airlines, Flight 11 crashes into the North Tower of the World Trade Centre.

At 0846 hrs, FDNY 1st Battalion Chief, Joseph Pfeifer, called in the first message to the Manhatten Fire Dispatch Office.

Half an hour later Moley telephones again to break the news of the second impact.

At 1403 pm (0903 am US time), United Airlines, Flight 175 hits the South Tower.

This terrorist action galvanised fire brigades worldwide; every Country, Brigade or Station have had their tragedies but 343 colleagues lost in one incident is impossible to comprehend.

On Saturday, September 22nd, we spent the day collecting at the Howard Centre in aid of the fallen firefighters and with other collections around the town we brought in over £7,000, fantastic. Money continued to flood in for another two weeks.

WGC Sub Officer Steve Cartwright told the *Welwyn and Hatfield Times*: "This tragedy has had an effect on everybody, we're just doing our little bit to help them out."

Down the road, the lads from Old Welwyn held a car wash and raffle.

Welwyn and Hatfield Times: "Welwyn's station commander David Smith said; 'God knows how many cars we cleaned but we didn't stop'."

On Monday, 29th October I am off to the Fire Service College, in Moreton-in-Marsh, Gloucestershire to attend Crew Command Course 07/01.

It is a three-week course designed to equip me with all the theoretical and practical knowledge I should need to be a leading fireman.

Each candidate had their own room and the facilities at the college were great. Restaurant, bars, gym, volleyball etc.

The incident ground training areas were also fantastic with a train crash set-up, high rise block, ship, aircraft, domestic houses and a motorway.

I also had a compatriot on the course, Paul Stephenson from Hatfield.

I really enjoyed the course, more so the practical elements, which included; operational command, basement firefighting, hazardous materials, railway incidents, heat and humidity, high rise and aircraft incidents.

Theoretical lessons included; fairness and dignity at work, communications, health, safety and risk management, leadership and report writing.

Another good thing was the mix of firemen from all over the country, from Cornwall to the north of Scotland.

One night in the bar I was talking to two lads from Strathclyde: "How are you doing lads?"

"Aye, aye, awl gud aye, lot of blether in class but passin' a canny week, aye."

What?

In comes the fireman from Inverness, also on the course, wearing a kilt, he sits down with us and he is greeted by the Strathclyde boys: "Hou ar ye lad? Hou's it gawin aye?"

He replies, "Lang may yer lum reek! Dinnae fash yersel bout me, I'm givin' it laldy. It's a sair fecht."

The Strathclyde lads look at each other and shrug, wot?

In the last week we were each given an incident to be in command of. Bearing in mind the geographical location of Hertfordshire in the middle of country, guess which scenario I got? Yes, you've got it, a ship fire!

The course finished on Friday 16th November, great time.

So back I went to Welwyn Garden City with a head full of knowledge just itching to put it all in to practice.

Can't wait for my first ship fire!

I was back on duty on 21st November and had plenty of opportunity to try them out.

On Wednesday, 21st November we had five calls including two RTAs.

On Thursday we turned out four times, including a swan rescued from a culvert and assisted to open water.

On our first night shift, the Friday, three calls and on the second night, the Saturday, a further four calls. One worth a mention.

Over in Oaklands there is a party going on, and candles are so atmospheric!

2259 hrs, BEEP, BEEP, BEEP, "190 to attend Oaklands Rise, Oaklands, house fire, possible persons reported."

2300 hrs, mobile to incident, Sub O Morgan in charge, crew of five. Also mobile 201.

In attendance at 2307 hrs. "Make pumps 4."

230 and 231 mobilised, together with DO Connor and Stn O Pennyfather.

It is a detached, posh house and the ground floor is well alight, I go in as part of a BA team.

We take a jet, as does a second BA crew.

It's very hot and smoky and half of the ground floor is severely damaged in the fire. The rest of the house damaged by smoke and heat.

Outside, on the lawn, there is a group of five distraught, young teenagers suffering from slight smoke inhalation and a sincere wish to be somewhere else!

The stop was sent by DO Connor at 2350 hrs, "a detached house, five children involved, 2 x jets, 1 x HRJ, 5 BA, PPV, TIC in use, Papa 01 86 95."

An ambulance was ordered to attend for the kids and the property was ventilated.

We make up and are back at WGC by 0016 hrs.

The fire was attributed to candles igniting curtains.

The parents were on holiday in France!

DO Dave Connor, the officer in charge of this incident was the current DC of C Division. Nice man, he helped me and Trig out a lot on our trip to Germany the previous year.

On the 2nd December, I was in charge.

The bells went down at quarter past seven in the morning, which meant I probably had to turn out without my morning cup of tea!

The call was to "Howlands House, Howlands, WGC, kitchen fire, possible persons reported."

The fire was extinguished with a HRJ. A man suffering from smoke inhalation was treated using the MARS resuscitator.

As an officer of the watch, I now had my own room at the station, which I shared with the other three watch L/Fm.

When I arrived we had four old metal lockers for our kit.

I designed a new range of bigger, wooden lockers and submitted it to the Station Commander, Martin Graham (I think), for approval.

All accepted and the Brigade odd job man Mick "Toosaux" Saunders duly arrived to build them.

Toos had been a fireman at St Albans but, unfortunately, had fallen off his motorbike in the early 90s and was retired early with dodgy legs.

He made a great job of them anyway and we all moved in.

How do you spell Toosaux I wonder?

I spent many a happy hour in my room; some good nights sleep and, at seven thirty, Molly the Station cleaner, would wake me with a nice cup of tea.

It's funny how tragedy seems to strike over Christmas, and this year is to be no different.

Just after 5.30 p.m., on Christmas Eve, an eighteen-year-old lad is driving his blue Peugeot 206 along the A414, Hertford road, towards Hatfield.

Judging by the crash scene, he was driving quite fast.

Near to Mill Green Lane, and just before the Hatfield House turn-off, he loses control. The vehicle leaves the road and crashes into the woods alongside the carriageway.

1740 hrs, BEEP, BEEP, BEEP, "190 to attend A414 westbound, near Mill Green, RTA persons trapped."

Also mobile are 180, crew of five, 185, crew of two and an ADO, Charlie 6.

We are in attendance at 1750 hrs.

The car has travelled at least ten metres into the trees, and has come to rest down a small dip and completely tangled in the branches of the trees.

Some of the trees have been cut by the car two metres from the ground.

The first task is to cut a path to the crash site using our various saws.

The car was badly damaged in the impact and the driver well trapped.

As the evening light was fading we set up several lights to illuminate the area.

The paramedics started to work on the casualty but he was declared dead at the scene.

Lukas cutting gear was used to open up the car and a winch and strops were used to pull the car back.

The driver was removed on a spinal board and taken to the ambulance.

Stop sent at 1831 hrs.

Home station at 1903 hrs.

Sue, the station cook, had invited us round to her house for Christmas dinner.

We took the appliance and parked on her driveway. Alan rigged up a connection to the radio and ran a wire into the house to a speaker. Sue gave us a fantastic dinner and after we retired to the lounge for coffee. One by one we all dozed off and asked Sue to wake us if she heard our callsign, 190, mentioned on the radio.

What a great afternoon.

Back to the station for the change of watch at six o'clock.

So that's it, another year gone and only six and a few months to go before retirement.

2002. STRIKE!

Welwyn Garden City was in B Division.

It had a wholetime pump, a Dennis Dagger, (KF02 UZT) and a retained pump, a Dennis, (P247 VMJ). Also on station was a utility van.

As a non-mobile special we had the listening equipment for detecting sound in collapsed buildings etc.

Early on in the year we had our first RTA.

On 10th January, just after quarter past eight in the evening we went out to the northbound slip road of junction 3 of the A1(M).

One van had overturned with one person trapped and five others requiring first aid.

Also in attendance 180, 185, 201 and Charlie 5.

After an hour we were back at home station.

Remember a while back I made the comment that the right people should get the job?

The height requirement of five foot six was removed in 1999, is it just me or is this a case of equal opportunities gone mad. To her credit this girl came 16th out of 400 applicants, presumably in the theory tests.

This article appeared in the Wednesday, 30th January edition of the *Daily Mail*:

"I was a laughing stock, sobs the five foot one firefighter.

She had to wait weeks for a made to measure uniform.

She needed a step ladder to clean the appliance.

On her training course, a five foot ten colleague hurt his back as they tried to remove a forty-foot ladder from the appliance roof.

During a chemical drill, the suit was too large, the legs too long, the gloves too large and the view panel too high.

A second firefighter was injured removing a ladder."
Despite all this she passed out and was posted to a station!

"Eventually her bosses told her she was too small to do the job. She is now suing the East Sussex Fire Authority for sexual discrimination, demanding that equipment be modified to allow her to do the job.

The brigade claims that, if she gets her way, a redesigned fire engine will have to be ordered with the longest ladders mounted underneath – at a cost of £140,000."

The hearing continues.

Would a 5ft 1in "fireman" have progressed so far?

Co-incidentally, I read in today's *Dorset Echo* (April 1st, 2015), at a presentation given by an area manager of the Dorset F&RS, a woman Councillor asked "how many of Dorset's 350 retained fire staff were women?"

The Area Manager said the figure stood at just five per cent. He added "In Dorchester there are two female firefighters out of a retained crew of thirty."

I wonder if the woman from East Sussex is still available.

On 4th February we went out at 0016 hrs to smoke issuing from the roof of the Co-Op in Stonehills in the Town Centre.

It was a false alarm.

At 0024 hrs we had another call, this time to smoke issuing from the Pizza Hut in Howardsgate, just over the road.

It was a false alarm as well.

Police on scene questioned a man who was at both incidents, and we went home.

At 0014 hrs on the 21st February we had a call to smoke issuing from Favourite Chicken in Church Road, Town Centre.

Guess what, another false alarm.

An eagle-eyed copper recognised the same man at the scene and this time he was taken away by the police.

This was a busy year at WGC.

Early on, on 26th February, I was in charge at a serious bedroom fire in Ingles, WGC. 2 BA put out the fire using a hosereel. Also in attendance were 191 and Station Commander Graham.

We assisted the police with a woman attempting suicide in Hertford Road at eleven p.m. on 7th March.

On 8th March, a person with their arm stuck in a letterbox.

A cooker on fire in Wheatley Road, on 17th March.

And on 29th March at the junction of Bessemer Road and Digswell Road, WGC a head-on collision occurred at 11.05 a.m., involving two cars.

A fifty-six-year-old woman was left in her damaged Toyota car with a broken sternum, broken ribs and severe bruising.

Two men from the other car, a Peugeot, fled the scene and were being hunted by the police.

We rendered first aid before the woman was taken to the QE II hospital by BHAPS.

Going back a couple of weeks I remember a lad in difficulties at the University of Hertfordshire in Hatfield.

At 0136 hrs on 9th March, we were called to an AFA.

We arrived there at 0143 hrs together with the pump from Hatfield.

We had a small fire in a communal kitchen.

The funny bit happened after we left. As we left the site there was a lad, clearly the worse for wear, leaning drunkenly against the University sign.

As we pulled out onto the road we were called back to the University to a reactivation of the alarms.

We turned around and headed back to the campus. This time, as we pulled in, the lad had been sick all down his front.

Twenty minutes later as we left for the second time, we passed the boy, this time, still covered in sick, he had his trousers round his ankles and he had crapped himself as well!

Great fun.

Do you think when he was picked up his mum let him get in the car?

At 6.37 a.m., on 16th April a Land Rover and trailer overturned on the A1(M) between junctions 5 and 6.

We booked in attendance at 6.42 a.m.

The WGC and Hatfield Herald of Thursday, 18th April, carried the headline: -

ESCAPE FOR MEN AS VEHICLE FLIPS

And went on: "Two men in a Land Rover were lucky not to be squashed when their vehicle, which was pulling a trailer, rolled over on the A1(M). One of the men was cut free by firefighters, who said the accident could have been much worse."

Gary "Spindle" Sanderson, from the BHAPS, said: "Both were very lucky not to have sustained serious injuries, due to the roof being flattened by the impact on the road."

The stop was sent at 7.18 p.m.

16th and 17th May, and two decent house fires for Sub O Payne to deal with.

On Thursday, 16th, in Shortlands Green, WGC, trouble is in the air.

The Welwyn and Hatfield Times of Wednesday, May 22nd reported that a neighbour and her partner "saw the blaze" and said "I saw some kids smashing the place up. There was a lot of noise from the inside around midday."

A Hertfordshire Constabulary spokesman later told *The Times*; "Neighbours have said the house has had problems with vandalism and there have been reports of parties."

1343 hrs, BEEP, BEEP, BEEP, "190 to attend Shortlands Green, WGC, house fire."

1344 hrs, mobile to incident, Sub O Payne in charge with a crew of six.

1347 hrs, in attendance.

We are confronted with a serious fire, with smoke issuing from upstairs and downstairs windows at the front and a large pall of smoke rising from the back.

A local resident runs up and tells me that they thought there may be someone inside so at, 1348 hrs, I sent "make pumps two persons reported."

1348 hrs, 191 mobile, L/Ff Harper in charge, crew of three.

A forced entry was made to the front door by removing the lower door panel and the first BA team (firefighters Baker-Croft and Kimber) entered the house with a jet and a TIC, with instructions to search the ground floor and carry out fire-fighting operations as appropriate.

1350 hrs, "a mid-terrace house – well alight – 1 jet - 2 BA in use."

Firefighter Ward had checked the back of the building and reported that the kitchen and rear of the house was well alight.

1351 hrs, "make pumps 3."

191 in attendance, and I committed a second crew (L/Ff Harper and Ff Firmin) to the building with a jet, via the front door and tasked to search the upstairs.

1351 hrs, Stn O Graham in attendance.

1352 hrs, 180 mobile, Sub O Hunt in charge, crew of four.

1356 hrs, 201 mobile, Sub O Stagg in charge, crew of four.

201 had been mobilised to back-up 191 as they only had a crew of three.

1359 hrs, I send an informative message "4 BA – 2 jets – all persons not yet accounted for."

1359 hrs, 180 in attendance.

Conditions inside were severe. Ff Kimber said in his statement for the fire investigation report; "as we moved around the rooms, extinguishing various areas that were alight, the TIC began to completely white-out with the heat. Ff Baker-Croft informed me that he was about to give the ceiling a few bursts with the jet as we had a lean flashover above us."

The first BA team left the building and reported; Ff Baker-Croft told me (as per the fire investigation report), "I said that I was not one hundred per cent confident that the house was clear of casualties as visibility was poor and due to the "trashing" of the upstairs, searching was difficult."

These two had been subjected to punishing conditions and I stood them down and ordered a third crew, Ff's Haque and Cowens from Hatfield, to search the first floor.

This team reported the house clear after an exhaustive search.

1403 hrs, 201 in attendance and released at 1411 hrs.

The property had obviously been the subject of vandalism, forced entry, paint thrown up exterior walls, damaged fixtures and fittings and two petrol cans in the garden. Coupled with the evidence of local people, I sent the message at 1406 hrs; "Fire Investigation Support Officer (FISO) required."

1413 hrs, C5, Stn O Stokes mobile.

At 1416 hrs, following a final inspection by myself and Stn O Graham, I sent the Stop message; "papa 01 86 94 – all persons accounted for."

1425 hrs, Stn O Stokes in attendance.

I handed control of the incident over to him pending his investigation.

At 1433 hrs, he requests the attendance of the Fire Investigation Dog Team, and they arrive at 1520 hrs.

Stn O Stokes report stated; "we cannot rule out the careless disposal of smoking materials. However, the evidence of vandalism and the absence of smoking materials in the area in which the fire is believed to have started leads us to believe that the fire was started deliberately."

Paula Pond's (Fire Investigation Dog Team) report states; "the FI dog was deployed to carry out a search of all areas of the ground floor and garden. The FI dog gave no indication of ignitable liquids present during the searches."

1800 hrs, 190 mobile returning. 1804 hrs, home station.

The following day, the 17th May.

Not far from the station a fire has started in a garden shed behind another mid-terraced house.

1045 hrs, BEEP, BEEP, BEEP, "190 to Verulam Close, WGC, fire."

1047 hrs, we are mobile, Sub O Payne in charge with a crew of five.

1049 hrs, in attendance, "make pumps 2."

1050 hrs, "a mid-terraced bungalow well alight – make pumps 3."

1051 hrs, 191 mobile, L/Ff Harper in charge, crew of four.

1052 hrs, 180 mobile, Sub O Hunt in charge, crew of four.

The fire has spread from the shed at the back into the roof space and across two properties; it has also burned through into the kitchen.

A BA crew are deployed to the house with a jet.

1054 hrs, 191 in attendance.

At 1055 hrs, I send an informative message, "A mid-terraced bungalow well alight – 2 BA- 1 jet, 1 hosereel, TIC-one elderly resident escaped prior to arrival of brigade."

1100 hrs, 180 in attendance.

1102 hrs, "make pumps 4."

Two more BA teams are committed to the fire with a jet apiece.

1102 hrs, 111 mobile, L/FF Doyle in charge, crew of 4.

111 had already been sent to standby at WGC.

1106 hrs, 111 in attendance.

1108 hrs, "mid-terraced bungalow – fire in roof – 8 BA, 2 jets, 1 hosereel, TIC in use."

1111 hrs, "Stn O Graham now in charge of incident."

1122 hrs, B1, DO Matthews in attendance.

Conditions are hard in the roof space but the fire is eventually brought under control and at 1135 hrs Stn O Graham sends "crews delayed sometime – cutting away and damping down in progress."

1211 hrs, stop message, "papa 01 86 95 – 1 person code 2 – 3 persons code 3."

1255 hrs, mobile returning.

The Welwyn and Hatfield Times of the 22nd May carried the headline: -

NEIGHBOUR HELPS VICTIMS TO SAFETY

And told us: "A mother and daughter were helped to safety by a neighbour as a fire engulfed their home.

A neighbour from Ludwick Way in WGC rushed to the pairs assistance as their bungalow went up in flames at 1045 hrs on Friday.

An asthmatic woman in her 60s from an adjoining property, was taken to the QE II hospital in WGC suffering from the effects of smoke inhalation."

Time for more honours to be heaped upon us.

Along with the Armed Forces and the other Emergency Services we are to be awarded the Queen's Golden Jubilee Medal.

The lads on the Watch were phenomenal eaters! I just couldn't keep up.

So much so that I was considered to be on half rations and subsequently only paid half the mess money.

Sometimes it took two of them to lift and carry a food-laden plate to the table.

Their eating prowess was only eclipsed by their capacity to drink.

They were quite a social Watch, playing golf together and meeting up at various places for a convivial get together, usually involving drink.

The early summer was busy with lots of incidents of varying interest: The generator of a set of temporary traffic lights on the B1000 on fire, a wok on fire at a local Chinese takeaway, girl stuck up a tree, car on fire under some flats, to mention just a few.

Then, on 22nd July, we were called out at 8.11 p.m. to Panshanger Airfield in WGC where a disused hangar had been set on fire by arsonists.

Sub O Morgan made pumps 4.

WGC retained WrL and two pumps from Hertford are mobilised.

The hangar contained rubbish and cylinders and was well alight. We used 3 jets, 1 hosereel and 2 BA to fight the blaze. During the fire we managed to remove four propane cylinders to safety and being in a remote location on the far side of the airfield we had to set up a water shuttle.

After a while someone noticed smoke rising from a second hanger and Control mobilised pumps from Hatfield and Old Welwyn to deal with it.

The stop message was sent at 9.27 p.m.

We had the usual false alarm regulars which threw up the occasional fire. The QEII hospital of course, the others being Gilbertson and Page and Cereal Partners.

A fire on 28th August at Gilbertson and Page gave me another new experience.

The Company had been making dog biscuits since 1883 and we attended their factory in Brownfields, WGC fairly regularly.

On this occasion a fire had broken out in the trunking of a biscuit oven.

Riding with us for the day was Samantha Buckingham from the Blue Watch who had swapped a shift with one of our lads.

Sam was a good firefighter and well thought of on the station.

We went out at 1402 hrs and in attendance at 1406 hrs.

The fire had travelled up the trunking and was smouldering at roof level.

We pitched the 464 ladder to the roof and Sam and I went up to have a look.

We needed to remove a plate in a rooftop box to access the fire so down I went for the hearth kit. Once removed, the fire was located and I considered the best option was to use the backpack sprayer to put it out.

So down I went again (ever the gentleman).

Using the long nozzle of the backpack sprayer Sam could extinguish the fire and that was that.

Mobile returning at 1455 hrs.

Another bonus of an incident at G & P was that we usually came away with a bag or two of dog biscuits.

On 30th September at just after a quarter past five in the evening, we were called to a fire at Cereal Partners, Hydeway, Broadwater Road, WGC.

This Company is famous for its Shredded Wheat and Shreddies cereals.

Also mobile is Bravo 191.

This call out involved a fire in a grain dryer and the area was heavily smoke-logged.

One BA team took a hosereel and the second the TIC.

I was in the hosereel team.

The sprinklers had also operated.

The stop message was sent at 5.59 p.m. and we were mobile returning at 6.09 p.m.

Around the beginning of August we were issued with some new kit.

The Hertfordshire on Sunday of 18th August had the following article.

ABLAZE WITH STYLE

"Hertfordshire firefighters are all lit up over their new kit.

The County's fire crews will get a fresh look this week when they are issued with new helmets, boots, smoke hoods and gloves to go with the tunics and trousers they recently received."

Earlier in the year events were underway that would have a big impact on the Country's fire brigades over the next few months.

On April 18th the Fire Brigades Union (FBU) leaders had agreed to press for an increase in pay for a fireman from £21,531 to £30,000 across the board.

At Annual Conference on May 15th, firefighters demanded a forty per cent pay rise with strike action to follow if the employers said no, which, of course, they did.

In June, pay talks broke down, and on August 28th the employers proposed a four per cent increase.

In September talks break down again and strike action was mooted.

An independent review of the fire service is launched, headed by Sir George Bain.

On October 18th FBU members voted nine to one in favour of industrial action.

Although I voted for strike action, in my mind I considered we had no chance of achieving the goal. Forty per cent was a massive amount and the impression I got from most of my colleagues was that the Government would just pay up.

The Hertfordshire on Sunday for October 13th carried a "special report" written by my mate Dave Rees, under the headline:

WHY I'M WORTH FORTY PER CENT RISE

Dave put forward a good case for our receiving the increase, and popped up again in the November 3rd edition to say "if nothing is done on Tuesday we will walk out on Thursday and it's an eight-day strike. We are worth £30,000."

In October the first two forty-eight hour strikes were called off and at the beginning of November the first of a series of eight day walkouts is postponed.

On November 11th the Bain report recommended a four per cent pay rise with a seven per cent rise the following year.

The FBU rejects the offer.

And so at 1800 hrs on Wednesday, 13th November at WGC fire station, we turn off the lights, close the doors and walk out for the first forty-eight-hour strike.

The fire service in Hertfordshire is handed over to 3rd Battalion the Parachute Regiment and 9 Squadron the Royal Engineers.

They had, I think, 13 Green Goddesses backed up by Royal Air Force BA Rescue and Rescue Equipment Support teams.

The nearest to WGC were based in St Albans and Hertford.

The second walk out took place at 0900 hrs on Friday November 22nd.

The Welwyn and Hatfield Times of Wednesday 27th said;

SHOVELLING ON THE MUD

"A Green Goddess crew shovelled wet mud into a burning car when the engine's water pumps would not work.

The fire, near the civic amenity site on the A414 Hatfield Road, happened at 3.20 p.m. Monday."

We did our normal shifts but instead of sitting in the warm station we had to sit out in the freezing winter weather.

We kept a fire going and had a caravan and gazebo for all those home comforts.

Well a kettle at least.

WGC November 2002: Seated L to R: Moley Kimber, Derek Macleod, Mark Saban, Alan Morgan. Standing Lto R: Martin Rodmell, ?, Gary Baker-Croft and Me.

Later on, a local company provided us with a portable building and the public were fantastic, bringing us all sorts of things. We were donated nappies, cash and food.

A five-year-old lad bought us a Christmas chocolate selection box with his pocket money and a woman dropped off her entire week's shopping. Although, to be fair, her husband turned up later to ask for some of it back!

One night Moley and me were "on duty" and our brazier got a bit out of control. We had stacked it with too many fence panels and the result was a great blaze that kept us very warm but melted and lifted all the tarmac from the pavement.

Of course, while all this political intrigue was going on, we were still going out to fires.

On the day shifts 21st and 22nd of September I was in charge at Watford fire station. Three calls, a false alarm, a rubbish fire and some undergrowth on fire.

And on 29th I spent the day in charge at Garston where I went out on a dumper truck on fire, an RTA persons trapped and a grass fire.

On 10th November at 11.03 p.m., we were called out to 25, French Horn Lane, Hatfield to "smoke in house, persons reported."

We turned out with Sub O Morgan in charge with a crew of five.

In attendance before us was Hatfield WrL with a crew of six.

As we pulled up the occupants abandoned the building, eight of them, climbing out of all the doors and windows simultaneously.

A fire in the kitchen was tackled by removing the burning pan to open air and the eight casualties were treated outside, five of them taken to hospital suffering from the effects of smoke.

We were back at WGC just before midnight.

At 2341 hrs on 5th December, another call took us over to Hatfield.

BEEP, BEEP, BEEP, "190 to attend BAE, Bishops Square, Hatfield – fire."

I am in charge with a crew of five and in attendance at 2350 hrs, joining 180.

The fire is in a ground floor bin store underneath a four storey office block. All four floors are smoke-logged.

The fire is extinguished by the Hatfield crew using a hosereel and the building is vented using our PPV and the internal venting system.

Mobile returning at 0019 hrs.

Back at WGC at half past midnight.

Guess what I introduced to the boys at WGC?

Yes, that's it, the Gibber Book!

These six lads turned out to be Masters of Gibber.

I'll show you what I mean.

THE ALL NEW BOOK OF VERBAL BOLLOCKS. 2002.

Alan: "Is it the spare filing cabinet key or is it the key to the spare filing cabinet?"

Sabes: "Is euthanasia alive and well?"

Sabes: "I got a hole in one with my second shot."

Crofty: "She's married to a copper, and her old man's a copper as well."

Daz: (Talking about the long jump). "I've often thought it would be better to dive into the pit and do a sort of jam roly poly at the end."

Rodders: "OCTOPUS, that's OCT as in five!"

Moley: "It's all make pretend."

Alan: (Watching football). "Is it two yellows and you're off or is it one yellow and the next one you're off?"

2003. A NEW ROLE.

Fire Service operations occasionally include the requirement to rescue casualties from height, or depth, where access is limited or difficult.

To that end, last year, the Brigade took delivery of some new equipment. As part of Health and Safety (I suppose), we were to have Rope Access Teams around the County, with WGC being designated as one of the Rope Access stations.

The idea was to make working aloft safer.

Our Watch co-ordinator/instructor was to be Moley, and he was duly sent on a number of training courses.

Following his return, we started our in-house training.

We were trained in the use of the specialist equipment, we could descend or ascend with or without a stretcher and once all the training was completed, we became operational and were mobilised to assist other crews to carry out safe rescues from height, shafts, sewers, wells, silos etc.

On Tuesday, 21st January, we had another twenty-four-hour strike.

The Final Outcome: Win, Lose or Draw? I'm not sure.

Our Strike officially ended on the 26th of August with the final agreement settling on £25,000 which was a sixteen per cent pay rise overall. However, it was negotiated that the pay rise would occur over a period of time starting with a four per cent rise from November 2002, a seven per cent rise in November 2003 and finally another four point two per cent rise by July 2004, and, **an understanding that modernisation measures would be subject to some measure of local negotiation!**

For me the worst thing about the strike, was the loss of our Sub O Alan Morgan.

Alan was on strike with us initially, but his conscience led him to return to work early.

The Watch took his decision very badly and for the most part ignored him in varying degrees.

For my part, I stood by Alan and became, to all intents and purposes the go between in all matters between the Watch and him, a fraught situation for all of us.

Things did start to get better but the mistrust and uneasiness eventually led to Alan leaving the Watch.

In order to alleviate the situation, he left us later in the year, moving across to Blue Watch and Steve Cartwright transferred over to us from Blue Watch.

Anyway, back to more interesting things.

0400 hrs of 15th February, and the bells go down, turning us out to "Bishops Rise, Hatfield, RTA persons trapped".

In attendance with 180 at 0408 hrs.

One car is in collision with a road sign and one male person is trapped inside.

We use Lukas to free the casualty; he is removed on a spinal board and is taken to the QE II hospital in WGC by BHAPS ambulance.

The stop is sent at 0422 hrs.

Our appliance is back on station and ready for redeployment at 0445 hrs.

Six days later an RTA on the A1 (M), had us rushing to junction 1, on Potters Bars ground.

One person trapped and eight others involved.

Back to WGC at 11.35 a.m.

8th March, A414, van well alight, 2 hosereels and 2 BA in use.

29th June, Mill Green Golf Club, Gypsy Lane, Hatfield, relief for a six pump fire.

17th July, a call to Bandicott House, Bandicott, WGC. I was in charge when we received a call to a kitchen fire where an elderly person was found inside and rescued by crews.

Back in June I had visited Germany again. It was the sad occasion of the funeral of an old friend, Karl Heiser, where I was to represent the Service.

I drove down to Ingelheim on 10th and I think the funeral was on the 11th.

I stayed at Pension Waldeck, up in the hills above Ingelheim and just behind the Bismarkturm, a tower built in honour of the first German chancellor Prince Otto von Bismarck (1815-1898).

The owner also kept on site, two tigers called Bengal and Fluffy, it was a great place to stay and the Ingelheim fire brigade sent a van to ferry me around.

On 12th I drove up the Rhine Valley to meet up with Wolfgang Dörsch at his home in Marienhausen.

On the 13th we headed back to Koblenz where Wolfgang shows me around the new training centre, what a great facility.

Next on my agenda is a trip down to Viernheim that evening, to visit my friends Norbert and Karin Maliske.

The next day I went to see more friends, this time Roland and Regina Ullmann in Edingen-Neckarhausen. This visit coincided with the open day at the Edingen fire station so more beer and sausages.

Edingen Fire Staion Open Day.

Exercise in Ingleheim.

I left Viernheim on the Sunday, 15th to drive back to Ingelheim.

Finally, on Monday, Martin Oudôt took me to visit the fire station at Wiesbaden on the opposite side of the Rhine and later that afternoon I watched the Ingelheim fire brigade on exercise.

Home on Tuesday, 17th, June.

For my shift of 30th July to 2nd of August I was sent to St. Albans.

I hadn't done anything wrong, they just needed an Officer in Charge.

St Albans had a brand new station, the old one in the town centre having closed some years ago.

It had two pumps, a hydraulic platform and an incident response unit.

Eleven calls in all, but only one decent job.

On Wednesday, 30th, we joined Garston for a false alarm in Bricket Wood.

Thursday, 31st, and we started off with a false alarm at Sainsbury's in London Colney.
Next up, both pumps were mobilised to two large rubbish fires in Parkbury Lane, St. Albans.

1646 hrs, BEEP, BEEP, BEEP, "110 and 111 to attend the Pasta Bowl, High Street, St. Albans, fire."

Both appliances with a crew of four, in attendance at 1651 hrs.

I am confronted with a narrow shop front, inside it is heavily smoke logged.

"Make pumps 4."

100 and 221 mobile to incident.

I get the crew to break in the front door and commit a BA crew with a hosereel to the building.

A second crew is deployed to the rear of the premise to check for fire and access.

From the front door, the restaurant stretches back a long way to the seating area and kitchen.

As soon as reinforcements arrived I committed a second BA team to the building.

The source of the fire was located in the kitchen and dealt with by the BA teams.

> I sent the stop message at 1718 hrs.
> There was some smoke damage to an adjacent clothes shop.
> We were back on station at 1747 hrs.

Friday night shift, 1st August.

2107 hrs, St Albans City Hospital, false alarm. 110 crew of five. Also mobile 111, 100.

1200 hrs, St Albans City Hospital, false alarm. 111 and 121 also mobile.

0218 hrs (2nd August), St Albans City Hospital, false alarm. 111 mobile.

In the morning, Red Watch had a standby Sub O coming in so I stayed on.

0933 hrs, Losnors Bridal Shop in Victoria Street, St Albans. The call was to a fire all out, PPV in use to clear the smoke.

Saturday night, 2nd July.

2048 hrs, both pumps mobile to an Italian Restaurant in Christopher Place, St Albans. 110 with a crew of five, 111 crew of four.

2120 hrs, same again.

0544 hrs (3rd), Reunion Waste, Appspond Lane, Chiswell Green. Both appliances mobile to a large quantity of compost alight. We spent an hour on site using jets to extinguish the blaze.

Arriving on station at WGC is another new vehicle, a 4x4, Ford Ranger (AJ03 AAZ).

So more off road training for the station personnel.

12th September, on the A119 at Waterford a car left the roadway leaving the female driver trapped inside. She was released using the Lukas cutting gear. Also in attendance two appliances from Hertford.

I think Alan left the Watch around now and the first call with our new Sub O, Steve Cartwright, took us to the QE II hospital for a false alarm on 3rd October.

6th October, at half past midnight, a car overturned on the Great North Road, Hatfield, trapping the driver.

Again we used the Lukas to free the casualty who was taken to the QEII by ambulance.

Hatfield's WrL and ERT were also on scene.

The middle of October saw a bit of a heat wave and started a spate of grass fires.

On 19th alone, a three pump fire in woodland in Essendon followed by three grass fires in WGC.

I used to enjoy my sea fishing and went on a few brigade trips and one year even took part in the Nationals at Weymouth.

On 20th and 21st November the Brigade Sea Fishing Section went Bass fishing at Weymouth.

Me and Trevor Evans with a couple of nice Bass.

And that's it for another year.

Due to the fraught situation on Watch, the Gibber Book didn't get many entries, only fourteen in fact.

Anyway, here's some from THE ALL NEW BOOK OF VERBAL B*LLOCKS. 2003.

Alan Morgan: "His old gloves aren't good enough according to the new standards which says they aren't good enough and his new one's don't fit which isn't good enough."

Sabes: "Well, join the boat, we're all in the same one."

Daz: "We're all in the same bowl."

Rodders: "Derek spoke to someone and they said that some rank or some position or some job there has changed or something so he'd have to speak to someone."

Crofty: "I ran my tits out."

At some point during the year I think Tony Morrison arrived to become our Station Commander as he is in the Gibber Book.

2004. A VERY LONG SHIFT.

Can you believe it, New Year's Day and I'm off to St Albans again.

Two suspicious car fires, one in St Albans at 7.18 p.m., and another in Chiswell Green at 10.13 p.m.

What's going on I'm all over the place.

At the end of the month, on 31st, I was in charge at Stevenage where we had to assist the Ambulance Service to recover the body of an elderly man from a house in Valley Way.

In charge at Hemel Hempstead on the night of 20th March. 11.13 p.m. Two cars in collision on Belswains Lane, 1 person trapped, code 2, 1 person code 3.

3.37 a.m., car on fire following an RTA on High Street, Apsley. One person code two.

Back home on the next night shift, 21st March. A call at 8.45 p.m. takes us to junctions 6 to 7 of the A1 (M). Two cars have collided, with one person trapped and two others injured.

14th May. A mile or so from the station a nurse with butter fingers is at work at the hospital.

BEEP, BEEP, BEEP, "190 to attend QE II Hospital, Howlands, WGC, chemical spillage."

1224 hrs, 190 mobile, Sub O Payne in charge, crew of five.

1227 hrs, in attendance.

On arrival, I find we have a situation on the sixth floor. I go up with one firefighter to assess the incident.

In a room adjacent to the operating theatres, there is a spillage of four litres of formaldehyde.

Following a consultation with Control, I asked for a full chemical response and both Hemel Hempstead pumps and the Chemical Incident Unit were mobilised.

I evacuated several rooms including one theatre surrounding the incident room and involving thirty-one people, three of whom needed first aid.

Formaldchyde is toxic if inhaled, swallowed or through contact with the skin.

With the arrival of the Hemel crews and the setting up of the decontamination area we started to deal with the spillage.

Four BA teams in chemical suits worked in relay to recover the liquid and clean the area before proceeding to the CIU for decontamination.

We got back to station at 1543 hrs.

Around this time we got a new DCFO, Roy Wilsher. I think previously he was an Assistant Commissioner with London Fire Brigade.

In July, comes some sad news from Germany, my old friend Hans Neumann passed away.

He died on 9th July.

Hans was in at the start of the exchange visits and was on the founding Board of the Mainz-Bingen Association.

White Watch, WGC, July/August 2004
Back row L-R M. Rodwell, Ward, M. Saban, S. Cartwright
Front row L-R Me, A. Kimber, G. Baker-Croft

The Officer in Charge.

Ford Ranger, AJ03 AAZ and Dennis Dagger, KF02 UZT.

I had a mate in Codicote, Paul, who ran the Shire Park Club, off of the Mundells, WGC.

I was never too happy with the fire safety there and on a Sunday afternoon I would take the appliance over to conduct an inspection on the snooker room.

After an hour or so once I was happy, we headed back for tea.

It's the early hours of the morning, Monday 19th July, and just over from the fire station, some lads are up to no good.

0241 hrs, BEEP, BEEP, BEEP, "190 to attend the Trades and Labour Club, Bridge Road, WGC, fire."

0243 hrs, mobile, crew of five.

The building is under refurbishment and is well alight.

"Make pumps 3."

Control mobilise 191 and 201. One of these pumps only had a crew of three and so 240 was also sent.

Initially the building was too dangerous to enter and so jets were got to work from the outside. As the fire was knocked down BA crews were committed to continue the fight.

The stop message was sent at 0403 hrs, with 4 BA, TIC and PPV in use.

Home station at 0423 hrs.

However, it was not over yet.

At 0850 hrs we were mobile again, a smouldering fire, missed the first time, had caught in the roof and it was well alight for the second time.

We were joined by Hatfield WrL, Old Welwyn WrT, St Albans WrL and HP.

We were relieved by our Red Watch after nine and headed off home.

Red Watch sent their stop message at 1045 hrs.

I had a short break in Koblenz over the weekend 13th to 16th August. I went with a friend, Patsy and I had unfortunately parted company, to see the 'Rhine in Flames' firework festival.

To cut down on costs I decided to contact the fire station to see if we could stay there. I telephoned them and amazingly spoke to Roland Kluth, who was the officer in charge of Watch 2 when I worked there in 1988 (see page 94). He sorted everything out and we duly arrived in the afternoon of Friday 13th.

Roland met us, settled us in and invited us over for tea. An hour or so later he drove us to his house in the Niederwerth district, where we met his wife Evelyn and spent a very pleasant afternoon in their company.

Me, Evelyn and Roland.

17th and 18th August, I did my two day shifts and the following day I went in on nights for a mammoth shift.

I had been asked to do an extra shift for a Red Watch fireman which meant that I started at 1800 hrs on the 19th and finished at 0900 hrs in the morning of the 21st.

We had ten calls altogether including a person shut in a lift, a pigeon trapped on a window ledge, a couple of floodings and a car fire.

So after thirty-nine hours at work just as we were preparing to go off duty, a final call came in at five to nine in the morning, giving me an hour's overtime as well!

It's 28th September, around eight p.m. and over in Cheshunt, at the Magistrates Court in Arthur Court, there is a scene of chaos.

The prisoner at the bar has escaped from his escort and is smashing up the courthouse and is currently up on the roof!

Due to the age of the building, asbestos is suspected and the police request the attendance of the fire service.

Control mobilise Cheshunt, the nearest station, Hemel with their WrL and CIU, and us as a rope rescue team.

We are mobile at 2021 hrs and in attendance at 2045 hrs.

I don't think we were needed but the CIU decontaminated one prisoner, one security guard and ten police officers.

The following morning at 0741 hrs, we are called out to an RTA outside Edgel Cottages, Holwell Lane, Essendon.

In attendance at 0746 hrs along with 180.

A flatbed truck has been in collision with an articulated lorry. The driver of the flatbed was released prior to our arrival, and taken to hospital by BHAPS.

We tidied up a bit and were at WGC at 0824 hrs.

On 29th November we had an RTA on the A1(M) with a car overturned.

On 7th December another RTA, this time on the Hertford Road, Mill Green with a woman injured after her car left the road, overturned on a grass bank and finished up in some trees.

As part of the rope rescue equipment we had an item called a Quadpod. It had four legs and could straddle trenches or manholes and allowed us to raise or lower personnel or equipment.

On 8th December we met up somewhere on Potters Bars ground for a training exercise with them.

RTA Essendon.

The scene in Harmer Green Lane.

18th December I was in BA at a three pump fire in the roof of a house in Hornsfield, WGC.

191 and 201 also in attendance.

We used a hosereel to extinguish the blaze.

And finally for the year 2004.

A call at 1229 hrs on Christmas Eve took us to the front garden of a house in Harmer Green Lane, Welwyn.

We had a crew of five as did the crew from Old Welwyn.

Two cars had collided in the narrow lane. A BMW, hit on the front nearside finished up on the road, and a Renault, that had ended up in the front garden with the driver trapped and his "fluffy dice" hanging on a branch three metres above ground!

He was released using Lukas cutting gear and taken to the QE II by ambulance.

MORE VERBAL CRAP 2004

Crofty: "He looked like a residential sergeant major."

Les Jones (Green Watch?): "I've heard the council are closing the public toilets… or is that a load of crap!"

Alan Morgan: "The pass mark is fifty per cent so you can get nil and still fail."

Course tutor: "A woman was hit on the head with a cricket ball and she was out."

Moley: "They wanted to put fifty pounds behind the bar, but I said it would just be swallowed up."

Me: Tony Morrison, "We've got Martin Graham, Martin Arrowsmith and Martin Rodmell on the station."

Me: "Ah, a trio of Rodmells."

Daz: "I've had about four second opinions!"

Daz: "I'm as sharp as a marble."

Crofty: "Down by the coastline was the sea."

Spindle: "He's got a urinary infection and he can't shake it."

Crofty: "Apparently this glue sticks shit to a blanket."
Rodders: "So how did that snake catch the gazelle? Surely it didn't run after it!"

Tony Morrison: "I wouldn't like to be sitting in their shoes."

Steve Cartwright: "We should be able to get in two rounds of golf, it stays dark quite late."

Sabes: "We're buttering as fast as our little knives will carry us."

Daz: "The other half was even bigger."

2005. THE BIGGEST FIRE IN EUROPE SINCE 1945.

The *Welwyn & Hatfield Times* of Wednesday, 19th January carried two articles of interest.

Firstly, it covered the arrival of our newest acquisition, a £165,000 WrL, a Scania 94D 260 with bodywork by John Dennis Coachbuilders (EU54 ZVD). New innovations included shelves in the lockers that pulled out and tilted and also a locker to contain the BA sets. And, as can be seen from the photograph below, it also had provision for a spare fireman in a sliding tray in the front offside locker!

Secondly, it had the headline:

FLYING CAR CRASHES INTO WALL OF HOUSE

It covered an incident that took place three days earlier.

Around twelve thirty a speeding, silver Peugeot 206 car flew off the road, cleared a hedge and struck a house, eight feet up the wall, knocking the porch three inches sideways.

BEEP, BEEP, BEEP, "190 to attend Mount Pleasant Lane, Hatfield, RTA persons trapped."

1234 hrs, mobile to incident, Sub O Cartwright in charge, crew of five.

1238 hrs, in attendance.

Also there were Hatfield's WrL and ERT.

The car has come to rest between two houses with the driver trapped in his seat by the collapsing roof of the car.

He is being treated by a paramedic and two ambulancemen.

Fire crews are stabilising the vehicle and preparing the Lukas equipment. The house also needed shoring up to prevent collapse.

To enable us to gain access to the casualty we had to remove the roof completely. Once that was achieved we could ease the man onto a spinal board and slowly remove him from his seat.

He had suffered multiple injuries to his head, chest, abdomen and legs. He was taken to the QE II by BHAPS.

The stop message was sent at 1317 hrs.

We cleaned up and were back at WGC at 1340 hrs.

Gary Sanderson, Acting Communications Manager for BHAPS, who was at the scene, said; "The driver's side of the car roof had collapsed."

"Our crews were faced with a very delicate incident, the male was well trapped in the wreckage and the building had suffered significant damage."

Mr Sanderson said; "He was full of praise for the staff who got the driver out quickly and safely to hospital."

Good old Spindle!

Crews at work with Lukas at Mount Pleasant Lane.
Pictures: Gary Sanderson

2nd February 2005. A terrible day for all of us in the Hertfordshire Fire and Rescue Service.

I arrive at work for another day shift.

The atmosphere on the station is palpable, a feeling of shock and disbelief.

Blue Watch have been on nights.

During the night we have lost two of our firefighters in a fire in Stevenage. At around three in the morning Stevenage station had received a persons reported call to a fire on the fourteenth floor of Harrow Court, in Silam Road.

The pair, Jeff Wornham and Michael Miller had died trying to rescue a thirty-two-year-old woman from an intense fire in her flat.

They had already saved a thirty-seven-year-old man from the blaze and had returned to rescue the woman.

Jeff was rescued by colleagues and taken to hospital, Michael was found in the flat with the female victim.

At the height of the blaze, fifteen fire appliances were in operation along with the other emergency services.

The fire involved the 14th and 15th floors and eight people were taken to hospital, including the critically ill man who was rescued. In all seventy-two other people were evacuated.

At 1.34 p.m. we were sent to the incident on relief along with Potters Bar.

We arrived there at 1.51 p.m.

On our way up to the fire floor the body of the woman was being brought down.

The fourteenth floor was a mess and the flat destroyed.

One of the saddest things I saw in my career were the metal plates from Michael's fire boots lying there on the floor.

So sad.

This time it was DCFO Wilsher who said, "These firefighters gave the ultimate sacrifice. They were trying to save someone else from a fire and they did their best to achieve that."

Over the years I was based at Stevenage I had been to these high rise blocks dozens of times on various incidents. A real case of "there but for the grace of God go I."

I didn't know these lads, they had arrived at Stevenage after I left. Always in our thoughts.

On Saturday 27th we held a "car wash" at the station in aid of the fund for the fallen Stevenage firefighters.

We did a six-hour stint, raising more than £3,000.

The Welwyn & Hatfield Times of the 2nd March headlined with;

FIREFIGHTERS SCRUB UP WELL FOR CHARITY

They managed to get a celebrity quote. "Leading firefighter at WGC, Sid Payne, said the group were kept busy by a constant stream of cars throughout the day. He also thanked the landlords of the Rose and Crown in Welwyn and the Globe in Codicote who held collections at their pubs towards the fund."

On 25th March at 0355 hrs, we used Lukas to release a young Fallow deer that had become trapped in a metal fence.

Around April time (I think) Roy Wilsher was promoted to CFO and a new DCFO arrived, Mark Yates.

This man was a real politician.

I had invited him to the station to meet the crew and talk about brigade matters in general.

I was in charge when he came to visit us on the 16th May and despite a barrage of questions from the lads he spoke at length on all types of subjects.

At 4.16 p.m. the bells went down and we turned out to an RTA persons trapped in Knightsfield, WGC.

We had two cars in collision with one female trapped.

201 and 185 were also in attendance.

We also had a very senior officer turn up – DCFO Yates came to see how we performed.

We used Lukas to free the casualty, the DCFO left and we returned to station at 5.10 p.m.

Over a cup of tea, we discussed the DCFO's visit and came to the conclusion that, given he had spoken at such length, he actually hadn't told us anything we didn't already know… it was a typically good politician's performance!

On 11th June I went, with my scuba diving club, to Sark in the Channel Islands.

The previous Sub O at Old Welwyn, Trevor Kendal, had retired there and undertaken to reorganise the fire service.

I was shown round the small fire station. The two appliances are trailers and the ambulance a vehicle body, all three with a towing bar. There are no cars on Sark and in the event of a call the appliances are hitched up to tractors and taken out.

Sark Fire Station.

A few incidents to report on prior to the big one.

6th September, 1408 hrs. A lorry trailer alight on the A1 (M), junctions 3 to 4. 2 jets in use.

15th October, 1712 hrs. A child suffering from the effects of smoke following a kitchen fire at his Heronswood home.

26th October, 0719 hrs. Relief for a four pump fire at Oakmead Lodge, Cottered. 400 tons of baled straw on alight.

31st October, 1750 hrs. A fire in the storeroom of the Post Office in Moors Walk, WGC. 2 BA, 1 hosereel jet, the TIC and the PPV in use to extinguish the blaze.

On the 27th November we were called to a house in Hedgebrooms, WGC.

We had been called by neighbours who could smell smoke.

We were mobile at 2059 hrs and in attendance at 2101 hrs. I am in charge with a crew of five. As it is a house fire, 191 are also mobilised with a crew of five.

Looking through the letterbox of the first floor flat, I can see light smoke and smell burning. Banging on the door brings no response. I get one of the lads to pitch the short extension ladder to a slightly open first floor window from where he can see the occupant asleep on the sofa.

Despite our banging on the door and shouting through the window we cannot raise the man.

We have a megaphone on the pump and even though most of the street could hear, we couldn't wake him up.

Eventually, with the police, we make an entry to the flat. No one can get through to this man; clearly he's had a really good afternoon session.

His dinner is turned off and the pan removed to fresh air.

We leave him, still sound asleep, with the police and return to station at 2122 hrs.

It's 11th December and it's going to be a day to remember!

I am woken just after six o'clock in the morning, at my home in Codicote, by a loud bang. It sounded like something had fallen off the wall. A search of the house revealed nothing.

Anyway, back to bed.

When I got to work at nine o'clock I learn that a huge fire is going on at the Buncefield Oil Terminal which exploded just after six that morning! It has been made a major incident.

At 1104 hrs, we are tasked by Control to standby at St Albans fire station. Sub O Cartwright is in charge, Crofty is driving and Darren Ward and I are in the back.

At St Albans, other crews were mustering awaiting orders. Among them were 310, 280, 201, 160, 251 and 140.

We were on call covering St Albans station ground.

There was an air of excitement; I think everyone wanted to get involved.

1227 hrs, we are called to St Annes Road in London Colney. We are in attendance with Radlett WrT at 1232 hrs. The call is a false alarm and we return to St Albans.

At 1302 hrs, we are off again, this time to Jennings Road, St Albans. The Radlett pump is also mobile. In attendance at 1308 hrs, we find a small fire in the living room. The fire is extinguished, the female occupier is treated by BHAPS for slight smoke inhalation. We cut away around the window frame to ensure all is cool, the cause of the fire is an overheating Christmas light. Back to B11.

At 1413 hrs we are mobile to the big one. We are mobilised by telephone and we leave St Albans station in convoy with several other appliances for the fireground at Buncefield, oil terminal, Green Lane, Hemel Hempstead. The roads are cleared for us and the M25 had been closed. A huge pall of thick black smoke is rising from the terminal and spreading out southward towards London and the southern counties (and hopefully France).

Convoy of Pumps on Route to Buncefield.

The Loading Gantry on the Evening of the 11th.

In attendance at 1426 hrs.

We pull up next to the site in Green Lane to await instructions.

There is a huge cloud of black smoke above us, drifting off south, the noise of alarms sounding and the red glow of the fire flickering in amongst the smoke.

We were there for a couple of hours before we received orders to proceed to the emergency water supply by Buncefield Lane. We positioned our pump and set into the EWS.

I was tasked, together with Dave Williams (who must have been there all day as he was on Green Watch), to supply hose lines to protect the tanks not yet involved. We had every length of hose off of every appliance and still struggled.

We ran out six lines of hose towards tank 910 and another six lines towards tanks 301-304, where Stn O Stokes was trying to set up a huge curtain spray to keep them cool.

We just didn't have nearly enough hose or other equipment to do the job, but we managed as best we could.

Light was fading as we got water on.

The fire took on a new aspect in the darkness, very eerie.

Welcome additions to the attendance were the canteen vans from the Women's Voluntary Service and Bedfordshire Fire and Rescue Service.

We worked on into the night, past our clocking off time.

Finally, we were relieved. However, it was impossible to get our appliance as it was blocked in by dozens of others. I think in the end we went home in Kings Langley's pump.

Other Hertfordshire appliances in on scene were; 010, 011, 031, 061, 070, 090, 110, 111, 140, 150, 160, 171, 180, 191, 201, 231, 240, 241, 251, 261, 271, 310, 320, 185, 189 and IR78 (a government supplied vehicle for chemical protection and decontamination and based at St Albans).

We arrived back at WGC at 2115 hrs!

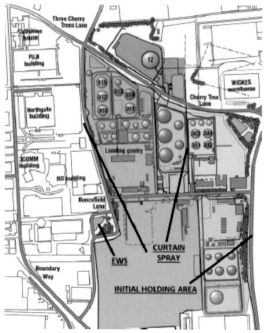

Map of Buncefield Oil Terminal, showing operations on 11th December.

Map: The Health and Safety Executive

We left the Blue Watch with the almost impossible task of trying to re-stow the appliance.

The Monday newspapers were full of the story.
The Daily Express headlined with:

12M BRITONS IN PATH OF BLAST CLOUD

- Children and elderly at risk
- Massive blaze will rage for days
- Clean-up bill put at £½ billion

"The biggest explosions ever seen in peacetime Europe rocked Britain yesterday, turning a fuel depot into a flaming hell.

A thick shroud of smog smothered much of southern England after three huge blasts shattered the dawn silence at the plant in Hemel Hempstead."

As a Brigade we had trained for an emergency at Buncefield, but only with one or possibly two tanks on fire. We now had twenty-two alight!

The following night shift, 12th, we were back on duty and at 0500 hrs on 13th we are on our way back to Buncefield as part of the relief.

Mobile at 0532 hrs and in attendance at 0550 hrs.

All through the day, more and more resources had been arriving. The government supplied High Volume Pumps were beginning to set into a lake a mile or so from the site, each one pumping 7,000 litres per minute through their 150mm hose to the fireground.

We couldn't start to fight the fire proper until we had enough foam concentrate on site and it was coming from all over the country.

We were involved in setting up foam equipment prior to starting firefighting operations.

As dawn breaks I went off to find some cigarettes for one of the lads. I found a van and set off. Not knowing Hemel very well I stopped to ask a copper where the nearest shop or garage was, he looked at me vaguely and said, "Buggered if I know mate, I'm from Kent". I assume the police needed some back up as well.

By the time we were relieved some firefighting had begun, with foam monitors and branches being got to work.

We got back to WGC at 1107 hrs.

Back on duty at 1800 hrs and another fun filled trip to Buncefield.

We are off at 2208 hrs and arrive at 2229 hrs.

Other Hertfordshire pumps in attendance are 041, 061, 131, 160, 161, 180, 201, 211, 231, 240 and 261 and 310.

We are now firefighting, using foam branches to extinguish the fires in the oil tank bunds, (a wall around the tank to contain spillages). This means we are up close and personal with the oil tanks, it's hot work and to make matters worse, when the wind gets up the smoke plume was forced down, surrounding crews in the oily smoke.

I go off for a well-earned cup of tea.

Walking between the burning tanks, fire is everywhere; thick, black smoke covers the area. It's all a bit surreal, like walking through Hades!

Coming in the opposite direction is a grimy, foam covered fireman from another brigade.

As we draw level he stops, touches my arm, raises his head, sniffs the air and says...

"CAN YOU SMELL SMOKE?"

And almost without breaking stride he heads off back into the inferno.

Working with a bulk foam carrier from another brigade.

The fire continues to rage during the night of the 13th.

The A Team.

The fight begins.

Dawn breaks on Tuesday 13th
revealing the build up of
resources and the HVP hose
lines.

We are relieved and still unable to get to our own fire engine; we head back to WGC in Rickmansworth's arriving there at 0349 hrs.

Wash, tea and a couple of hours sleep.

On Wednesday, the 14th December the stop message was sent: -

"An oil storage depot comprising of forty-one oil storage tanks, storing approx. 100 million litres of oil products and a residential and commercial area comprising numerous buildings of 1, 2, 3 and 4 storeys. Twenty-two storage tanks severely damaged and four storage tanks moderately damaged by fire. All buildings in storage depot and commercial area severely damaged by blast. Various levels of damage to residential areas. Multiple foam making equipment, high volume and fire service pumps and associated equipment used. Sixty persons code 2, 100 persons code 3, 3000 persons code 4."

And here's some information to give you an idea of some of the national response to Buncefield.

Bedfordshire: Potton Welfare unit, Dunstable WrT, Leighton Buzzard WrT, foam tender, explosimeter.

Berkshire: HVP.

Buckinghamshire: Aylesbury and Olney foam tenders, pumps from Amersham and Great Holm (Milton Keynes), explosimeter.

Cornwall: Foam tender.

Derbyshire: HVP.

Essex: Hose layers from Billericay and Hadleigh, WrT, foam tender and rescue tender from Grays and a lorry and support rescue pump from Epping.

Greater Manchester: HVP.

Hampshire: Foam tender and WrT.

Kent: Bulk foam carrier.

London: 2 x HVP's, Feltham PL, Bethnal Green PL, Sutton and Finchley bulk foam lorries, Southgate and Beckenham hose layers, Wembley gas explosimeter.

Norfolk: HVP.

Northamptonshire: Flatbed foam lorry.

North Yorkshire: HVP.

Oxfordshire: Flatbed foam lorry.

Somerset: Wellington WrT, HVP.

Staffordshire: 3 x pumps.

Surrey: Foam tender from Leatherhead.

As well as:

3 x 75,000 l foam tankers from Angus.

Foam and monitors from Lindsey Oil Refinery, Lincolnshire.

A foam pump from RAF Croughton, Northamptonshire.

Foam tankers from ESSO Fawley, Hampshire.

Foam from USAF Mildenhall and Lakenheath, Suffolk.

Additional foam stocks were sent from Hampshire, Humberside, Kent, Staffordshire, and Warwickshire.

Other supplies were diverted from Scandanavia.

And the cause? As I understood it, a delivery of unleaded fuel to tank 912 was underway when a fault in the system indicated that the level in the tank was static at two thirds full. The tank continued to fill and overflowed, resulting in a vapour cloud spreading out a kilometre or so over the surrounding area.

The ignition source hasn't been identified, but at 0601 hrs the vapour cloud exploded.

Views around Buncefield. Monday 19th December.

Well the fire was out but the incident wasn't over by a long chalk.

We were back on our next tour of duty on Monday 19th, 1000 hrs – 1428 hrs.

Tuesday 20th, 0153 hrs – 0733 hrs.
Tuesday 20th, 1831 hrs – 2254 hrs.
Our last visit was on 28th December.

The relief was gradually reduced and the job was just to make sure nothing else flared up and taking explosimeter readings.

There was a big tented burger bar set up which was open twenty-four hours a day where we could sit out of the cold.

On the afternoon of the 19th I wandered around the fireground looking at the total destruction.

We were so lucky that the depot exploded on a Sunday, a weekday would have resulted in many more casualties.

Infinite wisdom or absolute bollocks? 2005

Spindle Sanderson: "I was here ten minutes before I arrived."

Crofty: "I think that's a red heron."

Sabes: "The Royal Albert Hall was built to commemorate George V."

Steve Cartwright: (Crofty: "Giraffes eat eucalyptus leaves.")

"No they don't, they don't even live in a eucalyptus tree eating country."

Steve C: "It is permanent, albeit that it will unpermanent itself later."

Crofty: "They're both off sick, Steve's got the shits and Moley's got a loft hatch."

Ernie Hunt (Hatfield): "Water rescue incidents tend to be in or near the water."

Rodders: "Steve's having his watch mended; I hope they don't fob him off."

Me: (Crofty: "Did you see the headline in the Sun, 'Elton John takes his partner up the aisle')."

"I can't be arsed with all that."

Daz: "The officers are feathering their caps."

Daz: "Hark at Sabes, rattling some feathers."

Moley: (Fish tank): "It's exactly the same as the other one; I've just got to measure it to see if it's the same size."

Crofty: "I can't do predictive text in German… because I can't speak German."

2006. OUR OWN HIGH VOLUME PUMP.

7th January, 0440 hrs.

BEEP, BEEP, BEEP, "190 to attend the Haldens Club, Margery Wood, WGC, fire."

WrL mobile to incident, crew of six.

In attendance, 0444 hrs.

The clubhouse is well alight. A jet is got to work from the doorway and Sub O Cartwright sends "make pumps 4."

Control mobilise 191, 201 and 180.

The fire is through the roof and it isn't safe to send BA teams inside so two more jets are got to work from the outside.

Sub O Cartwright, HP required.

234 and 231 are mobilised.

The battle is joined from above by a monitor from the HP.

Eventually the fire is knocked down and the stop message is sent at 0651 hrs, "a social club approx. 15m x 15m, one hundred per cent severely damaged by fire, cylinders involved, 3 x jets, HP monitor, 2 BA, TIC and SHT/EX in use."

Crews can at last enter the building and extinguish the fire.

It looks like another arson job and two FISOs and Browza are sent to investigate.

Back on station at 0733 hrs.

The Welwyn and Hatfield Times of January 11th told us;
"It is understood a board and possibly a wheelie bin had been propped against the front door to start the fire."

19th January, 1549 hrs. We are driving back to the station.

Our call sign; "VI calling 190, over" – "190, go ahead, over" – "VI, 190, order your appliance to an RTA persons trapped, Green Lanes, Lemsford."

Also mobile are 180 and 185.

In attendance at 1553 hrs.

On scene, we have a school coach that has been in a head-on collision with a Ford Mondeo estate car. The coach has left the road and ended up in some bushes, the car across the road. There are ten school girls and a driver on the bus, shaken but not injured and the sixty-one-year-old driver of the car is trapped and in a bad way.

I am sent on to the coach to check on the girls, the others get to work with two sets of Lukas.

We have to get the girls off of the bus but don't want them to witness the casualty in the car. The solution is to line up the firemen as a screen in front of the car and the girls are taken into the nearby kennels to play with the dogs and await their parents.

The driver is released and taken to hospital by ambulance.

The stop message is sent at 1624 hrs.

Home station at 1639 hrs.

By this time the ERT based at Hatfield had become the Rescue Support Unit and the HP's based at Watford, St Albans and Stevenage are now Aerial Ladder Platforms.

Forty-eight High Volume Pumps were provided to selected Fire and Rescue Services as part of the Government's National Resilience Programme in 2004.

The New Dimension programme was set up to help fire brigades cope with the threat of terrorist and other major catastrophic incidents. It provided the vehicles and training for the crews in such things as; urban search and rescue, mass decontamination from chemical, biological, radiation and nuclear materials, command and control as well as the high volume pumps.

Now, as part of the programme we were to get an HVP in Hertfordshire, and it is going to be based at WGC.

So, I volunteer to train as an HVP Instructor and together with John Bone (Red Watch) and Sam Firmin (retained) we head off to the Fire Service College on 23rd January for a couple of weeks.

Early training with the HVP on the Watch.

A great course, I really enjoy being at the college.

The highlight, going to the pub and finding the course leader, an ADO, wearing a dress and serving behind the bar!

Each HVP consisted of a prime mover and demountable module containing a submersible pump, one kilometre of 150 mm hose and all ancillary equipment. Alternatively, two hose boxes with two kilometres of hose.

We eventually mastered it and returned to station to train everybody else.

Our HVP, PM 083 (WX54 VNL), arrived and once everybody was trained we were "on the run" and available to go to any incident, anywhere in the country.

5th February, 12:48 pm. Fire, the Crooked Chimney PH, Lemsford.

24th February, 1:17 am. Car Fire, Digswell Lane.

Industrial action loomed its ugly head again in May.

This time the problem was within the brigade.

In March the County Council had drawn up plans including: -

- Closing Radlett fire station.
- Reducing firefighters at St Albans and Stevenage.
- Increasing first and second engine response times to incidents.

The first strike took place between 1400 hrs and 2200 hrs on Saturday 20th May with further action planned for 26th and 31st.

I don't remember any of these things coming to pass at the time, but I see now during my research for this book that not only Radlett but also Bovingdon and Bushey fire stations seem to have been lost.

It was around about now that we were called to another bizarre incident. I don't remember the exact call because it is listed in my notes as a false alarm and I don't recall the address.

One afternoon the bells go down and I rush to the printer. The tip sheet states, "kitchen fire – occupier doesn't speak very good English."

We head out; I am in charge with a crew of five.

We pull up in front of the middle terrace house, outside are a family, a man, woman and child, all very animated. I go over to them, all I can get is "fire, fire, big fire".

Erring on the side of safety I get the boys to rig in BA and lay out a hosereel.

Inside the house I can detect no sign of fire. The man is pointing to a door… "big fire!"

Feeling the door with the back of my hand, no heat, anyway I back off and let the BA team open it… nothing.

The BA team back up and I get the occupier to come with me into the kitchen. He takes me over to the wall mounted gas boiler and points, excitedly, through the little window at the pilot light! "Big fire!"

We make up and head home.

It transpires that this family had only been in the country a few days, got a council house and had never seen a central heating system.

In my BA crew, ready to do whatever is needed, is Sabes, who has been on the Council house waiting list for years.

A six pump fire in Hoddesdon High Street on the 7th June had us turning out at 1830 hrs.

Steve Cartwright was in charge, with a crew of five.

We were on scene at 1903 hrs and were confronted with a number of shops well alight. I was in BA with Crofty I think. We took a jet up onto the first floor to find that the fire had vented out through the roof.

Other appliances in attendance were; 261, 150, 321, 241, 231, 234, 189 and 323.

Stevenage's HP was got to work and the fire is slowly knocked down.

The stop message was sent at 2018 hrs; "a range of shops 20m x 20m, first floor and roof well alight, make pumps six, 3 jets, 6 BA, HP in use, 8 persons code 4."

We are back on station at 2040 hrs.

I was in charge on the 9th July when we got a call to a car fire at Jordans, WGC at 3.15 a.m.

In attendance at 3.18 a.m., to find a motor car, well alight, under a block of flats.

The blaze is brought under control by a BA team with a hosereel and is then pushed out from beneath the flats which are all affected by smoke.

Stop at 3.45 a.m. and back to base at 4.07 a.m.

An unfortunate call on the 31st July, at 1500 hrs, had us rushing to Woodside House, WGC to an elderly lady in a bit of trouble.

I am in charge with a crew of four.

The lady had confused a metal waste paper basket with the toilet and sat down on it. She had been there some time before she was discovered by a visiting District Nurse, who called us.

The thin metal rim of the basket had pressed into the casualty's skin and was stuck there.

After a delicate, dignified removal of the object, we left the lady in the care of the nurse.

Stop at 1513 hrs and home station at 1528 hrs.

10th August at 9.39 p.m. I am in charge and we are off to rescue a puppy that has trapped its head between a radiator and the wall in a house in Maple Grove, WGC.

The bells went down at 10.46 a.m. and we turned out to Comet Way, Hatfield, RTA persons trapped.

In attendance at 10.51 a.m. together with 180 and 185.

The Welwyn and Hatfield Times of Wednesday, August 16th:

LUCKY ESCAPE AS VAN OVERTURNS

"A woman had a miraculous escape after her van flipped over in the path of an oncoming lorry."

The woman was released very quickly and we left Hatfield to it, returning to station at 11.12 a.m.

Over the last few years the rank names had been changing, again I'm not sure why. I went from being a Leading Firefighter to a Crew Manager to a Crew Commander. However, it had taken me so long to become a Leading Fireman and being a bit old school, I always referred to myself as a Leading Fireman when booking out on the radio etc.

It's almost a quarter to eight at night on Monday, 18th September.

The call comes in for "a flat on fire at Guinness House, Little Hardings, WGC."

Steve Cartwright is in charge with a crew of four, and we are in attendance at 2046 hrs.

Also mobile is 191 with a crew of five.

I head off to try and find the flat.

The flat is difficult to find in the labyrinth that is Guinness House.

Once tracked down I find a ground floor, smoke-logged flat, and am told that the occupier may be inside.

The BA crew is running a hosereel from the pump into the building and preparing to make an entry to the flat. I check the outside and find an open window so I lean in and call out. Immediately under the window is a settee and laying there I can make out the face of a casualty, I wasn't expecting to see that and it made me jump back! The BA crew arrive and I indicate the position of the casualty and head back round to the front door to help with the victim.

The BA crew emerge with my casualty... a bloody cushion with a photograph of the face of the occupier printed on it!

No one was in the flat; he was already in hospital, having been beaten up earlier in the day, the fire was set as an ongoing feud.

As you can imagine I came in for a bit of ribbing!

It's October, it's Crofty's birthday, and he's forty!

We are all off to Fuengirola in southern Spain to celebrate.

Finishing nights, we head off to Bishops Stortford fire station to leave the cars and get a lift to Stanstead Airport.

He has booked us an apartment, all very nice. I don't remember how many of us went but I will guess at ten? The days were taken up with them playing golf and me finding the local dive centre, with evenings spent in the bars and clubs.

I had a good couple of days diving. There is nothing of any note at Fuengirola and so we drove all the way, and hour and a half, nearly seventy miles to Gibraltar one day and a further fifteen miles to Tarifa on the other.

Steve Cartwright and I found time to visit the Moorish Castle of Sohail in Fuengirola (to get out of one of the afternoon drinking sessions!).

A great break, all good fun.

Back four days later in time to start the next day shift.

Back at the sharp end, at 2318 hrs on 5th November we went over to Valence Road in Cheshunt for a relief at a house fire.

I don't remember but it must have been a big house, because joining us there were Stevenage's WrL and HP, St Albans WrL and a WrL from Watford.

We got back to WGC at 0132 hrs.

On Tuesday, 5th December at a quarter past four in the afternoon the bells went down and we were mobile to Howardsgate, WGC to a fire on a balcony.

As can be seen in the photograph here, I think I was one of the last firemen to keep his original axe and belt.

Fire at Howardsgate, 5th December.

Personal axes were removed many years before in favour of two axes supplied as part of the appliance equipment.

I put mine on every time we turned out and used it on numerous occasions.

Almost the end of another year.

It's Friday, 29th December, and on the A414, Hertford Road, two cars, a blue Peugeot 407 and a black Volkswagen Golf are travelling towards Hertford.

At the station at 1554 hrs, BEEP, BEEP, BEEP, "190 to A414, Hatfield, RTA persons trapped."

We are mobile; I am in charge with a crew of four.

In attendance at 1601 hrs.

The two cars had collided on the roadway with the Golf ending up on the opposite carriageway.

Also in attendance are 180, 185, and 240, an ambulance fast response car and four further ambulances.

Two men and a woman, all in their seventies are trapped in the Peugeot and a twenty-four-year-old man is trapped in the wreckage of the Golf.

Crews get to work with two sets of Lukas cutting gear.

The first male casualty is released but pronounced dead at the scene, he is covered with a salvage sheet.

Our station vicar, Dennis, turned up and gave him the last rites.

The two other elderly occupants are finally cut free and taken to the QEII hospital.

The driver of the Golf is released after removing the roof of his car and also taken to the QEII.

We make up the gear and return to base at 1739 hrs.

Ambulance spokesman Gary Sanderson told the *Welwyn and Hatfield Times:* "The fire service did a great job assisting us removing our patients smoothly from the wreckages."

The second elderly man died later in the QEII and the woman was "comfortable." He had been picked up from the hospital by the couple to be taken home after suffering a heart attack!

The twenty-four-year-old was transferred to the University College Hospital in London.

BORE MOLLOCKS – 2006.

Sabes: "That reminds me of someone I can't remember."

Me: "That's not the only spanner in the ointment."

Molly (the cleaner): Daz, "I got cod and chips for £2.50. "That's dear, I only paid £5 for me and Bert."

Sabes: "He played a round of golf but he had a couple of bumholes."

Crofty and me: Crofty; "Look at Rooney, he can thread it through the eye of a blunt haystack."

Me; "The saying is 'shit through the eye of a camel'."

Crofty; "No, you mean 'a poke in the eye with a blunt needle'."

Steve C: "Bearing in mind that two weeks ago was a couple of weeks ago now."

This one just had to go in:

Crofty: Darren; "Why do we wear a poppy on Remembrance Day?"

Sabes; "Because during the shelling it was the only flower that would still grow."

Crofty; "I thought it was because they grew in some fields owned by a bloke called Flanders and there was a fight there!"

2007. "THANK GOD YOU'RE HERE."

My last full year as a fireman.

The first part of the year brought a number of rescues.

On the 6th January, at a ground floor flat in Chambers Grove, WGC, we rescued a woman and her two cats after a gas leak caused the flat to fill with gas.

On 31st January, two more rescues.

At 1245 hrs, on Essendon Hill, Essendon, we cut a woman from her car following a collision.

Followed by a call at 1423 hrs to Colgrove, WGC, where two young children had become locked in their house with mum outside.

At Elizabeth House Care Home, off Moors Walk, WGC, on 11th February twelve people had become trapped in the Dementia Unit when the door stuck.

Fire, 15th April, at Gasdesden Grove, WGC.

Compare this photo to the young fireman on Red Watch, Potters Bar, 30 years ago on page 33.

How time flies!

12th April, an RTA, with two persons trapped in Wheathampstead, followed by a call for the Rope Rescue Team to Hitchin, where a worker had fallen from scaffolding.

End of April and the first of the White Watch old timers has decided to move on.

After years on the Watch Mark Saban is transferring to Hatfield.

In his place comes a new recruit, straight from Training School, Shane Killick.

Shane is twenty-two years old, the same age I was when I joined.

I think his first duty day was 28th April.

As a Service HVP Instructor and Watch co-ordinator it had fallen to me to arrange some on-going training.

I had made contact with Sergeant Major John Pedley at Bassingbourn Barracks near Royston with a view to using their site for training. It had a huge lake, perfect for us.

I planned a big exercise.

I had arranged with WM Richard Litson, Green Watch, Kempston, Bedfordshire and Luton Fire and Rescue Service

(BLFRS), to meet and try to deploy the HVP submersible pump using the HiAB crane on their Specialist Rescue Unit.

I had also spoken with WM Jon Frame from Huntingdon fire station, Cambridgeshire Fire and Rescue Service (CFRS) to invite them to attend with their HVP.

Also there as observers were, Tony Morrison, Station Commander at WGC; Mick Richardson, Resilience Officer with CFRS; Andy Dunlop, New Dimension co-ordinator, Eastern Region and Paul Dudley, Training, HFRS.

The plan was drawn up and approved by HFRS on 10th January and by early April all participants had confirmed their attendance and final instructions and risk assessments had been issued.

It's got all the makings of a good day.

And so we all met up at Bassingbourn on 29th April for:

EXERCISE "TRIPLE CHAOS"

A great day out, operationally and socially, it's not often we got together with other brigades.

The attendance was as follows:

BRIGADE	STATION	APPLIANCE	CALL SIGN
HFRS	WGC	WrL	Bravo 190
HFRS	WGC	RUV	Bravo 197
HFRS	WGC	HVP	Mike 82
HFRS	WGC	WrL	Bravo 191
HFRS	Hatfield	RSU	Bravo 185
HFRS	Hatfield	RUV	Bravo 187
BLFRS	Kempston	WrL	2 Alpha
BLFRS	Kempston	SRU	Kempston 5
CFRS	Huntingdon	WrL	Alpha 274
CFRS	Huntingdon	HVP	Alpha 27 Hotel

The exercise commenced at 1045 hrs.

The exercise was to site two HVP hydrosubs in a confined area and deploy two submersible pumps over an obstruction utilising Kempston 5 HiAB and Hatfield's WIU boat.

Pumping from the HVP's via two lines of twinned 150 mm hose over 500m to supply four appliances, each supplying two ground monitors each.

At 1145 hrs we all stopped to take lunch in the Barracks canteen.

The last appliance left the site at 1614 hrs.

Hatfield's WIU boat is launched using the Hiab on Kemston's SRU.

Crews from WGC and Huntingdon prepare the submersible pumps
for deployment.

Deploying the submersible pumps using the Hiab.

A HVP laying the hose to the pumping appliances.

Bravo 190, Bravo 191, HFRS and Alpha 274, CFRS pumping.

Kempston 2 Alpha supplying a ground monitor.

Making up the hydrosubs.

Recovering the hose into the hose Box.

Firefighters from the three counties pose for a group photograph.

Firemen from four different stations and three different brigades all working together, love it. The best exercise ever (even though I did organise it).

22nd May, 1144 hrs; BEEP, BEEP, BEEP, "190 to attend Sir Frederick Osborn School, Herns Lane, WGC, chemical spillage."

Mobile to incident at 1145 hrs, WM Cartwright in charge with a crew of five.

In attendance at 1146 hrs; "make pumps 3, chemical unit required."

Control mobilise 240, 180, 018, 010 and 011.

A quantity of an unknown chemical has been released in the science block. Four people have been affected by the fumes, crews treat the casualties with oxygen, one of whom is taken to the QEII by ambulance. Once the CIU is in attendance and set up to receive contaminated firefighters, we start the clean-up operation.

> A crew wearing BA and gas-tight suits enter the building, secure the chemical, clean up the spillage and remove the contaminated materials.
>
> They undergo decontamination by Hemel crews and the stop message is sent at 1440 hrs; "unknown chemical release in science block - 4 persons affected by fumes - 2 LLGTS and BA in use – decontamination set up – 1 person code 2, 4 persons code 3, 30 persons code 4."
>
> Mobile returning and back at station at 1510 hrs.

My great recollection of this incident is the three officers who came with the Hemel crew.

All three were big men standing together, looking like a trio of firemen weebles!

CM Dave Humphries, WM Chris York and CM Gene Cutler.

Three great lads; Dave had a flat in Mallorca in the same town that I moved to when I retired.

I remember when he retired a year or so later, all of White Watch, Hemel came out to Port Pollença to celebrate.

I met up with them in the afternoon and the drinking went on for two and a half days. They even managed an early morning game of beach volleyball! A great few days, I am sure some of them didn't sleep at all!

Dave and I had many a *cerveza* around the Port watching the Spanish, zero health and safety festivities.

At some point the station received a second HVP, PM 086, (WX54 VNO). This one carried two hose boxes i.e. two kilometres of 150mm hose.

Two RTAs at the end of May.

On Wednesday 30th May at 11.11 a.m. we are called out to Burnham Green Road, Welwyn, where two cars have been in collision. Both drivers, a man and a woman, are injured.

Together with the Old Welwyn crew, we use two sets of Lukas cutting gear to release the driver of a black Mini Cooper.

Both casualties are treated on scene by BHAPS paramedics and taken to the QE II.

The following day, Thursday 31st, we join Hatfield WrL and RSU at junction 3 of the A1(M).

Around 5.30 p.m. a car left the motorway and hit a road sign, resulting in a female driver needing to be cut out of her car.

In attendance at 5.49 p.m.

Again, we use two sets of Lukas to free her.

Another customer for the A&E Department of the QE II.

More tragedy for the Hertfordshire Fire and Rescue Service.

On Saturday night, 16th June, Blue Watch Stevenage have responded to a car on fire near to junction 8 of the A1(M).

With the blaze extinguished, the OiC, Sub O Paul Mallaghan is taking details standing in front of the SAAB, when a VW Golf crashes into the back of it.

Paul is dragged along under the car and injured.

Another fireman is also hit.

Both are taken to the Lister Hospital where it is confirmed that Paul has died from his injuries.

This incident brought fresh misfortune to Stevenage, coming just a couple of years after Paul's colleagues Jeff Wornham and Michael Miller, also of Blue Watch, died in a fire.

The CFO Roy Wilsher told the *Stevenage Comet* of 21st June: "This is an absolute tragedy and we are completely devastated. Paul was a dedicated and professional firefighter and was well known and respected by his colleagues in Hertfordshire."

Summer 2007 was the wettest on record. The Met Office said 414.1mm of rain fell across England and Wales in May, June and July - more than at any time since it began compiling rainfall figures in 1766.

On 24th-25th June heavy rain brought flooding to parts of Yorkshire, Derbyshire, Lincolnshire, Nottinghamshire and Worcestershire. Wet weather earlier in the month meant water levels were already high and the ground quickly became saturated when the second downpour began.

It's 26th June and I have started another shift at nine o'clock in the morning.

Shortly after we are contacted by Control to inform us that the National Resilience Team has asked us to mobilise our HVP to South Yorkshire.

Stn O Morrison and I start to organise a team to deploy to the incident. This involved contacting off duty personnel as well as the crew on duty.

I went home to pack a bag and returned to station.

A crew had been assembled and issued with an HVP individual welfare pack. The pack consisted of a kit bag, towel, spare clothing, food and my personal favourite, paper pants!

I think we had a new or spare HVP, PM 036 (WX54 VKE).

The crew was Stn O Morrison in overall charge and liaison officer, myself as officer in charge of the HVP, together with Ff John Bone (Red Watch) and retained Ff Sam Firmin (both Service HVP instructors) and Ff's Martin Rodmell (White Watch), Phil Hill (Blue Watch) and Guy Phillips (RedWatch).

At 1100 hrs, HVP, WrL and RUV are mobile to Aston fire station, Sheffield, South Yorkshire, crew of seven.

On route, Phil Hill, ever the comedian, telephoned me on the HVP from the WrL, pretending to be a senior officer and asking where the hell we were as the floodings were getting out of control. I remember saying we were coming as fast as we could and perhaps they could get some more buckets until we got there.

After a four hour drive on the blues we are in attendance at 1457 hrs.

The fire station at Aston was a kind of holding area for resources. Tony Morrison heads off to find out the plan and we settle in up on the mess deck with a cup of tea.

1623 hrs. We are mobilised to the Ulley Reservoir, Sheffield.

We are in attendance, along with dozens of other appliances from brigades from all over the country.

The thirty-five-acre reservoir contained 580,000 m³ of water and it had been noticed that because of the unprecedented rainfall, a wall had collapsed and the clay bank of the dam was eroding.

Engineers signalled a warning of a possible imminent failure of the dam, endangering everything downhill in the water's path.

Overnight, police officers had cleared about 100 homes in the villages of Catcliffe, Whiston and Canklow and closed the M1 motorway between junctions 32 and 36. Also threatened was the electricity substation at Brinsworth; if it flooded, power would be lost for over 500,000 homes in the area, as it supplies the whole of Sheffield with electricity.

So it became the priority task to pump as much water from it as quickly as possible and try to relieve the pressure of water on the dam wall.

We didn't deploy our HVP but assisted with others and managing the hose.

When a commercial salvage company arrived we helped to unload their large bore suction hose and couple it up to several big pumps on shore.

Also there was a continual stream of sandbag lorries to unload.

We are released and return to Aston fire station to standby at 1844 hrs.

Earlier, as we had pulled into the car park at the reservoir, I met an old friend. Striding towards me was none other than Biggles!

He had transferred to South Yorkshire a while back, what a great surprise and nice to see him. We were having a catch up chat until I was called away to do a bit of work.

Submersible pumps set in at the Ulley Reservoir.

Pumping water from the reservoir.

Setting up the industrial pumps.

Fire brigade personnel pump water from the reservoir while engineers
shore up the dam wall.

Picture: The Enviornment Agency

At 2245 hrs we are taken to Sheffield City centre fire station where we park our appliances. We are accommodated in a nearby multi-storey hotel. My room had great views of the City.

At 5.29 a.m. I am woken by Tony Morrison and we are sent, with an officer as escort, to Doncaster fire station. More dozing.

We have been supplied with food for breakfast and use the kitchen to cook it. I recall an awful lot of smoke as the station changes watch. At ten fifteen a.m. Tony gets a phone call and we are mobilised. We pack up and wait for our officer escort to arrive to show us the way to the incident.

1024 hrs. Mobile to "Darfield, Barnsley."

I decide to site our HVP hydrosub in Riverside Close and deploy the submersible pump in the street behind, Church View, which is flooded and the lowest point, hoping that all the streets will drain towards us. We run a line of hose to the end of the street, over a wall and into the River Dearne.

The hydrosub is fired up and we start to pump 7,000 litres of water a minute away from the houses.

The locals start to appear so pleased to see us. One tearful lady says "thank God you're here!" We are the first emergency crew they have seen and are astonished that we have come all the way from Hertfordshire to help them.

All the surrounding streets are flooded and throughout the day we continue to pump and the water levels slowly start to fall.

Firefighters Bone and Phillips rescue two dogs from one of the houses after the owner turns up to ask for our help to get them out.

Every now and then a van would arrive with refreshments for us, burgers, tea etc.

Later on in the afternoon a South Yorkshire pump turns up and starts to pump out flooded houses in Riverside Close using their major pump. It is well into the evening before the streets are clear and we start to make up our equipment, finally leaving at 8 pm.

Church View, Darfield, Barnsley.

Rescuing the dogs from a house in Church View.

We realised that during this incident we would need to rethink our personal protection equipment. We spent the day in the flood water which was contaminated with sewage and all sorts of rubbish, not good.

I think we bedded down at Rotherham fire station for the night.

Thursday, 28th June dawns, the last day of our deployment.

At 0830 hrs our HVP is sent to the village of Bentley to help crews there.

Bentley is a couple of miles north of Doncaster, near to the river Don, which had burst its banks.

At 1100 hrs our relief arrived in a PCV and took over from us.

We headed home after a very hard but interesting few days.

The *Welwyn & Hatfield Times* followed our exploits, with headlines on the 27th June:

WGC CREW OFF TO HELP WITH FLOODS

And a quote on 4th July:

OUR CREWS JOIN FLOODS BATTLE

"Sid Payne, a HVP instructor at WGC fire station said: 'A year-and-a-half ago the people of Hertfordshire were faced with the explosion and resulting major fire at Buncefield oil terminal.

On that occasion fire services from around the UK responded to our call for help. This time it is the people of South Yorkshire who are desperate for assistance and we are pleased that we at WGC fire station were able to do something positive to help them during this difficult time'."

"Four relief crews from WGC have so far completed shifts in South Yorkshire. A fifth is due to take over today (Wednesday)."

And I am to be part of that fifth relief crew.

A few days earlier on Monday, 2nd July we have another solemn duty to perform.

The funeral of Paul Mallaghan took place at St Andrew and St George's Church in Stevenage. His coffin was borne on the Aerial Ladder Platform and passed between rows of hundreds of firefighters, not just from Hertfordshire but from all over the UK.

Yet another sad day for us all.

Also on the crew travelling back to South Yorkshire are Stn O Dave Harding, Liaison Officer, Moley and Paul Enever (I think); can't remember who else.

We are mobile in a PCV and head straight to Toll Bar, a village one mile north of Bentley, where the Ea Beck had overflowed and flooded the village.

The town is centre is flooded with a number of HVP's working along Askern Road, the main road through the village.

We also take note of the location of the large, mobile canteen.

We get our orders and are in attendance at Manor Estate, at 1203 hrs and take over the operation of a hydrosub at the junction with Askew Road.

The road is flooded and opposite, the houses, shops and businesses are also all flooded. Beyond that the playing fields and flood plains are under water; the water level halfway up to the crossbar of the rugby posts.

Over the next few hours three more hydrosubs are delivered by a tractor with a forklift for us to manage.

We have to lay six lines of hose, at least 800m (half a mile), a lot of it by hand, up the road and across some fields to a dyke to allow us to pump away the water. That's ninety-six lengths of 150mm hose and we had to ramp them where they crossed roads to enable the traffic to flow.

We are relieved by a night crew around 2000 hrs.

I think our accommodation was the Holiday Inn at Doncaster.

The place was packed with firemen from all over the place. I would very much doubt if the Holiday Inn has sold as much beer before or since.

Thursday, 5th July; breakfast.

Toll Bar, looking along Askew Road. Our hydrosubs were located to The left near the light brown building.

Car showroom opposite our location. It can be seen on the right hand side in the photograph above.
Pictures: Ben Gurr, the Times

0959 hrs we are mobile back to Toll Bar to take over our four pumps for the day.

As time goes on the water levels continue to fall, we seem to be winning. Cars in a garage compound, the roofs of which only were visible yesterday, start to appear and by the end of the day are very dirty but water free. Houses opposite are free of water and the occupiers start to clear them out.

During the course of the day we get to talk to some of the locals. It appears that some of the flood-devastated residents of Toll Bar have become convinced that their homes were sacrificed to the floods, blaming the Mayor, to save Doncaster's town centre!

The day is taken up redeploying the submersible pumps into deeper water as the floods recede and moving the hydrosubs accordingly, interspersed with regular visits to the mobile canteen.

We got a good reputation for hard work and knowledge among the other HVP crews and South Yorkshire officers.

> So much so that our advice was sought on various matters including sorting out problems with hydrosubs and pumps.
>
> Our shift ended at 1700 hrs and we returned to the Holiday Inn.

I slept well after dinner and a bit of socialising.

We are again mobile to Toll Bar at nine thirty a.m. for our last morning.

We man the pumps until eleven o'clock when our relief from Hertfordshire arrives.

We drive home stopping for lunch at an M1 service station.

After a couple of weeks of a different type of firefighting, it is back to normal and a night shift at WGC fire station, the 19th July.

Almost as soon as our watch starts we are turned out 6.06 p.m. to "Green Vale, WGC, house fire, persons reported."

Also mobilised are WGC retained.

We are in attendance at 6.11 p.m.

We are confronted with a serious fire, I don my BA set and we make an entry into the house with a jet.

In the hallway, on the floor, is a ninety-four-year-old man, we pick him up and take him from the house and hand him over to BHAPS. Returning to the building we find that the blaze is in the kitchen and it is extinguished, leaving the room severely damaged by fire and the rest of the house by smoke.

The casualty is suffering from smoke inhalation and is taken to the QE II hospital.

The stop message is sent at 6.27 p.m.

Back at the station we get a cup of tea and start to prepare the dinner.

At 9.02 p.m. the bells go down and we are mobilised as a rope rescue team to "Old Rectory Lane, Hatfield, child trapped in a tree."

Hatfield are in attendance and have sent the message "Aerial Ladder Platform required."

The girl had climbed a tree to look at a magpie's nest, quite high up and had got her hair tangled in the branches.

We are in attendance at 9.07 p.m.

We pitch a ladder up to the girl and put her into a support harness and secure her to the tree.

She is brought to the ground on the ALP and the stop is sent at 9.38 pm.

We are back for dinner at 10.02 p.m.

The flooding's continued.

On 24th July the Thames in Abingdon rose three feet (0.9 m) in less than twelve hours to a "perilously high" level and the Thames and the Severn were expected to rise to twenty feet (6.1 m) higher than normal.

So on 24th July we were requested to deliver a hydrosub to Oxford fire station.

I drove it down and left it there, returning the same day. I thought I went with Moley but he's not sure.

A crew of seven from WGC were deployed there around now.

The next day, 25th July we had a chemical incident behind Poundstretcher, Church Road, WGC.

We were called at 1243 hrs. In attendance at 1245 hrs.

Also in attendance were 180, 010, 018 and a number of officers including Dave Stokes.

A large unmarked drum leaking an unknown liquid was made safe by a BA crew in LLGTS.

Home station at 1426 hrs.

At the beginning of August, we had two visits to the station.

Firstly from an old friend, Martin Oudôt and his colleague Michael Gottschalk from Ingelheim, who came to see the HVP.

Michael, Shane, Daz and Martin.

Secondly from a group of visiting Japanese girls from the Miyazaki Nichidai School. They watched the crew drill and looked over the fire engine.

On 21st August the Rope Team was mobilised to "Shaw Close, Cheshunt, person stuck in a tree."

I am in charge. Mobile at 9.51 p.m., in attendance at 10.11 p.m.

A woman has tried to get her cat which had been up the tree for some time. Both were now stuck at the top of a large pine.

Using a ladder to get part way up the tree, and then cutting away branches as they went, I think Darren and Crofty climbed the rest of the way using a harness, attaching to the tree as appropriate.

The woman was put in a harness and brought to safety.

The cat put in a bag and lowered down to the ground where it promptly escaped and ran off! (I let the cat out of the bag!)

Stop sent at 10.49 p.m.

Home station at 11.10 p.m. It's way past my bed time.

I am on standby, in charge at Stevenage fire station, on 20th September.

A pretty uneventful day until at 1711 hrs we are turned out to "Danecroft, Letchworth, house fire, make pumps 4 – ALP and salvage tender required."

We are in attendance at 1723 hrs, along with 310, 311, 320, 321, 323 and 234.

Stop message sent at 1740 hrs: "fire in roof of end of terraced house – 4 BA, 2 x J, HRJ, ALP in use – 3 persons code 4."

Thursday, 27th September and a busy day.

At 10.48 a.m. we are mobile to "Coursers Farm, Colney Heath, fire, make pumps 10."

In attendance at 10.57 a.m. Also there were 110, 111, 180, 011, 150, 091, 140, 100, 201, 189 and a hose-layer from London.

Stop message sent later that night: "Haystack 50m x 15m well alight – 1 yard containing plant and machinery also involved – water shuttle, 2 x J, HRJ, 6 BA in use."

Then at 3.57 p.m. we are on our way to "junction of Hatfield Avenue / Coopers Green Lane, Hatfield, RTA persons trapped."

In attendance at 4.01 p.m. with 180.

Stop message sent at 4.14 p.m.: "Two cars in collision on roadway – 1 female adult trapped – Lukas in use – 2 persons code 2, 2 persons code 4."

I am being promoted, albeit temporarily, to the rank of Sub Officer (Watch Commander) on the Blue Watch, WGC!

Twenty-nine years and six months too late but at least it will enhance my pension. Blues were a good Watch. My L/Fm was Liam Jackson with Fm Martin Arrowsmith, Phil Hill, Paul Gilmartin, Russ Osborn and Matt Taylor.

My first operational call in my new role was to a bin fire on 21st October.

It's Moley's fortieth and we are off on another jolly.

At the beginning of November we set off to Stanstead Airport and on to Madeira!

Nice hotel, but who cares, we are straight on the beer.

I find myself a local dive centre and head out on a RIB to dive a couple of pinnacles with lots of big grouper, one bright yellow one that allowed you to give it a scratch!

Moley wanted to go fishing so we found a boat and booked up.

We went out and through a rock wall and into the open ocean where it got quite rough.

We fished a deep drop-off. By the end of the day it was only the birthday boy who had caught anything; Moley had landed a 34lbs (15kg) Amberjack, a 20lbs (9kg) Red Snapper and a shark.

Back to port after a bumpy but great day.

When we got back the boat skipper arranged with a local, harbourside restaurant to prepare the fish for our dinner.

We went back to the hotel to change and then out for a fish supper. The table was packed with goodies and then the whole Jack and Snapper arrived. Fantastic.

A few beers afterwards to wash it all down.

The old town of Funchal made a very interesting visit.

Back to the UK and back to work. Well done Moley!

As we move towards the end of the year, one final rescue to perform before I retire.

It's 30th November and a night shift.

We are out on a false alarm call as the clock ticks over into December and I am back in bed at ten past midnight.

Forty minutes later the alarm sounds and the lights come on, the printer in the Watchroom tells us: "190 to attend Rupert House, Little Hardings, WGC, flat fire – persons reported."

We are mobile at 0053 hrs. Also on the incident are retained pumps from WGC and Old Welwyn.

As we pull up outside the building at 0056 hrs, smoke is billowing from the ground floor flat. I get a BA crew with a jet to enter the flat. The fire is in the kitchen and the occupier is found by the crew, asleep, and led from the flat to safety.

He is treated by other crews for smoke inhalation using oxygen.

A second BA team is also deployed to the flat; the fire is extinguished, a cat is recovered and the flat is ventilated.

I send the stop message at 0114 hrs. And crews begin to tidy up.

My secondment to Blue Watch came to an end on 31st December. A good couple of months for me.

2007 – A GOOD YEAR FOR THE SPOKEN WORD.

Moley: (Showing off his new grey trainers): "Great aren't they exactly the same as my green pair."

Steve: "Do you want any jam Jim?"

Jim: "Yes, that would be nice."

"We haven't got any!"

Steve: Crofty: "We've been really busy."

"Yes, a period of untranquility."

Martin Arrowsmith: "It will pump between 3,000 and 3,000 litres per minute."

John Bone: "The life jacket is designed to deflate on contact with water."

Shane: Darren: "What did you fail your driving test on?"

"Errr… erm… er… hesitation."

Tony Morrison: (On the phone): "Come for Sunday lunch… well about lunchtime."

Steve: "Mind your head… duck up!"

2008. GOODBYE!

I start the year back on White Watch. Thanks to the Blues for their hospitality.

Following our deployment to the floods in South Yorkshire, it became very apparent that our normal firefighting clothing just wasn't up to the job.

Hatfield had dry suits for use at water incidents and after some consultations it was decided to issue similar protective clothing to us for use with the HVP.

Under the tuition of the Hatfield crew we had some training at a local pool and the dry suits were issued some time later.

We also received new helmets and boots around now.

A few last incidents to record as I wind down to retirement.

On 5th February, I was rudely awakened (again) at 6.38 a.m.

190 with a crew of 6 was mobilised to "A1(M), junctions 5 – 4, RTA."

Also mobile were 180, 185 and 201.

We arrive on scene at 6.45 a.m.

A petrol tanker has been in collision with three other cars, causing all three lanes of the motorway to be blocked.

Four people have been injured and are being treated by BHAPS.

No one is trapped and after the stop has been sent at 6.54 a.m., we are released and return to WGC, leaving the Hatfield crew to finish up.

Five days later, 10th February, we are mobilised as the Rope Rescue Team.

> 1330 hrs, to "Lime Avenue, Wheathampstead, person fallen into basement."
>
> We are in attendance at 1342 hrs.
>
> The call was to a construction site. The concrete floor and first few courses of bricks had been built at ground level and below that was a basement.
>
> The casualty had fallen from the floor several metres into the basement, landing heavily on the concrete floor below.
>
> We lowered a nine metre ladder into the basement to allow paramedics to get to the casualty.
>
> Following an assessment of the situation it was decided to lower a second nine metre ladder into the basement and put the casualty into scoop stretcher (carried on the ALP). We would then use the two ladders as guides and lines to haul the stretcher up to ground level. Once everything was in place the stretcher was slowly pulled up with a fireman on each ladder following it up.
>
> Once at the top the casualty was moved to solid ground and handed over to the Ambulance Service for further treatment and conveyance to hospital
>
> We had a large attendance for manpower and the ALP if needed, as it could have also been used to raise the stretcher.
>
> Other appliances attending were 211, 221, 191 and 231.
>
> Once all the equipment was made up we returned to WGC at 1451 hrs.

And finally.

Around five in the afternoon, on 29th February, opposite the Chieftain public house in Cole Green Lane, a local woman looks out of her window.

She tells the *Welwyn and Hatfield Times* (Wednesday March 5th): "It was scary at first. I was in the kitchen and went to pull the curtains and then I saw smoke billowing out."

I come on duty at six o'clock and in charge for the night.

At 1813 hrs Control send us to The Chieftain, Cole Green Lane, WGC, on relief to take over from Blue Watch.

We are in attendance at 1818 hrs.

The front part of the disused building and roof is well alight.

Other resources start to arrive, relieving the day watch crews, including 191, 180, 201, 234, 240, 189, 150, 323, 111, 211, 321, 241, 110, 230, 094, 185 and 090, nearly eighty firemen.

10 pumps, 2 aerials, Control Unit, Rescue Support Unit and a salvage tender.

The fire is divided into four sectors and I am put in charge of the sector at the back of the pub.

BA crews have been withdrawn from the front part of the building. In my sector the building is not yet alight although smoke is issuing. I ask for permission to send some BA teams in to save the back half of the building but the request is denied.

We have jets in place and just have to wait for the fire to reach us. Even the crews on the platforms are withdrawn to keep them out of the smoke.

This is called "passive firefighting", stand back and pour water on it.

Oh well! We wait as the fire steadily burns its way towards us, finally bursting through with a blast.

We get our jets to work and continue to do so until at about 2245 hrs when we are relieved.

We are back for a late dinner at 2303 hrs.

The fire is finally under control at about one a.m. (1st March).

The stop sent: "An unoccupied public house – 50m x 60m – consisting of 2 floors well alight – 5 x jets, 2 x ALP's, 4BA in use."

So that is it, a few more jobs but nothing of note.

Sub Officer Payne posing at his last big fire!

Back Row: Gary Baker-Croft, Darren Ward, Shane Killick, Martin
Rodmell
Front Row: Steve Cartwright, Me, Adrian Kimber.

My last call in charge was to a false alarm at Brocket Hall on
1st April.

And my last call on my last shift, was to a false alarm at
the QE II hospital on 2nd April.

I am doing a last bit of paperwork before leaving the station for the final time. I notice the pump from Hatfield in the yard, nothing unusual about that; also there seems to be a lot of activity around the station.

At about a quarter to nine I get a message to go to the appliance bays.

There I find Tony Morrison, in full undress uniform, White Watch, the oncoming Green Watch, firemen from the two off duty watches as well as retained personnel and the crew from Hatfield, all lined up around the bays.

Stn O Morrison comes to attention and salutes me, calling the parade to attention.

Up until now I hadn't had any issue with retirement. However, I have to say that this fantastic gesture from my fellow firefighters brought a tear to my eye.

It took me by surprise, not knowing quite what to do; I shook hands with Tony and then went around the assembled crews thanking them for the support and friendship over the years.

And so I walked out of the station and into retirement.

I officially finished on 7th April.

The boys on the Watch had organised a retirement party for me. It was held at the Peace Memorial Hall in Codicote on Saturday 12th April.

The turnout was fantastic. A hundred firemen plus, past and present. From my first watch at Potters Bar, all through my time at Stevenage and WGC, just too many people to mention but it was great to see everyone.

Great to see family and friends as well.

Two fire engines turned up outside, bringing the on duty crews from Stevenage.

In true fire brigade form the bar was drunk dry.

I got some lovely presents to treasure.

I wanted a traditional style send off, and so Alan Morgan, Tony Morrison and Pete Hazeldine took it in turns to pull my career apart with some memorable anecdotes.

White Watch, WGC bought me an inscribed fireman figurine and the very traditional "fireman's axe on a plaque with my two cap badges".

Pete Hazeldine gave me my service certificate on behalf of the CFO.

White Watch presented Patsy with a bouquet of flowers, again a traditional gesture.

After all the mockery and presentations, I gave a short speech of thanks and I can't think of any better way to end this book than by repeating the words I finished up with on that night:

"Working in the fire brigade is unlike any other job. Whenever you are called to an incident you are expected to resolve any problem with four or five firemen and the equipment carried on the fire engine. If you need to call on additional resources, there is a wealth of experience and practical knowledge just a radio call away.

But every now and then you have to rely one hundred per cent on someone who you have no direct control over and trust that person completely to keep you safe.

So I would like to thank all of you for keeping me safe either directly or indirectly over the last thirty years.

As we know in Hertfordshire, not everyone gets to stand here having completed their thirty years' service. All very sad.

"Thank you, I love you all."

ABBREVIATIONS AND DEFINITIONS IN ORDER OF TEXT.	
Green Goddess.	A Bedford RL series fire engine originally built between 1953-1956 for the Auxiliary Fire Service and kept in reserve by the Government until 2004.
The Make-up.	See "Messages."
Porto Power.	A tool we used for road accidents.
Lower down.	To lower something from a height.
Escape ladder.	A 15m/50ft wheeled ladder that can be pushed with a crew of four or five.
464	A 14m/46ft triple extension ladder carried and operated with a crew of four.
BA	Breathing Apparatus.
RTA	Road Traffic Accident.
Appliance.	A fire engine, also called a pump.
Jet.	A hose line, usually consisting of a 1¾"/45mm hose with a branch and nozzle.
Watch.	When we worked a 48 hour week the shifts were colour coded so we had Red, White and Blue Watches. After 1979 we started to work a 42 hour week and Green Watch was introduced.
To drill.	To train.
The bells go down.	The alarm at the station sounds and the lights come on to alert the crew to a call.
Wholetime.	Professional full time station or fireman.
Watch room.	Kind of control room where we received our call out information.

Guvnor.	Any fire brigade officer but in particular a Station Officer on a Watch.
Retained.	A part time station or fireman.
Station ground.	The area covered by a fire station.
Tirfor winch.	A manually operated winch.
Out duty.	To spend a shift at another station if they are short of firemen.
OiC	Officer in Charge.
D Delta.	A fire caused by suspected arson.
FPO	Fire Prevention Officer.
HGV	Heavy goods vehicle.
Packset radio.	An early hand-held radio, enabling communication between radio sets.
Curtain spray.	A small piece of equipment that fits into the end of the hose. It has a number of holes which enables a spread of water, creating a water barrier between a fire and some unburnt area.
AFA	Automatic Fire Alarm.
DSU	Distress signal unit. Attached to a BA set. It activates if the BA wearer is immobile for a few seconds to alert fellow firemen to an emergency.
HRJ	Hosereel jet.
Salvage sheet.	A large tarpaulin used for sheeting up to prevent damage by rain or firefighting water.

FB 5X	Low expansion foam branch carried on appliances.
FB 10	Low/medium foam branch.
FB KR4-33	Medium/high expansion foam branch.
Round the pump proportioner and inline inductor	Two methods of drawing the foam concentrate into the water flow to produce the finished foam.
Rota book.	Every shift the firemen were given various tasks i.e. driver, BA wearer or number 5, also kitchen, petrol or watch room duty, as well as standbys. The Rota book made sure everyone did their fair share, (except the one who had control of the book of course.)
Hydrant.	Underground water supply with access for us to obtain water for firefighting.
BA Control Officer. BACO	A fireman who keeps check on the BA crews by recording them in and out of the incident.
Shear legs.	A metal tripod with a block and tackle for lifting.
Chocks.	Wooden blocks and wedges used to stabilise vehicles.

"A" post.	The posts supporting the roof of the car, containing the windows. From the front to the back they are the "A", "B" and "C" posts.
Beaters.	Pieces of hose nailed to broom handles and used to "beat" the fire out.
Standpipe.	A piece of equipment that screwed into the hydrant and then supplied water to the pump via a hose line.
Lightweight pump.	A lightweight pump that took four men to carry it! It could be removed from the appliance and carried to a remote water supply.
Tip sheet.	The incident printout.
Water shuttle.	One or more appliance filling its water tank from a water supply, delivering it to the fire ground and returning to fill up again.
WEDA pump.	Small submersible, electric water pump.
Off the run.	Not available.
Malicious false alarm.	A call put in by someone for fun, when there is no fire situation.
CPR	Cardiopulmonary resuscitation. Artificial respiration.
Short extension ladder, SHT/EX	A light ladder with three parts and can be pitched by one person.
Roof ladder, RF/L	A ladder with small wheels that can be run up the pitch of the roof and a hook for fixing it to the ridge.
Acro prop.	An adjustable metal post for supporting loads.

Running call.	A call that is reported to us directly without calling 999.
Line.	Fire brigade term for a rope.
Sprog.	The newest / youngest member of the Watch.
MARS	Manual and Automatic Resuscitation system.
Hot cans	Purpose made containers to enable us to train in real fire conditions, flashovers etc.
105	9 m or 10.5 m extension ladder.
PPV	Positive pressure ventilation to extract smoke from a building.
9l FX	9 litre foam fire extinguisher.
5kg CO_2X	5 kilogram carbon dioxide fire extinguisher.
Dry riser.	A pipe running up inside of a high rise building with a connection at ground level, which can be filled with water and accessed on every floor via another connection.
Strops.	Polyester webbing lifting straps with a loop at each end.
Flashover.	The temperature point at which the heat in an area is high enough to ignite all flammable material simultaneously.
Lean flashover.	The ignition of the gas layer under the ceiling, leading to total involvement of the compartment.
HiAB crane	A Swedish made, extendable crane.
Ground monitor.	A means of supplying a jet via a hose, fixed in place by using various equipment.
LLGTS.	Limited life gas-tight suits for chemical protection.
Major pump.	The pump on the appliance.

TYPES OF APPLIANCE.		
Water tender escape. Pump escape.	WrE PE	An appliance carrying an escape ladder.
Water tender ladder. Pump ladder.	WrL PL	An appliance carrying a 14m/45ft aluminium triple extension ladder.
Water tender. Pump.	WrT P	An appliance carrying a 10.5 m or 9 m aluminium double extension ladder.
Emergency Rescue Tender. (Later Rescue Support Unit)	ERT RSU	A vehicle containing specialist rescue equipment not found on an appliance.
Control Unit.	CU	A vehicle used at incidents involving five or more appliances to enable the OiC to manage the incident safely.
Salvage Tender.	ST	A vehicle containing pumps, salvage sheets etc. for the protection of property and goods from damage by firefighting or weather.
Hydraulic Platform. (Later Aerial Ladder Platform.)	HP ALP	An appliance with three hydraulically operated booms ending in a cage platform that can extend to 30m/100ft.
General purpose lorry.	GP lorry	A flatbed lorry used to transport the divisional foam stock and foam firefighting equipment or the shear legs.

Hosereel Tender	HrT	My old appliance with a 100 gallon water tank and hosereel drum fitted internally after 1948. It originally had a trailer pump.
Personnel carrier	PCV	15 seat transit van.
Turntable ladder	TL	A hydraulic, telescopic ladder rotating on a turntable normally extending to 100 ft/30 m
Chemical Incident Unit	CIU	An appliance containing the equipment to decontaminate firefighters at an incident.
High Volume Pump	HVP	A prime mover with a demountable module containing 1) a hydrosub with submersible pump and 2) a hose box with 1 km of 150mm hose.
Ranger Utility Vehicle	RUV	A general purpose vehicle with off road capability.
Water Incident Unit boat	WIU boat	An inflatable boat.
Specialist Rescue Unit	SRU	A vehicle containing heavy rescue equipment.
Incident response unit	IRU	An appliance designed to undertake mass decontamination.

STATION NUMBERS AND CALL SIGNS		
Fire Brigade Control	V1	
Stations	Call signs	Appliances
Hemel Hempstead, A11	010	WrL
	011	WrL
	014	Canteen van
	018	CIU
Tring retained, A03	031	WrT
Berkhamsted retained, A04	041	WrT
Kings Langley retained, A06	061	WrT
Rickmansworth, A07	070	WrL
	073	ST
Watford, A09	090	WrL
	091	WrL
Garston, A10.	100	WrL
St Albans, B11	110	WrL
	111	WrL
	112	WrE
	114	HP/ALP
	GH11H9	IRU
Redbourn retained, B12	121	WrT
Radlett retained, B13	131	WrT
Borehamwood, B14	140	WrL
Potters Bar, B15	150	WrL
Cheshunt, Cheshunt retained, B16	160	WrL
	161	WrT
Hoddesdon retained, B17	171	WrT

Hatfield, B18	180	WrL
	185	ERT/RSU
	OC (later 189)	CU
Welwyn Garden City	190	WrL
WGC retained,	191	WrL
B19	Mike 82	HVP
Old Welwyn retained, B20	201	WrT
Wheathampstead retained, B21	211	WrT
Harpenden retained, B22	221	WrT
Stevenage, C23	230 (later 232, 231)	WrE
		WrL
	231 (later 230)	
	234	HP/ALP
	237	Land Rover
	G4 (later G10)	GP lorry
Hertford, C24,	240	WrL
Hertford retained	241	WrT
Ware retained, C25	251	WrT
Much Hadham retained, C26	261	WrT
Sawbridgeworth retained, C27	271	WrT
Bishops Stortford,	280	WrL
C28, retained	281	WrL
Buntingford retained, C29	291	WrT
Royston, C30,	300	WrL
Royston retained	301	WrT
Baldock, C31,	310	WrL
Baldock retained	311	WrT

Hitchin, C32	320	WrL
Hitchin retained	321	WrT
	SI (later 323)	ST

RANKS.	
Fireman /Firefighter	Fm / Ff
Leading fireman / Leading firefighter	L/fm / L/ff
Crew Commander / Crew Manager	CC / CM
Sub Officer	Sub O
Watch Commander / Watch Manager	WC / WM
Station Officer	Stn O
Assistant Divisional Officer	ADO
Divisional Officer	DO
Deputy Divisional Commander (DO)	DDC
Divisional Commander (DO)	DC
Senior Divisional Officer	SDO
Assistant Chief Officer	ACO
Deputy Chief Officer	DCO
Chief Fire Officer	CFO

MESSAGES	
Mobile to incident	The appliance leaves the station en route to the incident.
In attendance	The appliance arrives at the incident.
Assistance	Request more appliances with a "make-up" i.e. Make pumps 2, ERT required.
Informative	A message to let Control what is happening.
Fire surrounded	Used at larger fires when the fire is under control.
Stop	No more assistance required.
Mobile returning	Appliance leaves the incident.
Home Station	Appliance closing down.

Published sources.

Allgemeine Zeitung.
Bexleyheath and Welling Observer.
Cheshunt and Waltham Mercury.
Daily Express.
Daily Mail.
Dorset Echo.
Hertfordshire Mercury.
Hertfordshire on Sunday.
Ingelheimer Zeitung.
Mail on Sunday.
Mainzer Rhein Zeitung.
Mainzer Zeitung.
North Herts Gazette.
Potters Bar Press.
Rhein Zeitung.
Royston Crow.
Stevenage Comet.
Stevenage Gazette.
Stevenage Herald.
Stevenage Mercury.
The Independent.
The Sun.
Trierischer Volksfreund.
Viernheimer Tageblatt.
Welwyn and Hatfield Citizen.
Welwyn and Hatfield Express.
Welwyn and Hatfield Review.
Welwyn and Hatfield Times.

PHOTOGRAPH ACKNOWLEDGEMENTS:

Hertfordshire Fire and Rescue Service:
Archant Newspapers:
The Stevenage Comet:
Hertfordshire Mercury:
North Herts Gazette Series:
Rhein Zeitung:
Allgemeine Zeitung:
Martin Oudöt:
Gary Sanderson:
The Health and Safety Executive:
The Environment Agency:
The Times, Ben Gurr:

THANKS FOR THE ASSISTANCE OF:

Hertfordshire Fire and Rescue Service.
Martin Oudôt.
Jane Rugg, curator, London Fire Brigade Museum.
Gary Sanderson, East of England Ambulance Service.
Roger Middleton, HFRS Museum
Current serving and retired HFRS members.